Mordaunt Roger Barnard

Sport in Norway and where to find it

Together with a Short Account of the Vegetable Productions of the Country

Mordaunt Roger Barnard

Sport in Norway and where to find it
Together with a Short Account of the Vegetable Productions of the Country

ISBN/EAN: 9783337107420

Printed in Europe, USA, Canada, Australia, Japan

Cover: Foto ©Andreas Hilbeck / pixelio.de

More available books at **www.hansebooks.com**

SPORT IN NORWAY.

REIN-DEER HUNTING ON THE HIGH FJELD.

To face p. 110.

SPORT IN NORWAY,

AND

WHERE TO FIND IT.

TOGETHER

WITH A SHORT ACCOUNT OF THE VEGETABLE
PRODUCTIONS OF THE COUNTRY.

TO WHICH IS ADDED,

A LIST OF THE ALPINE FLORA OF THE DOVRE FJELD

AND

OF THE NORWEGIAN FERNS, &c.

BY

REV. M. R. BARNARD, B.A.,
LATE CHAPLAIN TO THE BRITISH CONSULATE, CHRISTIANIA, NORWAY.

LONDON:
CHAPMAN AND HALL, 193 PICCADILLY.
1864.

[*The right of Translation is reserved.*]

LONDON: PRINTED BY WILLIAM CLOWES AND SONS, STAMFORD STREET
AND CHARING CROSS.

TO

PROFESSOR RASCH,

KNIGHT OF ST. OLAFS, ETC.,

OF THE CHRISTIANIA UNIVERSITY,

THESE PAGES ARE AFFECTIONATELY DEDICATED,

BY HIS SINCERE FRIEND,

THE AUTHOR.

PREFACE.

In the first part of this little volume it will be my endeavour to make the reader acquainted with the resources which Norway offers to the angler and the sportsman.

To do this the better, I have described each Amt (province) in turn; and have, moreover, as far as was possible, given the routes to the various rivers.

Hitherto a certain degree of mystery has hung, as it were, over the salmon rivers of Norway, and erroneous reports have, in consequence, been circulated concerning them.

These reports have assumed two opposite forms; the one, that every yard of water is leased, and is in the hands of Englishmen, and that a man "might as soon expect to get a seat in Parliament, as to obtain any salmon-fishing in Norway;" and the other, that he has nothing to do but to set foot in the country, when he will find salmon waiting to be caught in every **river**. I **need** not say **that** these " opposite poles of belief" **are** both of **them** erroneous. The first, I presume, owes its origin to those who, **knowing** well the magnificent sport that is to be had **in** some parts, have adopted the plan of keeping such **knowledge** to themselves **and their own** immediate circle; while the latter **is the natural** reaction of the former.

There **is no question but** that the *best* **parts** of the *best* rivers are **"taken up"** for longer or shorter **periods**; but that a man, **who is** blessed with a good constitution, who does not object to locomotion, and **who does** not mind " roughing it" a bit, cannot meet with **very fair sport**, experience has shown me to be a fallacy.

And, **what is more,** it frequently happens that the latter may meet with better sport than the former; for the one is necessarily a *fixture*, while **the** other can move from place to place, and try his luck in many waters.

It is more especially for this class of sportsmen that the following pages are intended; and while I **fear** some of the former will not be pleased at my revealing facts which have hitherto been kept very dark, I am inclined to think that **they** will **be** favourably received by many good and true men, whose knowledge **of** sport in Norway has hitherto been too **vague** and limited to justify them in incurring the expense and trouble **of** a trip there. Let me, however, seize an early opportunity of warning my readers against forming too exalted notions of the sport a visit to Norway may be likely to afford them, as a great deal of disappointment may thus be **saved.**

In a word, no " pot-hunter " should go **to Norway.**

On the other hand, **if** a man delights in glorious scenery, if the fresh mountain air **and the free life** form the principal charm, and he can be contented with a fair amount of sport, and will not grumble if "the water is in bad condition," or all the ryper gone **to** anywhere **else** but where he happens to be, then I think a trip **to** Norway will do him incalculable good **both** in body and **in** mind.

By the permission of my friend Dr. Schübeler, of the Botanical Gardens **at** Christiania, I am enabled to give my **readers** a short account of the " Vegetable Productions of Norway." And as many of those tourists who visit Norway have **no** one especial object particularly in view, but who **fish** a little when they can, take up gun or rifle when an opportunity occurs, or collect specimens of wild flowers and ferns when they can find them, I have added for their especial benefit, under the title of 'Botanical Rambles on the Dovre Fjeld,' (with the permission of the late talented Professor of Botany, Herr Blytt,) a list of the Alpine Flora that may be found growing there, together with *some tours which will be the most likely to repay the trouble of the collector;* and have also given a short account of the ferns of Norway, which latter I am glad to see Mr. Bennett is bringing before the notice of the English public in a very practical way.

In conclusion, I would only add that I can insure the authenticity of all that is herein stated, and that it has been my great object to avoid drawing too bright a picture of the resources the Fjelds, Forests, and Rivers of the country are capable of affording.*

* The Author will be much obliged for any corrections or alterations which personal experience may suggest.

GENERAL INDEX.

	PAGE
DEDICATION.	
PREFACE	ix
INTRODUCTORY REMARKS	1

CHAPTER I.

Finmarken Amt	7
Nordlands Amt	17
North Throndhjems Amt	23
South Throndhjems Amt	30
Romsdal Amt	35
North Bergenhuus Amt	46
South Bergenhuus Amt	53
Stavanger Amt	57
Lister and Mandals Amt	60
Nedenæs Amt	64
Bratsberg Amt	65
Jarlsberg and Laurvig Amt	69
Buskeruds Amt	70
Christians Amt	73
Hedemarken Amt	75
Agershuus Amt	82
Smaalehnenes Amt	85

CHAPTER II.

The Wild Reindeer and Elk of Norway, their History, Haunts, and Habits	86
Game Laws	157

CHAPTER III.

The Feathered Game of Norway	158

CHAPTER IV.

	PAGE
Bear and Lynx Hunting	180
Tabular form showing the number of bears killed in each Amt from 1846 to 1860	189

CHAPTER V.

On the Artificial Breeding of Salmon	193

CHAPTER VI.

Sketches from Sætersdal	207

CHAPTER VII.

The Vegetable Productions of Norway	236

CHAPTER VIII.

Botanical Rambles on the Dovre Fjeld, &c.	276
Appendix	331

ALPHABETICAL INDEX OF THE RIVERS.

	PAGE		PAGE		PAGE
Aardals Elv	47	Figge	58	Nid	32
Aarö	47	Fjelna	44	Nid	64
Aasta	79	Geiranger	38	Nord	32
Alten	13	Gjendals	19	Nordals	32
Andro	25	Glommen	75	Örkla	31
Augna	25	Gudvangen	48	Osen	79
Aurlands	48	Guul	30	Otta	73
Ausnæs	29	Hadelands	74	Otteren	64
Balsfjord	15	Hallingdal	70	Ougne	58
Bais	18	Hartvig	18	Öy	26
Bævra	44	Haukla	31	Pasvig	9
Bævra	74	Herdals	38	Qvinna	63
Beieren	19	Horningdals	50	Ranen	19
Bergsdal	55	Iisfjord	41	Rauma	40
Birkedals	37	Jacobs	8	Reisen	14
Bjerkedals	20	Jöstedal	47	Rena	77
Börs	13	Laagen	73	Rombaken	18
Braagna	26	Langdals	38	Rytsaa	20
Dalen	20	Lax	12	Salten	19
Dokka	73	Lerdals	46	Sanddola	28
Drammen	70	Lilledals	42	Skaugdal	32
Eina	31	Lira	63	Skjeggedals	54
Elvegaards	18	Logen	69	Skjeggedals	65
Enningdals	85	Maals	16	Sogndal	58
Eridsfjord	41	Maan	86	Sogne	62
Etne	53	Mandals	62	Sördals	32
Etnedal	73	Mista	78	Staavil	31
Exingdal	56	Namsen Elv	26	Staburs	13
Figge or Lods Elv	25	Neiden	10	Steenkjær	24

ALPHABETICAL INDEX OF THE RIVERS.

	PAGE		PAGE		PAGE
Steindals	32	Tabörsnæs	13	**Valdalen**	38
Steindals	54	Talfjord	38	**Valders**	73
Stor	19	Tana	10	**Vanelven**	37
Stor	50	Tengs	58	Vardals	21
Stördals	23	Thyda	35	Værdals	24
Stordals	32	Todalen	43	Vefsen	20
Stryen	50	Topdals	61	Vigelands	58
Suledals	58	Torrisdal	61	Vik	55
Sundals	42	**Trysil** or Klar	78	Vingdals	44
Surendal	43	**Undals**	62	Vosse	55
Svinna	43				

SPORT IN NORWAY, AND WHERE TO FIND IT.

INTRODUCTORY REMARKS.

THE tourist who visits Norway for the second time will in all probability omit to take with him some articles which he found encumbrances on his first journey, and bring others which he had previously omitted. I will therefore devote a few lines to the necessary "impedimenta" which my own experience and that of others has suggested to me, and which may prove of service to the new-comer.

But first a word or two as to the route.

Two steamers (screw) leave Hull for Christiansand and Christiania, one every Friday night; the "Scandinavian," belonging to Messrs. Wilson and Son, Hull, and the "Ganger Rolf," a Norwegian boat. Having travelled by both of these, I should give my preference to the former, though the latter is an extremely good and clean boat, and Captain Gloersen and the first mate are most gentlemanly and obliging officers.

Captain Fairburn, of the "Scandinavian," has been a sailor for upwards of sixty years, and is well up to his duties, and, what is more, extremely attentive to them. His employers will lose a good servant whenever he retires into private life. An attentive steward and stewardess will be found on board, and the *cuisine* is all that can be desired.

The average passage to Christiansand takes about forty-eight hours, and it requires from about seventeen to twenty more to Christiania.

The fare is £4; return tickets, available for the whole season, are £6. There are also two steamers running between Hull and Bergen, one every ten days, I believe. The fare, if I mistake not, is £3.

As most of the travelling in Norway is done *en carriole*, I should recommend a strong deal box in preference to a leather portmanteau, which does not get improved from the "skyts-boy" sitting on it. It should have a waterproof cover to guard against rain and dust, which latter enemy will otherwise penetrate through every little chink. Some leather straps should also be taken, sufficiently long to fasten the said box securely on to the dash-board behind, and leathern loops should be fixed on the covering for the straps to pass through. Next, a leather carpet-bag, which should be protected also with a waterproof cover, the opening being on the side, not on the top. This can lie between the traveller's **feet in** the bottom of the carriole. And lastly, a knapsack, which **will be** found very **useful** in making short **tours of a few days.** I have **seen some very** good ones in Christiania, fixed on a light wooden **frame, so** as to prevent them rubbing against the back, **and** thus allowing a free current of air to pass between.

A long waterproof **coat,** and fishing-boots, **or water**proof gaiters, and **a sou'-wester;** also a **brown holland** over-all, **to keep** the dust out in hot weather, should **be taken.** And lastly, the **services of a large-sized cotton umbrella,** to be used either as a *parapluie* or parasol, **will be found very** acceptable.

As to clothes, each one **must** please himself; only, it is **a great** mistake not to take warm clothing. And, if I may **be allowed** to add, every gentleman should provide **himself with** a presentable suit. I have **seen** some of our countrymen parading **the streets of Chris**tiania dressed **in the** most shabby manner. **Indeed, it** is a current joke among the Norwegians **that the** English come out there **for the** purpose **of** wearing out **their** old clothes.

Mr. Bennett, of **Christiania,** supplies tourists with carrioles, **harness,** bottle-cases, &c., at a moderate price, taking **them** back when returned at a certain deduction previously fixed upon. Thus all the inconvenience of having to shift carrioles at different stations in the interior, and of standing the chance of getting your inside shaken out in the rough peasant-carts will be obviated. It will be well to pay attention to the way in which he fastens the rods, &c. Mr. Bennett also provides bags for dogs, which, fastening underneath, form a very comfortable and convenient bed.

I would recommend the traveller to do without an interpreter, if possible. I fancy that by "cramming" up a hundred words or so of Norsk beforehand, the services of these expensive nuisances may be dispensed with.

As regards the battery, a double gun, large bore, and a rifle will be sufficient. They should both go in one case, which should also be protected with waterproof covering. The rods should be very carefully packed so as to prevent chafing; a leather case will be found very convenient, though I prefer a wooden one.

No tourist, be his object what it may, should go without a light trout rod; one that will do up in a small compass. I have bought very compact ones at Gowland's, in Crooked Lane, and have great pleasure in recommending this shop. The experienced salmon-fisher of course knows pretty well what he should bring, and I would only, therefore, take the liberty of recommending him to bring plenty of tackle, and to have an ample supply of line, flies, and *plaited* casting-lines. He will also bring a trout-rod or two. And I would further recommend every one to equip himself with spinning baits, &c., and to take a long and strong line for trailing out behind him when he is travelling by boat-skyts. I have known good sport to be had in this way, and it serves, moreover, to relieve the monotony of a long row.

As to dogs, I should fancy a setter in preference to a pointer; but this must of course be a matter of choice.

Provisions can be procured in all the large towns; but I should recommend any one who purposes to stay some time up in the country to provide himself with sundry essences of vegetables, such as celery, &c.; also cayenne, mustard, spices, &c. They can be procured at Fortnum and Mason's, and will be found extremely useful articles in the fisherman's *cuisine*, who will often (always is best) have to act as his own cook. For one soon gets tired of salmon, however diversified it may be in the manner of preparing it. By the way, a bottle or two of Worcestershire sauce,* &c., should not be omitted.

The steamer usually arrives in Christiania early on the Tuesday morning.

The Victoria Hotel is decidedly the best, and is, indeed, one of the most comfortable foreign hotels I ever put up at.

---

* The following recipe for sauce for cold salmon, copied from the 'Field,' will be found very good; *experto crede*. "Three tablespoonsful of cream, one ditto of vinegar, one ditto of Worcestershire sauce, one teaspoonful of mustard, one ditto of white sugar, to be well mixed."

I would venture to remind all tourists that Divine Service is performed every Sunday morning at eleven o'clock in a convenient building near to Mr. Bennett's house, and that the Church Establishment *is supported by voluntary contributions*.

Finally, I would strongly recommend every **one to** lose **no time** in consulting **Mr.** Bennett after his arrival in Christiania. **This gentleman, who has** for many years **studied the requisites of the** English **traveller, and who is** most **kind and courteous** (and therefore not unfrequently treated scurvily), will supply all the information that can be needed.

N. B. Every traveller should provide himself with **a good map** of **the** country, with Bennett's "**Handbook,**" price **two** marks, **and** with plenty of small change, before **leaving** Christiania.

CHAPTER I.

FINMARKEN AMT.

THIS Amt, which is the northernmost and largest in Norway, is bounded on the north by the North Sea; on the north-east by Russia; east by Sweden; south by Nordland, and west by the sea. It is divided into four Fogderies — Tromsen and Senjen in the south, Alten, Hammerfest, and E. Finmarken; and contains a superficial area of 59,778 square miles. Magnificent salmon-fishing is to be had here. But before beginning to speak of the rivers, it will be best to devote a few lines to the route.

There are two ways open to the traveller's choice: the first, by disembarking at Christiansand and waiting for a steamer to the north, for I do not think they correspond. It is a tedious and monotonous journey. In the first place, it occupies eight days and a half from Christiansand to Throndhjem. From this latter place to Hammerfest it takes a week, and from Hammerfest to Vadsö in the Varanger Fjord about three days. In all, therefore, about eighteen days and a half, *at least*; and this may be considerably increased in stormy weather.

Another route is by going to Christiania, and travelling by carriole across the Dovre to Throndhjem. And this part of the journey may thus be done in shorter time (and, moreover, give the traveller the opportunity of seeing Gudbrandsdal and the Dovre Fjeld) than by steamer northwards from Christiansand.

Thus, it requires but one day from Christiansand to Christiania—usually seventeen hours—and the journey from hence to Throndhjem can be done comfortably in four days.

Sportsmen bound for the northern rivers must bring tent and canteen with them all complete. A stock of provisions, tea, sugar, spirits, &c., had best be laid in either at Christiania or at Throndhjem. Musquito curtains will be found a luxury, and a veil and gloves are quite necessary for fishing. If the gloves, moreover, are too thin, they will not prove a sufficient protection. A friend of mine had the shape of the glove beautifully impressed upon his hand; for these plagues had stung it through every stitch.

I will begin at the extreme north-east of this Amt.

JACOB'S ELV is on the Russian frontier, and runs into the mouth of the Varanger Fjord. It is an excellent salmon river. As far as I can learn, *it has never been fished by any Englishman*. I have been informed that the river literally swarms with salmon; but as a set-off against this, that the Laps do a great deal towards spoiling the fishing by netting. It can easily be reached from Vadsö by boat-skyts, a distance of fourteen or fifteen miles. Here a tent is absolutely requisite; provisions, too, must be taken, and an interpreter, and an arrangement should be made with the same boatman before leaving Vadsö.

PASVIG ELV, a few miles to the west, runs into Kloster Fjord, a collateral branch of the Varanger Fjord. Capital fishing may be had here. Salmon are only able to run up about three miles and a half, as a foss prevents their further progress. But below this some excellent sport may be had. But few Englishmen have ever fished here, I am inclined to think. A tent is not absolutely necessary, though always desirable. Boat-skyts can be taken from Vadsö to Piselvnæs, where a hunter named Clark resides, who is, I believe, of English extraction. He is a prodigy of a linguist, speaking seven different languages, I have been told. He is also Lensmand of the district, and can give excellent information as to fishing and shooting in general in this Amt. The English sportsman who purposes fishing either in this or in Jacob's Elv, will do well to make Mr. Clark's acquaintance as soon as possible, and request him to make arrangements with the boatmen, &c. In general, the boatmen require about half a dollar a day each. The fish, with the exception of what is consumed, should be given to the inhabitants.

There are two small rivers on the opposite shore of the Varanger Fjord, south of Vardö, but I have not any information concerning them.

The NEIDEN ELV, on the same side as Pasvig Elv, can easily be reached from Piselvnæs. Tents are necessary. The river abounds with fish, and can be fished many miles up.

The TANA ELV. This magnificent river can be reached from Stangenæs, where the steamer stops. This station is one day's journey short of Vardö, and is about three miles distant from the mouth of the river. Boat-skyts should be taken from Stangenæs to Fjeldma, where it will be well to make inquiries of the Foged, Lensmand, or Kjöbmand (merchant). Boats peculiar to the river are used in order to pass the fosses. Arrangements, too, should be made with the Foged, or with Herr Schanke, Inspector of the Fishery, as to what payment will have to be made for leave to fish. This will probably not amount to more than a few dollars per week, unless the price has been raised of late, which is by no means unlikely. A tent is absolutely requisite, and a good stock of provisions should be taken. Fins should be employed for skyts-folk, and for interpreters. With these preliminary remarks, and only adding a recommendation *that it is best to* avoid landing a fish on the Russian *side of the river*, I will proceed to give a brief account of some of the best places.

Salmon run up to a distance of two hundred miles!

The first foss is Seida Foss, about forty miles up the river; the second, and the best on the whole river, is Galgo-guoika, or Kjæring Foss. The **next foss is** about seven miles higher **up**, at the **mouth of the Utsjok river,** where good **quarters may possibly be had at the house** of the pastor. **The next foss is at** the **mouth of** the Levvojok **river, and the next** at the mouth of the **Valjijok river.** After this, not many good places **will be found** till arriving at the Lappish village, Karasjok, **or** further **up,** in Anar Elv. At the above-named places magnificent sport may be had. Salmon of a very large size **are** taken, and long lines and stout tackle are absolutely requisite. At Karasjok a **visit will** probably be paid to the Lensmand, especially when **it is** mentioned that this gentleman has a capital cellar of **wine,** and, moreover, English beer and porter—no despicable treat in these northern latitudes. He is extremely hospitable. If he be not at home, the traveller has **still** permission to help himself, and can either leave the money there, **or** pay it to any Handelsmand or Lensmand in **Finmarken.** Such liberality is of course beyond abuse!

Above Karasjok good fishing may be had at Assebakte.

A friend of mine, who has had much experience on the river, told me that he found 9—11 P. M., and 1—6 A. M. the best times for fishing. It little matters when one sleeps in those sunlight nights!

In calm, sultry weather, the musquitoes are very troublesome: the atmosphere at times is so thick with them "that it is almost possible to cut your name out among them" a gentleman told me. It requires a little manœuvring to keep them out of the tent. The best plan is, on entering, to close the entrance as quickly as possible, and then to commence "blowing a cloud," when they will congregate in the top of the tent, and can thus more readily be disposed of with a damp towel, or bough of birch wood.

Lax Elv is at the bottom of the Porsanger Fjord, and is about eighty miles east of Hammerfest. It has not a very large body of water. The banks are but thinly inhabited, so that a tent is quite necessary. Salmon run up about thirty-five miles. The steamer stops at Kistrand, about twenty-five miles from the mouth. Men should be engaged at Kistra, and some arrangement be made about the fishing. Information can be obtained from the Pastor, Foged, or Handelsmand. This river will be too small to remain there all the summer. **The fishing commences about** ten miles from **the** mouth.

The STABURS ELV, about ten miles distant, can also be tried; and the TABÖRSNÆS ELV, **a** little to the left, about fourteen miles distant, can also easily be visited. And lastly, the BÖRS ELV, opposite to Kistra, will at least afford some first-rate sea-trout fishing.

There is a small river at the bottom of Rep Fjord, about twenty-five miles north of Hammerfest, which, **I am told,** is worth **trying.**

The ALTEN ELV **is a fine** salmon **river, running out into** Alten Fjord. Magnificent **sport has** been had in it. **The** whole of this river **is leased for a** number of years. **Salmon run up it for** twenty-five miles, to a foss, **which** obstructs their further progress. It is a populous district.

Little facilities have hitherto been afforded for fishing, as a portion of the inhabitants formed themselves into a community, and exercised a monopoly for a number of years. This right, however, is questioned, and will be probably ultimately abolished, as an appeal against it will be made to the higher courts, if not otherwise set at rest. **Like most of the** rivers in Norway, **this** splendid stream is greatly injured by the selfish **and** destructive proceedings of the inhabitants in staking and dragging. The executive is now endeavouring, by means of enactments, to check this evil, but the remissness of the authorities who should see that the regulations are carried out is so palpable that the law is comparatively a dead letter.

There is a nice little stream about seventeen miles further out in the Fjord, by Talvig Præstegaard, where there are one or two good places. The fish do not run large there. Also two rivers at the bottom of Qvœnanger Fjord may be tried; they often hold good fish. Char will generally take a fly greedily in all these rivers.

Reisen Elv, to the south of Alten, is a fine river. It lies about fifty miles east of Tromsoe, in a valley running over that distance into the interior. It has a good body of water, with several fosses of no great height. Salmon run up a long way. Owing to the character of the stream, they will not take a fly, I am informed, though they are exceedingly abundant.

An acquaintance of mine travelled by land, in 1859, from Bosekop to the Reisen Elv, or rather, by land to Qvœnanger Fjord, about fifty-five English miles, and thence by boat by the islands of Spilderen and Kaagö to the Reisen. "I reached Reisen," he informed me, "at 6 p.m., and got excellent quarters at Landhandler Lund's; at ten, walked about two English miles up the river to investigate it (in fact, the main reason of my expedition). The water was very thick, and they told me it was often so in summer. The first fishing place is about fourteen English miles up the river, and there is a still better one at from twenty to thirty miles up. At a distance of about sixty to seventy miles from the mouth, there is a foss where I heard that salmon were very plentiful, and that the river was always clear there; but that unluckily it cannot be fished from a boat, and the rocks are so high that if you hook a fish from land you cannot gaff him. Very few Englishmen seem to have tried this river. One has noted in the book at Lund's (1857) that he had had good sport. But nobody seems to have tried up by the above-named foss. The great drawback to the Reisen is evidently the mud. I know but too well from experience what a plague that is, especially in the short salmon season of the north. If I ever come back there I will try and get above the source of the mud, up to the foss, and see whether it be not possible to fish the pool. I should think there would be but little chance of sport before the end of June."

The steamer stops at Skjerve Island, about twenty miles from the mouth of the river. This island is of tolerable size, containing the parish church and the parsonage house. There is good ryper shooting in the neighbourhood.

SKIBOTN ELV, in Lynge Fjord, is a nice river, and is well worth a trial; there is a station here. Also BALS FJORD ELV, not far distant. They are both small rivers, but hold salmon.

The **Maals Elv** is a fine salmon river, south of Tromsoe. Its banks are thickly inhabited. I believe the greater part, if not all of it, to be engaged. Salmon run up thirty miles. The steamer stops at Maalsnæs, at the mouth of the river. It is one of the best-cultivated districts in **Finmark**.

A few miles to the south of this there are two **small rivers**, running out into the Fjord opposite to Klöven, two stations short of Maalsnæs.

The northern rivers are of course later than those in the south. I believe the best time for the Alten and the Tana is about the second week in July.

"A knowledge of the waters, which experience alone can give, is needful to insure success in the northern rivers, otherwise days are lost in fishing places where there are no fish. Early in the season the deep pools below the fosses and **rapids are best**. Later on the fish take to the strongest streams, and in autumn lie above the largest falls and rapids. Here it **requires nerve**, good **boatmen, and stout tackle. In such places**, by a skilful stroke at the moment of hooking your fish, you **may succeed in** turning him up stream, otherwise you **lose him to a certainty**. It is hazardous work, and requires experience."

Game in Finmarken is principally confined to ryper, hares, and ducks. The reindeer, of which many will **be seen, are for the** most part tame, the property of the

Lapps. Elk are not found. Excellent ryper-shooting may be had on Karlsö, Loppenö, Hadselö and Houkö near Tromsoe. As many as fifty brace a day have been bagged! I am of opinion that but very little shooting is to be had now-a-days on the mainland. Some twenty years ago black game were numerous, but they are certainly not so at the present day. On the islands, however, wonderful sport may be had. The steamer stops at the first two islands, where tolerable accommodation may be found.

Bears are numerous, the average number killed being $22\tfrac{8}{15}$ per annum. Some parts of Finmarken are first-rate for bear hunting. A Norwegian pastor who resided in the N.E. towards the Russian frontier, told a friend of mine that "there was a hill in his parish where I might feel certain of seeing a bear any day I went there. The people," he added, "were afraid to meddle with them."

The island of Senjen is noted for bears; and I should say there possibly might be some fishing to be had there. The valley of the Reisen also is good for bears.

NORDLANDS AMT.

This large province is bounded on the south by north Throndhjems Amt, east by Sweden, north by Finmarken, and on the west by the sea. It is divided into three Fogderies—Helgeland in the south, Salten in the north, and Lofoten, Vesteraalen, including the islands. It contains 31,376 square miles.

Unfortunately, my information concerning this Amt is very scanty; in fact, north of the **Vefsen** river it is comparatively a "terra incognita." **The means of communication in the interior are but small, there being scarcely any** roads at **all; so that there is but** little wonder that sportsmen have frequented places in preference which were more accessible, and which afforded fewer impediments to locomotion.

But that a visit **to** Nordland **would be found extremely remunerative I entertain not the** slightest **doubt;** though, at the same **time, I do** not think any **single river,** with the **exception of the** Vefsen, to be capable of showing permanent sport.

In the **extreme north,** in Ofoten Fjord, there are one or two small rivers which may possibly afford sport; but I am afraid to **say** that such will be the case. I will, however, name them.

The first is **Hartvig Elv,** a small river running into Harjangen Fjord, a branch of the **Ofoten Fjord.** A few **miles south of this come** Rombaken Fjord and Bais **Fjord, into which two rivers** of the same names respectively flow. Again, a little to the south is Elvegaards Elv, running into Sjomen Fjord. Between the mouth of the Ofoten Fjord and Tys Fjord there are several small rivers; but I regret to say I can give no information about them. But for those who wish to explore in these parts, Lödingen would be the station at which to quit the steamer.

In **Tys** Fjord there **is a** small river **at the bottom of** Kjöbs Fjord. **In North** Folden Fjord there are also a few small rivers; and the GJENDALS ELV, STOR ELV, in South Folden Fjord, and one or two others, may be tried. I should imagine that these rivers have in all probability never been fished by Englishmen.

The steamer stops at Bodö, at the mouth of the Salten Fjord, whence the BEIEREN ELV **can** easily be **reached** by boat-skyts. Though a small river, it is **said to be** a very good one. It has been **fished** by Englishmen; but whether taken up **or not I cannot** say with certainty. **A little to the east** of this is a small river running **out at a** place named Sandvig, and again to the east, SALTEN ELV. I believe that very good sport may at times be had in this river. Between this and **the** Ranen Fjord there are several small rivers, but concerning which I know literally **nothing.**

Kobberdal is the stopping-station for this **fjord,** whence boat-skyts can **be** taken. The RANEN **ELV** at the extremity of this fjord **is,** I am informed, **an** excellent **river** in comparison with its size. Salmon, however, are **only** able to ascend a very inconsiderable distance; in fact **not** more than one mile. Within this space the fishing **is** said to be something marvellous.

My informant, a Norwegian pastor, a skilful fisherman himself, tells me that he is of opinion that no Englishman has ever fished here. I have since learnt that this river was fished by an Englishman about ten years ago, but with what success I cannot say. I believe, however, that he considered the state of the water extremely variable. Above the foss, which prevents the fish going higher up, there is very superior trout-fishing to be had. The DALEN ELV, BJERKEDALS ELV, and RYTSAA, all in this fjord, are capable at times of affording fair sport. So that I am inclined to think, taking everything into consideration, the exploration of these rivers will not prove time lost. And lastly, there is a small river running into this fjord about one mile and a half above Mo Church. The property owning the fishing, which is well spoken of, is named Selfors.

Opposite to the mouth of the Vefsen, a small river named the DREVJE may be tried.

The VEFSEN ELV, which runs into Vefsen Fjord, is a good salmon stream. The salmon go up it only about seven miles, a foss preventing their further progress. I had been under the impression that salmon ran up this river to the distance of twenty-two miles. Indeed, I have repeatedly been told as much; and this but affords an additional proof as to how very guardedly one should receive hearsay information. The name of the second foss, which is, in fact, about that distance from the mouth, is "Lax Fossen;" and this has probably given rise to the idea that salmon may be found higher up the river. My informant, who has himself fished the river, tells me that he considers it next to impossible for salmon to get over the lower foss, though some of the inhabitants averred that they did so late in the season: this, however, he seems to doubt; and indeed the information afforded by the Bönder is seldom to be relied on. The fishing in the Vefsen is very limited in extent. There are only two pools of any consequence—one immediately below the foss, and the other about one mile lower down. Occasionally magnificent sport may be had; but it is a very uncertain river, and is very liable to be flooded, when it becomes so thick as to render fishing impossible. Moreover, during the latter part of July there is usually too little water, which, added to the quantity of timber that is constantly being floated down it, renders the likelihood of obtaining sport very precarious. The fishing is let on lease. Sannæsöen is the nearest station for the Vefsen.

In the extreme south there is a small river, VARDALS ELV, in Bindalen parish, also a small river at the end of Lang Fjord. There are several small rivers running into Vel Fjord, a little to the north, which hold salmon. I have, as it will be noticed, been extremely cautious about recommending rivers in this province, as my information has been so scanty; but there is nothing I would like better myself than to devote a summer or two to the Nordland rivers.

Some little salmon fishing may, I am told, be got in the Lofoten islands. Thus, in Dverberg parish, in Andö, near the church, fair sport may at times be got. In Sortlands parish, in Hindö, there is a tolerably sized stream running by a property named Osvold Gaard. Also in Vest Vaagen there is a small river running by Borgo parsonage, where the fishing is said to be good. I merely mention these rivers in case any traveller should find himself among these beautiful islands, where there is so much to admire in the grandness of the scenery.

The shooting in this Amt is not considered very good. And to begin with bears. Nordland stands at the head of all the Amts in the country in this respect. The average number killed is $34\frac{4}{15}$; but owing to the density of the forests it is almost impossible to find them. Elk deer are not found; and the same may be said of rein as in Finmarken, namely, that they are nearly all tame herds.

The shooting on the islands is well spoken of.

I have not been able to learn much about the shooting in Saltdal, and in the Ranen valley, but have been told that it is good. This, however, I cannot guarantee. A friend of mine who has shot for two seasons in the valley of Vefsen gives the shooting to be had there a rather bad character. "I have shot a few capercalzie, some woodcocks, ducks, plovers, &c., but I don't think, in two seasons, I saw more than a brace of ryper —no hjerper, though nearly every day I was through the woods or on the fjelds, and had good dogs. I once crossed the fjelds from the Vefsen to Hals Fjord, about twenty-five English miles, and saw no game of any description, though, I must add, I had no dog with me at the time. Very good ryper-shooting may, however, be had on the Lofoten isles."

North Throndhjems Amt.

This Amt is bounded on the east by Sweden, south and west by South Throndhjem Amt and the sea, and north by Nordlands Amt. It contains about 178 square miles, and is divided into three Fogderies— Stör and Vardals in the south, Inderoen in the middle, and Numedal in the north.

Proceeding from Throndhjem, which is situate in the extreme north of South Throndhjems Amt, the first river we come to is Stördals Elv. There is a station at Helle on this river, where also there is a ferry, about sixteen miles east of Throndhjem. It is an early river: the salmon go up about twenty-eight miles to Nustad Foss. It rises very rapidly, and is frequently flooded.

Properties **owning** the fishing are Værnæs Præstegaard, Hove, and Ofsti near the mouth. **The** inhabitants fish a good deal themselves, **both with** rod and net.

The next river of any importance **is VÆRDALS ELV, a short distance** to the north of Levanger, **between which** place and Throndhjem there is steam communication. Salmon go up to Vuku, where the road to Stockholm, running through the beautiful and well-cultivated valley **of** Værdal, **crosses it.** Here it commences to be **precipitous.** The best time for fishing in **this river** is **early in July. It is about thirty miles** distant from Helle, mentioned above.

The best fishing **is high up in the river.** The trout-fishing is said to be **very good in this river.**

About twenty-five or twenty-six miles to the north is the famous Stenkjær, where the river from Snaasen Vand empties itself into the Throndhjem Fjord. The scenery in this neighbourhood is surpassingly beautiful; and as the fishing is also first-rate, it cannot **be** too highly **recommended to the** notice of sportsmen. There is a good station **at** Stenkjær; and here **the** fishing is excellent.

The right of **fishing on this river** belongs to a Fru Gram, owner **of a property named** By, with the exception of the last mile and **a** half, which belongs to Hegge Gaard. The portion **of** the river between Fossum **Vand and** the lake above, though **short, is**

capable of affording excellent sport. Whoever fishes in this part will do well to secure the services of one Henrik, a Huusmand, living at **Fossum** Plads; he is a good fisherman, and is well acquainted with the river.

Every information about the fishing in this river can be obtained from Herr Moe, a merchant residing at Stenkjær.

The AUGNA ELV, running into the last a short distance above Stenkjær, will probably afford good sport. Salmon go a long way up it. Helge **will be found** a fair station to put up at.

The fishing under **Fossum** Foss is said to be very superior.

The FIGGE or LODS ELV is also a likely stream: the right of fishing belongs to the following properties— Bruun, Löd, and Ryg.

The ANDRO ELV, running in at the northern extremity of Snaasen Vand, which is forty miles long, abounds with trout of a large size.

There are several **small** rivers on the western coast of the Throndhjem Fjord, which may occasionally afford sport, *e. g.*, at Lexviken, Mosvik, and Östvik north of Stenkjær. This last-named place can be reached by carriole from Stenkjær in a very short time, and is on the direct road to the Namsen.

At Overgaard, two stations beyond this, at the

bottom of Lyngen Fjord, a branch of the Namsen Fjord, fishing can be had in the Öy river.

From this place, which is about thirty miles from the mouth of the Namsen, the traveller will meet a small river, the BRAAGNA ELV, running through Bangdalen. It is a nice little river, and is perhaps capable of affording occasional sport.

The NAMSEN ELV, so noted for its splendid fishery, rises in Nams Vand, 1,300 feet above the level of the sea, and runs with many bends and turns in a south-westerly, and subsequently in a westerly course. Its length is about 120 miles. It can either be reached by steamer from Throndhjem, or by the route of Stenkjær, just named.

As may be supposed, it is a very rapid stream, and very liable to be flooded. Indeed, the water will rise from twenty to twenty-four feet in an incredibly short time. At a distance of about forty-two miles from its mouth is the magnificent Fiskum Foss, one of the most majestic falls in the whole country, being 580 feet broad, and 156 feet high.

The fishing immediately below this is, beyond compare, superb.

The fishing in this river does not properly begin before arriving at Vie, about twenty-five miles from the mouth, the part below this being too deep to allow of salmon taking a fly. The middle of June is the earliest period at which one can begin fishing. I had thought July to be the earliest time, but have been told by a friend of mine, who has had much experience in the northern rivers, that he is of opinion that the best fishing may be had in the Namsen before July. "From my experience of the northern rivers," he writes me word, "I should say that in most of them the season begins about the middle of June, and fish may often be killed still earlier; and although you do not get nearly so many fish as in July, yet their average size is much greater. I have noticed also that the fish are usually better hooked in the earlier part of the season, and that the proportion of lost fish gradually increases as it advances. Another advantage of June fishing is that you are not troubled with grilse."

It is extremely difficult to say how much of this river is actually leased. It may be taken up from Fiskum Foss as far as Grongs Præstegaard; but I much doubt whether pastor Rambeck, who owns part of the best fishing near Fiskum Foss, has let his right away. All the way down to Vie the river abounds with magnificent pools, and as the road runs by it, information can be readily gleaned at the different stations. (For further remarks the reader is referred to Murray's 'Handbook,' p. 206.)

It is necessary to have experienced boatmen on this river, to insure sport, two for each boat. These have the privilege of claiming what they call their *specie fish*, *i.e.*, a dollar for every fish above a certain weight. Moreover, the tackle used must be **extra** strong, and the **lines** must be long ones. Plaited **gut casting** lines should always be used in preference to twisted **ones**. That distinguished fisherman, Sir H. Parker, killed **on** this river a salmon of sixty pounds weight after **a little** more than an hour's battle. "It was caught on a number six or seven **hook**; wings, two golden tippets **dyed** crimson, sprigged with mallard, teal, golden pheasant, and Argus pheasant; horns, blue macaw; head, black; **body,** claret pig's wool; tag, **red** mohair, ribbed gold **twist.** . . . **On the same** day he **bagged** nine others, one **of forty pounds;** one thirty pounds; one eighteen **pounds; one fifteen pounds;** and the rest from eight pounds downwards." Perhaps a better day's sport has never been known!

I believe that little of this river is *permanently* engaged.*

Should there, however, be no opportunity **for fishing** in any part of this noble river, which **I much** question, the SANDDÖLA ELV, which runs into **it near** Grong, should be tried: it is **a** fine river. **On** the opposite shore there is the BJÖR ELV, running out of Eids Vand. Good fishing may **be** had here. Salmon go up as far

---

* *Vide* Appendix.

as Höiland. The station at Romstad **above this** will be found to afford fair accommodation.

Proceeding northwards by the road **the Öy Elv,** near Öy station, should **be** tried.

On the southern shore of Indre Foldens Fjord there are several **small** rivers which no doubt will occasionally yield sport; but **I** have been unable to gather any certain information concerning them.

Fishing can be had **in** a river running into Oplo Fjord **in Kolvereid** parish; and there **is a nice little river running** in at the end of Sor Salten **Fjord.**

After leaving Öy **the** next station **is Kongsmoen** on **the** Öy river. The fishing **here is well spoken of.**

There is a small river I **omitted to** mention running into **Veterhuus Botn,** a little **north** of Namsos. I believe **its name** is Ausnæs Elv. I have heard that fair sport may occasionally be had.

I have heard **of** there being fishing in a river at Aafjord, belonging, **I** believe, to the pastor.

With regard **to** trout-fishing, it may be remarked that all the above-named rivers will show excellent sport, especially the Namsen, above Fiskum Foss. But **few,** however, would come so far merely for the sake of **such** small fry.

In Stordal and Værdal Fogderies black game, capercalzie, and **ryper** are plentiful, but reindeer are not so numerous.

In the **neighbourhood** of Snaasen Vand rein are **more** plentiful, and excellent capercalzie, black game, **and ryper** shooting may be **had**. On the islands duck and wild fowl are abundant.

In the northern parts of this Amt reindeer **are** abundant, but elk are scarce. Red deer may be **found** on Otteröen, which is **easily** reached from Namsos. The ryper shooting on this island is excellent.

Overhalden, in Grongs parish, is **a good neigh**bourhood for ryper, capercalzie, and black game; and tolerable ryper shooting **is to be** had on Gjed Fjeld in the same parish.

Bears are rather **numerous**; $30\tfrac{7}{13}$ being the **average number** killed **per** annum. Lynxes are also **often met with.**

South Throndhjems Amt.

This Amt borders on Sweden to the east: on the south it is bounded by Hedemarken and Christians **Amts**; on the west **by Romsdal** Amt; and on the **north by** Throndhjem Fjord and north Throndhjems **Amt.** It contains 143 square miles.

The Guul Elv is a renowned salmon river. It rises **to the north of** Roraas, and runs **with a** north-westerly course to Soknæs, where it crosses the Throndhjem **road** over the Dovre Fjeld; thence it turns to the north, **and** falls out into an arm **of** the fjord some few miles **to the**

south-west of Throndhjem. The steamer to the north touches at Throndhjem. (For other routes, *vide* Bennett's 'Handbook of Routes,' 1, 2, and 3.) Salmon go up this river about forty miles to Svelget in Aalen parish. A great portion of the fishing in this river is usually taken up, as, for instance, at Soknæs. At Bogen, a few miles east of this, the fishing is well spoken of, and at Rogstad. As the road runs by the river all the way, there may possibly be found a few places where leave to fish can be had. Its tributaries, the EINA ELV, running into it near Bogen, the HAUKLA, and STAAVIL, a few miles to the west, should be tried.

The ÖRKLA ELV had formerly a bad reputation, owing to certain parties having met with poor sport one season. It is, however, an excellent salmon river, and is capable of showing very good sport. Salmon go up in it to Havdals Foss in Rennebo parish, south of Meldal. A branch road from Flaa runs by it (*vide* Bennett's 'Handbook of Routes,' 2). At Fandrem, near its mouth, good fishing is to be had, and also in the neighbourhood of Gumdal, where there is an exceedingly good station. But perhaps the best place on the whole river is at Langsæter, about fourteen miles above Fandrem. Hereabouts there are at least twenty or thirty pools. Good quarters can also be had; but I believe most, if not all, of the fishing in this river to be taken.

The early part of July is the best season, I have been told, for fishing this river, but should think it might be tried earlier. At Kirkesæter there is a likely river running from a lake into Hevne Fjord.

The SKAUGDAL ELV, north-west of Throndhjem, is also a good river, though small, in Statsbygd parish. Good fishing may be had at Uddue station, where there is a foss, immediately below which capital sport may be had. Above the foss the trout-fishing is all that could be wished. The steamer from Throndhjem stops here. A few miles to the north of this there is a small stream named the NORD ELV, which may sometimes yield fair sport. Further again to the north are three small rivers close together, NORDALS ELV, STORDALS ELV, and SÖRDALS ELV. They may probably be worth trying. They can be easily reached from Valdersund, where the steamer to the north stops. Beyond this, again to the north, there is a small river running into the fjord in Björnor parish.

The steamer stops near this also. And in the extreme north of all is the STEINDALS ELV, which may perhaps at times be worth the fishing.

Returning now to Throndhjem there is the NID ELV, which, though it affords but small space for fishing, is yet, for that little, first-rate. Salmon go up to Leer Foss, about three miles and a half above Throndhjem. Immediately below the foss there is a magnificent **pool, and good** sport may be had here. The fish **run large, and** have been taken **up to forty pounds in weight.** The river in question belongs to a gentleman of the name of Overston. The trout-fishing in the above-named **rivers** is unquestionably good.

Good trout-fishing **may** be had in THYDA ELV, running into the east end of Selbo Söen; and as the road runs by it for a long way, fair accommodation may be obtained. The fishing also in Selbo **Sö** is highly spoken **of by Belton** in his 'Two Summers in Norway.'

There is also good trout-fishing to be had some few miles from Roraas. **The apothecary in** this (so-called) town, **who is an ardent disciple of the** gentle art, will give the stranger much useful information. If I remember right, he speaks English.

Ptarmigan are abundant in this neighbourhood. Drivstuen, on **the Dovre** Fjeld, will be found an **excellent** station to put up at. Good ryper-shooting **can** be had here, and reindeer are not unfrequent. At **Opdal,** a few stations higher up, where the road **branches off** to Sundal, the shooting is well-spoken of; also at Sogndal and Budal. Good shooting, too, can be had in Örkedal (Gumdal is a good station to put up at) and on the heights surrounding the Guul Valley. At Sælbö, also, good sport is to be had. Doubtless the **shooting over the** whole of this Amt is good; but I have confined myself to those localities concerning which I have reliable information.

On Hitteren, red-deer shooting may be had (*vide* Murray's 'Handbook,' p. 253); but they are rapidly diminishing in number, and will ere long, in all probability, become extinct on that island. "In 1861," a gentleman informs me, "I did not certainly see more than one-third of the number I had seen three years before. The reason evidently is, that they are over-hunted by the proprietors, whom the ready market afforded by the steam communication with Throndhjem tempts to convert their venison into dollars. It is on this account, also, that there are no good heads on the whole island."

Red-deer shooting is, moreover, rather expensive work. In the first place, leave must be obtained of the proprietor, who not only expects the quarry, but a payment of three dollars for every deer that may be killed, and one dollar for the guide; and after all it is but tame work compared with reindeer hunting. In the north-western part of this island a fair sprinkling of black game and capercalzie may be found. Ryper are scarce, though there may be some on the sea side of the island. There is a great deal of marshy ground, where one would naturally imagine snipe to resort in great numbers, but I am not aware that they do come there.

A friend of mine writes me word that in 1858 he

explored the valley of Örkedal to the source of the river, for the express purpose of investigating the shooting, and that he is of opinion that good general sport may be had in it. "Several points," he adds, "might be named as head-quarters. I think Kalstad might be as good as any, which, though not so good a station as Gumdal, is better situated for sport. At Haarstad, a small but pretty comfortable station, we were told that at Neerskoven, seven miles distant, there was excellent ryper-shooting, and a Sæter close by. Lower down the valley hares were said to be very plentiful, but we could not find any; perhaps because we had no "hare-hunde." Næverdalen * would, I have no doubt, be a very good point, and the station is tolerably comfortable. The trout-fishing ought to be particularly good there, and the river is close to the station-house."

The steamers to the north stop at Havn Hitteren. I forget what the average of bears is for this Amt, but in 1860 thirteen were killed; in 1859, nine; in 1858, five; in 1857, six; in 1856, fifteen.

Romsdal Amt.

This Amt is, I should say, held in higher estimation, both by tourist and sportsman, than any in Norway. Abounding in beautiful scenery of a varied nature,

* Næverdalen is, however, over the border, in Hedemarken Amt.

smiling and fertile valleys, lofty mountains, brawling cascades, and noble rivers, it presents to the tourist in search of the picturesque all that can be desired; while the ample facilities of its rivers and fjelds offer to the sportsman abundant employment. The valley of the Rauma is considered to be the most beautiful of the many beautiful valleys of Norway. Its noble mountains, with their alpine peaks, lend a charm to it which the tamer, though still lovely, aspect of Gudbrandsdal fails to impart. I doubt much whether any mountain pass in Switzerland can surpass it. Pages and pages might be written on it, and still signally fail to convey but a very feeble impression of what a personal inspection would produce.

But as in writing these pages it has been my determination not to be led astray by a love for the picturesque, but simply to confine myself to such facts as may be of use to the lover of sport, I must turn aside from such temptation, and endeavour to act up to my purpose.

Romsdal Amt is bounded on the north and east by S. Throndhjem Amt; on the south by S. Bergenhuus Amt; and on the west by the sea. It contains 125 square miles, and is divided into three Fogderies— Sondmör in the south, Romsdal in the middle, and Nodmör in the north.

If not pressed for time, the sportsman will do well

to travel *viâ* Christiania, so as not to miss the scenery of the Mösen and of Gudbrandsdal.

This Amt is intersected by three principal valleys—Romsdal, Sundal, and Surendal, named after the rivers flowing through them.

In the extreme south there are many small rivers, **which** may be worth trying, as sport is occasionally, though by no means always, to be had in them. And as many of them are **not** named in the map, I will, as far as I **can,** supply the omission by mentioning their names.

And first at Vanelven, in the extreme south-west of Sondmör, there is a small river, about thirteen miles long. **A little to the east of this is** Birkedals Elv, falling out into the fjord near Kile, where there is a station. It runs from a lake, and its course is only **seven** miles. It can easily be reached from Nöstad, near Horningdals Vand, which will be mentioned **in** the following Amt. **To** the west of this there is a small stream running into the bottom of a fjord.

In the Hjörrendfjord, to the west of the last-named fjord, there is a likely-looking stream running out at Öie, where there is a station.

All **these rivers** can be best and most easily reached by the steamer between Bergen and Throndhjem, which stops at Volden. Hjörrenfjord can be reached **by** carriole from **this place.**

To the east of this fjord is Nordals Fjord, which contains some likely rivers. At Strand, half-way down on the western shore, there is a good stream, and one also immediately opposite at Stordalen. There are stations in the immediate neighbourhood of either river. A little to the south the fjord branches off, one arm going to the right, the other to the left. In the former there is a very good river, VALDALEN ELV, running out at Sylte. It can be fished about seven miles up, and salmon will take a fly very eagerly here. At the extreme end of this arm there are two small rivers, HERDALS ELV and TALFJORD ELV; as they are within easy access from Sylte by boat, they might be tried. In the former of these, at about a distance of four miles from the mouth, tolerable fishing may be had. In the other arm, the Sunelven Fjord, the LANGDALS ELV, at the extreme end, is a good river. It is only about seven miles long. Stadeims Gaard owns the fishery. There is an excellent pool under a foss about two miles from the mouth. A little to the east is the GEIRANGER ELV; it is about ten miles in length. There is now steam communication between Hellesyldt at the end of this fjord and Aalesund. (For further information, *vide* Bennett's 'Handbook.') At Eidevik, a few miles due east of Aalesund, where the steamer stops, there is a small river which may be tried.

Let it be distinctly understood that **I by no means** wish it **to be** inferred **that** salmon-fishing can be enjoyed in all of the above-named rivers. But that fair sport is *occasionally* to **be** had in *some* of them, I **am** quite convinced. And **to** the **sportsman** who is possessed **of a good** constitution, and not adverse to locomotion, the proximity of the above-named rivers to each other may afford him an opportunity of **testing** the greater part of them. And as all the best fishing in this Amt is hired, he must be content to put up **with** what he can get, forming a residue, by **the way, by no** means to be despised.

We now come to Molde, **at the mouth of** the Romsdal Fjord, **a** stopping station **for** the steamers to the north. A small **steamer** runs up the fjord to its extreme **end at** Veblungsnæs, for the route of which, *vide* Bennett's 'Handbook.'

In the neighbourhood of Molde there is some good trout-fishing **to be had.** The view from this **place** over the mountains of Romsdalen is truly magnificent. Before arriving at Veblungsnæs there are one or two small rivers, which, I **am** told, occasionally will yield a little sport; thus **at Vold,** a few miles to the west of the above **village.**

"That **district** of the western coast of Norway which is bounded **by** Romsdal on the west and Sundal on the **east,** affords an unrivalled field to the sportsman, or to the tourist in search of the picturesque. Three noble rivers, equal in their volume of water, and in the length of their course, drain this mountainous region, and fall respectively into the Romsdal, Lange, and Sundal Fjords." We will first consider the RAUMA. This fine river rises in Læsjoværks Vand, near Holager. This lake, which is seven miles long, and 2,050 feet above the level of the sea, is the source of two rivers, the Laagen flowing to the south, and the Rauma to the north. This is a most remarkable instance, and is worthy of note; for not only is it a rare thing for two large rivers to flow in contrary directions from one and the same source, but the Laagen, by falling into the Miösen at Lillehammer, from the other end of which, at Minde, the Vormen ultimately flows into the Glommen, the whole southern part of the country between Frederickstadt and Veblungsnæs is rendered insular.

The RAUMA is a first-class salmon river, and abounds with salmon of a large size. Salmon go up to Ormen Foss, about twenty-one miles from the mouth: about fourteen miles lower down is another foss, below which the fishing is first-rate; for though many salmon do undoubtedly surmount this first obstacle, yet by far the greater part remain below. But for the last seven miles, down nearly to Veblungsnæs, the fishing is truly magnificent, and for four miles immediately below the foss, second, perhaps, to none in **Norway**. Thirty-two fish have been killed in one day by **two rods** immediately **below** the fall. The water is generally discoloured by snow, but this does not prevent the fish from rising. **Good and** cheap quarters **can** be had at Veblungsnæs; and if **the services of one** Jörgen Erichsen, residing there, can be obtained, he will be found a good pioneer. About half a dollar a day will be sufficient remuneration. He is well acquainted with every pool in the river. The greater part of this fishing is **taken up; but** there are still portions **where excellent sport can be** had by asking **permission of the proprietors, and** paying a small sum. **Landmark, who lives** a few miles above Veblungsnæs, and at whose house most comfortable accommodation may be had, owns a part of the Rauma, and will let the fishing.

A little to the north-east of Veblungsnæs there is a **small river, Iisfjord** Elv, running out at **Hein,** which may be worth trying.

About twenty miles to the east of the Rauma is the Eridsfjord Elv, **which** rises in the mountains about **Læsjöe,** and empties itself into an offshoot of the Lange Fjord. About five miles from the sea it passes through **a** lake fourteen miles long; and the fishing **lies wholly** between this lake and the mouth of the river. It abounds in fine **pools** and rapids. The fish **in** this river attain a large size, since, if they succeed in passing the few traps on the river, they obtain complete safety in the deep waters of the lake: thus a larger number escape, year after year, than if they had to run the gauntlet of every trap between the mouth of the river and its source. Only a few pass through the lake and find their way into the river above. In 1860, 2569 lbs. of salmon were taken here by one rod in thirty-nine days' fishing, giving an average of nearly 66 lbs. per day. In the month of August the river abounds in sea-trout, and in some seasons the large lake-trout find their way into it.

The scenery of this district is extremely grand. The valley is wider and more highly cultivated than Romsdal, while the mountains which enclose it are scarcely inferior in height. "For its size," writes my informant, "the lake is perhaps the finest in Europe, equalling in its whole extent the most romantic parts of the Lake of Lucerne."

Near Botten, on a branch of the Sundals Fjord, there is a small river running down from the Skaar Fjeld. It is best reached by carriole from Molde *via* Eide, on the Fanne Fjord.

LILLEDALS ELV, a small river a little to the northwest of Sundals Elv, may at times, perhaps, be found to show sport.

The SUNDALS ELV rises on the Dovre Fjeld, near Drivstuen, and falls into the Sundals Fjord. At Aune, two stations above Drivstuen, the road to Throndhjem branches off to the left, and follows the course of the river to its mouth. It abounds in salmon, sea-trout, and brown trout. After heavy rains, however, it is scarcely fishable, as it becomes discoloured from the marly character of its banks at a particular spot. Moreover, the pools are inconveniently distant from each other, and there are no opportunities afforded for the salmon to congregate in a small space. Salmon go up to Gjöra, about twenty miles up the river. They may, perhaps, get further up, but I am inclined to think there can be no fishing above this place, as here the river passes through a narrow gorge, and becomes, in fact, a torrent.

The scenery of this valley is very grand, though not equal to that of Romsdal or Eridsfjord.

The fishing by Hoaas is taken up; but I should fancy leave can be got to fish higher up stream. This, however, can be ascertained at any of the stations on the river.

North of this river are the TODALEN ELV, running out at Kværnsæt, and the SVINNA ELV; and between the former of these and Sundals Fjord is a river running into Ulvuna Fjord. They are, I believe, capable of showing sport.

Again further to the north is the SURENDAL ELV, a capital salmon river. From Honstad downwards, where it is joined by the Vingdals Elv, there is excellent fishing to be had. I cannot say what part of this river is taken up. The trout-fishing in this river and its tributaries is well spoken of. The road to Christiansund runs through Surendal, so that fair accommodation can be had on the route.

The Bævra Elv, a little to the north of Surendal Elv, is a likely-looking stream. It is about eleven miles long. There are also some smaller rivers running into the Vinje Fjord, in the extreme north of this Amt, of which the Fjelna Elv is the most likely.

From Vinje there is a direct road to Throndhjem, through Örkedal, from which it is distant about thirty miles.

Reindeer shooting may be had on the eastern fjelds in Söndmör Fogderie, in the extreme south of this Amt, called Lang Fjelds; and indeed all the terrain between Sunelven Fjord and Hjorrenfjord will well repay a visit. For those who purpose hunting in this district, Herdal will be found a good place for headquarters. The fjelds also between this and Nordals Fjord are said to be very good. Ryper and black game are abundant, and ptarmigan are always found on the heights. Red deer may be found on the islands Sulö, Hareidsland, and Gurskö. Larsnæs, on this latter island, is a stopping-place for the steamers to the north.

Reindeer shooting can also be had on the Romsdal Fjeld, Troltinderne, and Bröste Fjeld. On the fjelds opposite Veblungsnæs fair ryper **shooting may be** had **on the** low **scrub on** the mountain **side**; while **ducks, and occasionally** snipe, are to be found on **the** low marshy ground **near** the village.

Indeed, the whole terrain from Romsdal to Surendal consists of good shooting ground, and many opportunities for reindeer hunting may be had. It may be remarked that the **most** favourite localities for **reindeer are** treated of in a **separate** chapter **devoted to the** "history, haunts, and habits" **of this noble animal.**

Red deer may also be found on Smölen, the northernmost island belonging to this Amt, and on Erlvaagö. It is not unlikely that there may also be other islands, besides the above named, where these animals may be found; **but I** have **only** mentioned those concerning which **I** had certain and reliable information. **The steamer** to the **north stops** at Edö, a small island **a** little to the south of Smölen. In Surendal, ryper, black game, and hares **are** abundant.

The average number of bears killed in this Amt is $17\frac{4}{15}$ per annum. Veblungsnæs would be excellent head-quarters for any one ambitious of killing a bear; they are numerous in the neighbourhood, and there are several **good** hunters hereabouts. Lynxes, moreover, are not uncommon. It will thus be seen that good general shooting is to be had; but the sportsman must be prepared to rough it if he hopes to be successful.

North Bergenhuus Amt.

This Amt is bounded on the north by the last named; on the south by South Bergenhuus; on the east it touches on Buskerud and Christians Amts; and on the west it is bounded by the sea.

It is divided into two Fogderies, Yttre and Indre Sogn in the south, and Söndfjord and Nordfjord in the north. In the south it is intersected by the Sogne Fjord from west to east. This noble fjord, which has many collateral branches, is about 120 miles in length. The coast is fringed with numerous islands, between which and the mainland the steamers to the north wend their way.

Salmon are to be found in all the rivers running into the Sogne Fjord.

To begin at the extreme end. The LERDALS ELV running out at Lerdalsören, is a good salmon river, and abounds with fish, though they do not attain a very large size. Lerdalsören can be reached either by steamer from Bergen, or by the route of the Fille Fjeld, *via* Christiania. (*Vide* Bennett's 'Handbook,' pp. 18, 44.) The fishing in this river belongs to the properties Tinjum, Moe, and Lysne. That in the neighbourhood of Lysne Gaard is very good. The latter part of June will be found to be the best time for this river, and the fishing is best near the mouth. Lerdalsören is an excellent station, and the station-master is very civil and obliging.

AARDALS ELV, running into a fjord of the same name, a little to the north of Lerdalsören, is often capable of affording excellent sport; but the quantity of water in this river is very irregular. It is best after a good deal of rain has fallen. Fish have been taken, I am informed, up to forty pounds in weight. When the water is very low, salmon run up into a lake which is about five miles in length, and from thence find their way up a river running in at the other end for about three miles and a half. In the autumn the salmon-trout-fishing to be had in this river is exceedingly fine. I believe the fishing here to be engaged, but am not certain. I do not think it was in 1860. I do not know whether fishing can be had in the Jöstedal river near Lyster in the Gaupne Fjord; but it is a likely-looking stream, though, of necessity, a late one, owing to its running down from the glaciers. It is about thirty miles north of Lerdalsören, whence it can be reached by boat-skyts. (For an account of the glaciers *vide* Murray's 'Handbook,' p. 165.)

In Sogndals Fjord, to the west of this, is the AARÖ ELV, which, though not of great extent, yet has a large mass of water. Salmon of an unusually large size have been taken here. I have heard of fish weighing forty-four pounds being captured in this river. They are a beautifully clean fish. This also is a late river, and cannot be fished with success before the middle of July, as the water which comes down from the glaciers is so intensely cold that the salmon will not rise to the fly. I believe this fishing to be engaged.

AURLANDS ELV, running into a branch of the fjord east of Nærödal, abounds with salmon of a large size

SCENE IN AURLANDS FJORD.

The water in this river is very irregular, and the fishing is best after a flood. July is the earliest period at which it can be fished. Sea-trout of a very large size are taken here; and late in the autumn splendid sport may be had. This river is let on lease. There is a small river in the same fjord, at the extreme end, which should be tried. It is called the MOLDA ELV. Salmon of a large size may be taken here, but the water is very variable. It is only after a flood that fishing can be had. In a dry season the river would be a total failure. Moreover, it is terribly trapped. Most of the fishing belongs, I believe, to an "ex-M.P.," Thorstein Fretheim.

In Narödal salmon-fishing may occasionally be had. Gudvangen is a fair station, though not first rate. In the lower part of the Gudvangen river, late in the season, there are a great number of sea-trout, and indeed most of the rivers running into the Sogne Fjord and its branches will be found to afford good sea-trout fishing. A fly with a light-blue body and gold tinsel can be recommended for these fish. It may be remarked that the scenery about here is grand in the extreme. A little way up the valley, the traveller, who is making his way to Bergen by land, will pass Stalheim. The road up the mountain is of a most extraordinary "corkscrew nature," and is a fine specimen of Norwegian engineering skill. On either side of the road are two fine fosses which add considerably to the beauty of the landscape.

There may be possibly some small streams further seawards in the Sogne Fjord; but I think I have named all that are worth mentioning. There is a small river running out at Eidevik in Söndfjord, a little to the north; but I have not met with any one who has ever tried it. It may very likely hold fish.

There are some small streams between this and Nordfjord; and I much doubt whether they have ever been fished. I can hazard no information about them.

But in Nordfjord there are many good opportunities for the salmon-fisher. The steamer to the north stops at Bryggen at the mouth.

The river from Horningdals Vand, running into the fjord, is said to abound with salmon. The river running into the Gloppen Fjord at Sandene, a little to the south, frequently holds good fish. It is named STOR ELV. A little to the east, STRYEN ELV, coming from Opstruen Vaud, can also be conveniently tried. It is a likely stream, though small. There are several smaller rivers in this fjord and its branches; but I have been unable to gather any information concerning them.

In the extensive ranges of mountains in the neighbourhood of Lerdal, Jöstedal, Lyster, and Urland good reindeer hunting may be had.

Aardal would be a particularly good point from which to make expeditions after reindeer. A very clever and intelligent hunter named Hans Natvik, who lives near by, can be highly recommended. On the neighbouring fjelds he usually kills many deer himself every season, and is well acquainted with the whole terrain between this and Tyen Vand. Sletterust is the **best point from which to hunt this, which** is one of the best districts for reindeer in the whole country. Tents are, however, almost a *sine quâ non*, as the Sæters, as is universally the case in the Bergen Stift, are very bad and dirty. A friend writes me word that he crossed the fjeld from Lerdal to Aardal, and that in coming down through the thick scrub which covers the steep sides of the mountains above Vik, his guide informed him that very many bears had been killed there. On the whole there is scarcely a better prospect of sport anywhere in Norway than in the neighbourhood of Aardal. Elks are not found in this Amt.

In Indre Sogn ryper are numerous, and, indeed, abound on all the fjeld sides in low scrub. Capercalzie are common in the woods about Kaupangor and Fronningen on the opposite sides of the Sogne Fjord in Indre Sogn; and Jöstedal abounds in black game. Indeed, I do not hesitate to say that general shooting is pretty good in nearly every part of this Amt; and I have only given prominence to places where I have been informed it is superior. Near Horningdals Vand also the shooting is very fair.

Ducks and all manner of wild fowl will be found in plenty along the coast.

The average number of bears killed is $14\frac{7}{15}$ per annum.

For bear-hunting Lerdalsoren would be admirable head-quarters. In 1860 a hunter living at Qvikne, on the Lerdals Fjord, succeeded in killing in the spring of

GUDVANGEN STATION.

that year three bears at Aerdal. There is a great deal of thick wood here. Bears are also frequently seen in Tönjums Dal, about seven miles from Lerdalsören, and often commit havoc amongst the sheep and pigs. There are some stone huts in the valley; and if one were to establish oneself there for a while, say in May, before the people come up to the sæters, **an uncommonly** good chance of getting hold of a bear might be had. It is rather stiffish walking **on** the mountain-sides above Tönjums **Dal,** but the ground is **very** favourable for **seeing bears.**

South Bergenhuus Amt.

This Amt is bordered on the south by Stavanger **Amt**; on the east by Bratsberg and Buskeruds Amt; and **on** the west by the sea. It contains 141 square **miles,** and is divided into two Fogderies, Söndhordland **and** Hardanger, Nordhordland and Voss. **On the east it is** separated **from** Hallingdal and Nummedal **by a chain** of mountains, Langfjelde, **which** in places **attain** an altitude of 5,400 feet above the sea.

The magnificent Hardanger Fjord intersects this Amt from south-west to north-east, the scenery of which is perhaps the grandest and wildest in the whole country (*vide* Murray's 'Handbook,' p. 178; Bennett's ditto, pp. 25, 26); and as there is weekly steam communication with Bergen, a passage of but a few hours, **its** beauties may readily be explored.

The fishing in this Amt is by no means unimportant In the extreme south there is a small river called Etne Elv, which can be tried; and there is a likely-looking stream running out into a fjord at Fjære, a few miles to **the** north-east. But **neither** of these is of much importance.

About half-way up the Hardanger Fjord at Vikor, on the northern shore, there is a small river, the STEINDALS ELV. As the steamer from Bergen, from which it is about fifteen hours, stops at Ostensjö, a few miles to the north, it might be tried.

Here is the magnificent Ostud Foss, a waterfall of about 700 feet in height (*vide* Murray's 'Handbook,' p. 170).

In Sör Fjord, a collateral branch of the Hardanger Fjord, some fishing may at times be had near Kinservik, on the eastern shore. The steamer stops at Utne, at the mouth of this fjord, whence boat-skyts can be taken. At Odde, the extreme end, there is a small river which may hold salmon. This place may be reached in thirty hours from Bergen by the steamer.

The Folge Fond is in the immediate neighbourhood. The SKJEGGEDALS ELV, running out at Tyssedal, a very few miles higher up, is a nice little stream.

Much sport with salmon in the above-named rivers cannot be guaranteed, but there is little doubt that they may occasionally prove worth trying; and as they are in the midst of the most glorious scenery imaginable, the casual tourist may find it worth while to bear them in mind. From their nature, and owing to the irregularity of their water, they must be best after heavy rains.

The river at Vik, running out in Eidfjord, the

extreme end of the Hardanger, is a nice little river. Good sport has often been had here. This place is within easy distance of the magnificent Vöring Foss, and the scenery in the neighbourhood is of that savage grandeur which can rarely, if ever, be seen in any other parts of Europe (*vide* Murray, p. 169). At Ulvik, where the steamer also stops, a little to the north of Vik, and at Ose, between the two named places, the rivers may be tried.

Proceeding down the fjord again in the direction of Bergen, there are one or two small rivers which may perhaps at times afford sport, *e. g.*, at Strandvik, Haalandsdal. A small river running out at Samnanger, a few miles east of Bergen, in a branch of the Strande Fjord, may also be tried.

In BERGSDAL ELV, a few miles to the north of Bergen, salmon-fishing may occasionally be had.

The VOSSE ELV is a remarkably fine stream. It consists of two arms, one rising near Opheim, and the other near Lange Lake. These meet at Vossevangen, near the church, and pass through Vangs Vand, and Evanger Vand. Capital salmon-fishing may be had at Bölstadören. This latter is a good station, and the river has been much fished by Englishmen. Whether it is leased now I do not know; when I was there five summers ago it was open. Salmon of a large size may be taken, and the trout-fishing is first rate.

Further northwards is the EXINGDAL ELV; it is a very likely-looking stream. There is also another river a little above this running out at Mo. In both of these I believe fair fishing may be had.

Some of the best reindeer ground is to be found in the eastern parts of this Amt. The neighbourhood of Vikör, on the Hardanger Fjord, at Graven, Ulvik, Kinservik, and on the large and extensive range of mountains towards Hallingdal and Nummedal, and to the east of Vossevangen, will be found usually to abound with these animals. Red deer are found on some of the islands off the coast. Ryper, too, are generally plentiful. As the forests in this Amt are comparatively of small dimensions, black game and capercalzie are not so numerous as elsewhere. Of elks, I believe there are none. The average number of bears annually killed is small, being only $1\frac{1}{5}$.

I had always been at a loss to understand why the number of bears killed annually in this Amt was so small; but I have been given to understand, on good authority, that the smallness of the returns must not in this case be taken as any evidence of their scarcity. "On the contrary," writes my informant, "I am inclined to think that in some parts of the Hardanger country, they are more numerous than in any other part of Norway. The reason is, that the peasants here know nothing at all about bear-hunting, and, in fact, seem afraid to venture on it. In one part near Ulvig, where I hunted bears unsuccessfully in 1860, I learnt that a year or two before a bear had been committing **great** depredations; and that the farmers had actually subscribed and sent all the way to Romsdal for an experienced hunter, **who** remained there all the summer. He was, however, no more successful than myself.

"Every year the bears commit grievous havoc in many parts of the Hardanger country. There is no difficulty in *hearing of them* almost anywhere; **but** without a regularly trained bear-dog, which **is not to** be had in that part of the **country**, it is almost hopeless to think of finding them, at least in summer.

"Properly prepared for the campaign, and able to devote plenty of time to it, the bear-hunter would, I am confident, find the mountains bordering the Hardanger Fjord a noble field for operations."

Stavanger Amt.

This Amt is bounded on the south and west by the sea; on the north by South Bergenhuus; and on the east by Lister and Mandals Amt, and Nedenæs Amt. It is divided into two Fogderies, Jædderen in the south, and Ryfylke in the north. Its superficial area is about 76 square miles.

This Amt will be found to present but few attractions.

to the salmon-fisher; but still some sport may be had with a little looking for it.

Beginning in the extreme south, there is a small river running through Sogndal, a few miles north of Hekke Fjord. Salmon-fishing is to be had here at times; it belongs to Eeg parsonage. Salmon may also be found in TENGS River, and in OUGNE River, in the parish of Ekersand. They had better be fished near their mouths.

In FIGGE ELV, a little to the south of Stavanger, some fair fishing may occasionally be had. It is a small river, but the fish go up it for a long distance. Schjefveland will be found to be a comfortable station to put up at.

In SULEDALS ELV, running out at Sand into one of the arms of the Bukn Fjord, fishing may be had. Salmon go up to the extreme end of Suledals Lake.

VIGEDALS ELV, a little more to the west of this, is said to hold salmon.

To the north-east of Stavanger there are several small streams in the parish of Strand and Hjelmeland; but I have been able to learn but little concerning them. Those who wish to try their luck hereabouts had best inquire of Dr. Stang, or of Herr Candidatus Juris Baade, who is a government inspector of salmon fisheries. Both these gentlemen live in Stavanger.

It may, however, be remarked of all the rivers in

this Amt, that they are very short, and that they rise very suddenly after rain. Moreover, the timber-floating which is constantly going on in them will be found such a serious annoyance as to render the fishing anything but profitable. And even when the water may be clear of such impediments, the fish are so extremely shy as to take a fly very unwillingly.

The neighbourhood of Stavanger being totally devoid of wood, much shooting cannot be expected in this part. Hares are, however, tolerably plentiful. In the autumn immense flocks of snipes visit the neighbouring marshes, when excellent sport may be had.

Reindeer are found in the neighbourhood of Höle, south-east of Stavanger, and of Aardal and Suledal, and on the fjelds forming the eastern frontier. Red deer may be found in Skjold, on the borders of South Bergenhuus Amt in the extreme north, also in Hinderaa, Vikeland, and Imsland parishes near Sand. In these districts ryper are generally plentiful, black game not abundant, but a good sprinkling of snipes, plovers, and hares may be found. Here also the white, black, and blue fox may be met with. All along the seacoast good opportunities for wild-fowl shooting may be found. In the spring, shortly before breeding-time, thousands of eider-duck congregate in the fjords.

Bears are not numerous, the average number killed amounting only to two a year. In the summer of 1862 two young lads managed to kill a bear under rather peculiar circumstances in the neighbourhood of Stavanger.

A bear had been committing great havoc among the sheep and cattle for some time past, and had somehow managed to elude the hunters. So the two youths in question determined to try their luck, and see if they could not bring Bruin to book for his misdeeds. Armed with two old rusty fowling-pieces they set off one morning in quest of him, and after searching about for some time were fortunate enough to espy the bear. When within about thirty yards they each let fly. One of the guns, however, refused to go off, but the other fortunately inflicted a mortal wound, or else they might not have escaped so easily. Finding that the animal was unable to attack them they now advanced, and one of them, picking up a good-sized stone, hurled it at the beast, intending, if possible, to kill it. Meanwhile, the other one had reloaded his piece, and, discharging it in Bruin's ear, put him *hors de combat*.

Lister and Mandals Amt.

This Amt is bounded on the north and east by Nedenæs Amt; on the south by the sea; and on the west by the last-named amt.

It contains about 43 square miles, and is divided

into two Fogderies, Lister and Mandal. Its principal towns are Christiansand and Mandal.

Five valleys intersect Mandals Fogderie—Topdal, Torrisdal, Sogndal, Mandal, and **Undal**—all running nearly parallel with each other, and separated the one from the other by mountain ranges of no great altitude.

Mandals Fogderie contains many and very important salmon fisheries. And first, the TOPDALS ELV, a continuation of OTTEREN ELV—the river which runs through Sætersdal—is **a fine** salmon stream. Salmon go up in it to Boen Foss. A part **of this river is** owned by an Englishman who has **a property** on it; but whether all the fishing is taken **up, or not,** I cannot say with **certainty.** It abounds with fish, but they are generally of small size, and of poor quality.

The names of the several properties which have the right of fishing on this river are Gustnæs on **the** western shore **of Topdal** Fjord, Tved, Boen, Kjevik, **and** Drangholt. More accurate information can, however, be obtained in Christiansand. It is an early river, and can for the most **part** be fished **from** land. Bright-coloured flies are recommended.

The TORRISDAL ELV, **a** little to the west, is a large river. **Salmon** go up to Vikelands Foss, beyond which they cannot pass. Quarters and fishing may be had at Vigelund, which is an exceedingly good station. The fishery belongs to Consul Vildt, a Swiss gentleman, who takes great interest in the propagation and breeding of salmon. This **gentleman resides** in or near to the town, and will, I am told, give **permission** to fish. A **small** payment will, however, probably have **to be** made. **It is a very** rapid stream, and the fishing is principally **from boats**. It is, moreover, somewhat later **than** the **Topdal Elv.** Large dull-coloured flies, with a little tinsel, **are recommended.**

The Sogne Elv is a small river, but is, perhaps, worth trying.

The Mandals Elv, running **out by** Mandal, was formerly a very celebrated salmon river; but **bag-nets, poaching,** &c., have considerably deteriorated it. **It might** however, with good management, be still made one of the best in the south of Norway. Some fair fishing may still be had on it. The principal fosses are Kjole Foss, Aase, Noddings, and Skjærveland. Quarters and fishing may perhaps be **had at the properties Holme, Osteboe, Skinsnæs,** Langelund, Möe, and Hesaae. **Mr. Lloyd** recommends B or B B **hooks, fur bodies, with** mixed wings. **In many** parts a boat **is not** requisite. It may be **fished up** to Næs Vand, a little above Lövland, where **there is a** good station.

About seven miles from Mandal to the west is Undals Elv. Salmon go up in it to the upper Öidne Lake. It is an early river, **and** abounds with fish. Quarters and fishing may probably be had at Vigeland,

Skofteland, and Vigmosstad. It may be remarked that it is not a large river, and has not many casts.

About ten miles to the west of this is LYNGDAL ELV. Salmon run up a distance of about eleven miles, to a foss named Qvas Foss. Properties owning the fishing are Qvævik, Qvelland (about a mile and a half above the church). Bergsaker, where the road crosses it, is a fair station. The accommodation in this district is not all that might be desired; but if lovely scenery can in any way make up for this deficiency, there is abundant compensation.

Further to the west is the QVINNA ELV. Salmon can go up in it to Rafoss. The road to Hekke Fjord crosses it at Fede, a good station, where fishing can be had. It is a fine river, and has many likely-looking pools. I do not know whether it is engaged.

The LIRA ELV, a little to the west, is noted for its fine trout-fishing. It is more than probable that salmon may be found in it, but of this I am doubtful. I may remark that all the above-named rivers will afford good sport to the trout-fisher.

Elk are not found in this Amt.

In the fjelds around Siredal reindeer hunting may be had, and good ryper and black-game shooting. On many parts of the coast, snipe and woodcock shooting may be enjoyed. Towards the end of May and beginning of June, myriads of barnacle geese may be found along the coast, and in the fjords. The best general shooting will be found in Siredal. The average number of bears killed in this amt is $2\frac{1}{13}$ per annum.

NEDENÆS AMT.

This Amt is bounded on the north and east by Bratsberg Amt; on the south by the sea; on the west by Lister and Mandals Amt; and on the north by Stavanger Amt, and a small portion of South Bergenhuus Amt. It contains about 90 square miles. The principal rivers are the Nid, Topdals, and the Otteren. The latter of these, as mentioned above, flows into the sea at Christiansand, under the name of the Torrisdals Elv. It is divided into two Fogderies, Nedenæs and Raabygdelag. The salmon and trout fishing in this Amt are very insignificant. The NID ELV, near Arendal, used formerly to be famous for its salmon-fishing, especially below a foss named Rygende Foss; but of late years it has much deteriorated, and I should scarcely think it worth while going out of the way for, to try.

The OTTEREN ELV, in Sætersdal, is said to afford good trout-fishing; but the fact is, Sætersdal has been so little *be-travelled*, that even Norwegians know but little about it. The inhabitants of this valley are a very peculiar race of people, totally unlike what are met with in other parts of the country.*

The TOPDALS ELV, and its tributary the SKJEGGE-DALS ELV, will also afford tolerable trout-fishing, while the lakes are said to abound with good fish.

The shooting in Sætersdal is exceedingly good; ryper, black game, and hares are abundant, while the quantum of bears it yields is by no means insignificant, the annual average throughout this Amt being $21\tfrac{3}{5}$.

The scenery in this valley is very wild and romantic; but the dirty habits of the Satersdölen (the inhabitant of a valley is called Dölen) are proverbial, and have tended, almost as much as its previous inaccessibility, to render it comparatively an unknown district.

BRATSBERG AMT.

This Amt is bounded on the north and east by Buskeruds Amt; on the east and south by Jarlsberg Amt and the sea; and on the west by Nedenæs, and South Bergenhuus Amts.

It is divided into three Fogderies—Nedre Thelemarken, Bamle, and Övre Thelemarken; and contains some of the most picturesque scenery in Norway.

Being but a poor district, the accommodation to be met with is none of the best; and as poverty and dirt

* The habits and customs of this peculiar people will be treated of in a separate chapter.

F

seem generally to bear a direct proportion to each other, neither can be said to form an exception to the rule.

The salmon-fishing in this Amt is extremely unimportant. In fact, I believe the river running up by Skien is the only place where salmon are taken; but I feel pretty confident, from the nature of the water, that no rod-fishing is to be expected here.

On the other hand, it offers numerous facilities to the trout-fisher.

A glance at the map will show that it abounds with lakes large and small, and tributary streams; but I shall confine myself to those in which I have fished myself, or of which I have reliable information.

The eastern end of Bandags Vand by Strængen, where there is an exceedingly comfortable station, and where the landlady thoroughly understands how to make an Englishman comfortable, will be found to afford some excellent sport. The shortest route to this place is by steamer from Christiania to Skien, thence by carriole to Fjærestrand, a distance of only a few miles, on Nordsöen, and by steamer to Ulefoss, which place is only a two to three hours' journey, along one of the best chausées in the country, to Strængen. A steamer goes from this place to Dale, the extreme end of Bandags Vand, along the wildest and most desolate scenery imaginable. The river running into the lake here is a magnificent trout-stream, and has some pools which an ardent fisherman will rejoice to wet his line in. Very large trout can be taken, and those fond of spinning will find good sport by rowing to and fro across the mouth of the river where it debouches into the lake.

The famous Mjös Vand can be reached in one day across the mountains from Dale, and in July will afford excellent sport; but as it is nearly 3000 feet above the level of the sea, it is extremely cold up there. Most of the "Rak Örret" is made from trout caught in this lake; which article of food, perhaps, vies with "Gammel Öst" in its smelling qualities, but is considered a *bonne bouche* and "appetite tickler" by most Norwegians.

Excellent trout-fishing, too, is to be had in Nisser Vand, a large lake running nearly at right angles to Bandags Vand. The direct road from Thelemarken to Arendal runs along its eastern banks. The fish here are as pink as salmon, and are most delicious eating.

Of the lakes and rivers in the extreme north of this Amt I know nothing, but they must afford good fishing; but lying so far from any road, and the want of anything like decent accommodation, must prove a serious drawback to the tourist sportsman. In fact, all through Thelemarken, the stations are, with but few exceptions, disgustingly dirty, and deficient in aught to stay the traveller's stomach but flad-bröd and gröd. Even the mere tourist in **search of** the picturesque will find a light trout-rod an excellent accompaniment. Only, *verbum sap.*, when he catches **his trout, let him,** unless he has a very powerful stomach, **superintend the cooking of them himself.**

The MAAN ELV, flowing from the Mjös Vand into Tin Soen, is a good river. On this, and nearer to Mjös Vand, is the **famous Riukan Foss.**

Near Hitterdal, **famous for its quaint** ship-like church, good trout-fishing may be had.

I have mentioned but few of the lakes and rivers in this province; but those I have named are the most accessible, and are generally considered the richest in fish. (For routes to Thelemarken, *vide* Murray, p. 195, and Bennett's 'Handbook,' p. 28.)

The shooting **over the whole of this Amt is generally good.** The neighbourhood of Strængen **abounds with** hares, snipe, and black game. Ryper are plentiful on all the fjelds. Reindeer are numerous **on the** fjelds about Tinds, Vinge, and Moe **(a few miles** west of **Dalen), and** in the northern **parts of** Övre Thelemarken.

The magnificent Gausta Fjeld, **the** highest mountain in the south of Norway (6000 feet), is never without **a good** sprinkling of rein.

Bears **are** numerous throughout the province; the average number killed **being** $33\frac{11}{13}$ per annum; and I would almost recommend any one desirous of enjoying some bear-hunting to select this Amt in preference to any other in the whole of Norway.

JARLSBERG AND LAURVIG AMT.

This Amt is bounded on the east by the Christiania Fjord; on the south by the sea; on the west by Bratsberg; and on the north by Buskærnds Amt. It contains $18\frac{1}{2}$ square miles.

The only river of **any importance is the LOGEN**, which enters this Amt **on its north-eastern** frontier, and flows into the sea near **the town of** Laurvik. The Logen **is an** excellent **salmon stream, and** was considered by Sir H. Parker **to** be second **to** none in the whole country. Salmon run up to Vittingfoss, in Sandsvær, Buskeruds Amt, their further progress **up the river being** impeded. Kjæro Foss and Vigelstad Foss are considered the best places on the whole river. The water hereabouts is somewhat later than it is lower down. Some portion of this river is taken up by an English gentleman who has bought a property; but there **are** still places, I believe, open to engagement.

The shooting in this Amt is not good, as it is one of **the most** populous in Norway. Reindeer are not **found, for the** country **is flat**; neither, I believe, are **elk**. In the wooded parts of Laurdal some black game may be found; but unless bound for the Logen, the sportsman who expects to find much employment for rod or gun will be disappointed both as regards the fishing and shooting.

Bears are not often met with, the average number killed being only $2\frac{1}{13}$.

BUSKERUDS AMT.

This Amt borders to the north on Christians Amt and North Bergenhuus Amt; to the west on South Bergenhuus Amt; to the south on Bratsberg and Jarlsberg Amts; and to the east on Agershuus Amt and the Christiania Fjord. It is divided into three Fogderies —Buskerud, Ringerike and Hallingdal, and Nummedal. Its superficial area is about $105\frac{1}{2}$ square miles.

With the exception of the Drammen river and the small portion of the Logen river alluded to in the last, salmon are not found in this Amt. A great many salmon go up to Hougsund, a few miles above Drammen; but from the nature of the water I should scarcely think it possible that they will rise to a fly. I have been told, but will not vouch for the truth of it, that some salmon-fishing may be had in a small river running out by Lier, about seven miles east of Drammen.

There is, however, excellent trout-fishing to be had

in many parts of this Amt. And first I would name Hönefoss, about thirty miles from Christiania. The road to it runs by the beautiful Tyri Fjord, at the foot of the famous Krokleven.

At Hönefoss there is a comfortable little inn, a little below the last foss. Two rivers meet here, the one coming from the Rands Fjord, and the other from Spendilen, and united, flow into the Tyri Fjord.

Some very nice fishing may be had at this place, both with fly, and—later on in the summer—by spinning. Trout of a large size are often taken. The fishing all the way up the Spendilen river is good. The other river, from the Randsfjord, will well repay exploring. About ten miles up from Hönefoss there is an excellent part near a flour-mill, situate in the middle of a forest. Both above and below the foss, by which the mill stands, good fishing is to be had.

Being within such easy distance from Christiania, these rivers cannot be too highly recommended to the fisherman who has not much time at his disposal in the country.

The HALLINGDAL RIVER runs some miles west of Hönefoss, and enters the Tyri Fjord a little below Modum. It is a fine river, and abounds with trout. And as the road runs near it up to the Kröderen lake, about fourteen miles from its mouth, accommodation (such as it is) can readily be found.

A short distance below Modum is Björndal, where

fair fishing can be had on the Drammen river. From this place skyts should be taken to Tingelstad, on the Eggedal river, which may be fished up to Medalen. The road runs by it all the way. Good trout-fishing may be had in the Logen river, already spoken of, all the way up to Opdal: the road runs by it to this place. And further up this river the fishing is good, but the accommodation very inferior. The north-western part of this Amt, owing to its inaccessibility, is but little known to the fisherman; but should dirt, fleas, and poor fare not prove insuperable impediments, there is little question but that capital sport may be found.

In the southern part of this Amt the shooting is poor; but both in Hallingdal and Nummedal excellent ryper-shooting may be had. Opdal will be found a tolerable and convenient station as head-quarters.

In the north and north-western parts reindeer are numerous, especially on Reensfjeld, Hemsedals Fjeld; in the extreme north, Nystols Fjeld and Hallingskarven.

Elk are rare. Bears, principally in the northern districts, are not uncommon. The average number killed is $14\frac{10}{13}$. In 1860, however, 23 bears were killed in this Amt.

CHRISTIANS AMT.

This province borders on the Miösen lake, Hedemarken, and Agershuus Amts, on the south and east; on the north it is bounded by Romsdals Amt, and part of South Throndhjem Amt; and on the west and south by Romsdals and Buskeruds Amt. It is divided into three Fogderies—Thoten, Valders, and Gudbrandsdal. Its principal rivers are the Laagen and Rauma, which have their source at either end of Læsje Vand, as mentioned above.

The Laagen, which flows into the Miösen at Lillehammer, has many tributaries; among the most important of which is the Otta Elv, which falls into it at Kringelen, a mountain pass, famous in the annals of Norwegian history for the massacre of Colonel Sinclair. (*Vide* Murray's 'Handbook.') The trout-fishing in the Laagen is not held in high esteem. A great quantity of the large lake-trout are taken in traps at Hunnerfoss, about ten miles north of Lillehammer.

Valders is situate in the southern part of this Amt, and is extremely rich in vegetation and smiling landscape. The beautiful Randsfjord, formed by the confluence of the Dokka and Etnedal rivers, is about 50 miles long, and 290 feet above the level of the sea.

The Valders River rises near Nystuen, the extreme top of the Fille Fjeld, and flows with a south-westerly course through Aadalen, Spendilen lake, and joins the Hadeland river, as mentioned above, at Hönefoss in Ringerike.

Fair fishing may be had in the Etnedal and Dokka rivers.

In Vaage Vand, and its tributary the Bævra Elv, some very superior trout-fishing may be had, especially in the neighbourhood of Lom at its western extremity. Jerkin, on the Dovre Fjeld, will afford ample employment for the trout-fisher, though the fish do not generally run large. In fact, there is scarcely a lake or river in the whole of this large Amt but will afford some amusement.

In the fjelds around Læsje, Laurgaard, and Vaage, reindeer are numerous, and ryper abundant. Laurgaard and Brændehaugen are very comfortable and favourite stations for sportsmen. The Jotun Fjelds, a little south of Vaage Vand, were noted for their quantities of reindeer; and Lomseggen, at the western end of this Vand, is perhaps the best terrain of all. Reindeer used formerly to be much more numerous in the Vaage district of the Jotun Fjelds, but seem to have diminished of late years. Altogether, I should say, to insure success, Lomseggen and the western side of the Jotun Fjelds are the most likely places.

In the neighbourhood of Lille Miösen, a few stations short of Nystuen, excellent shooting is to be had.

Jerkin is a very favourite station for sportsmen, and good ryper-shooting is to be had here, and, in fact, at times all over the Dovre and its collateral branches. Indeed, the whole terrain between Gudbrandsdal and Valders will afford **ample sport**; but the accommodation to be got is questionable.

Elk were formerly numerous in this Amt, but are now only to be found in the largest forests, west of the Randsfjord. The average number of bears killed is $8\frac{11}{13}$.

HEDEMARKEN AMT.

This large and important province is bounded on the north by South Throndhjem Amt; on the west by Christians **Amt**; on the east by Sweden; and on the south by Agershuus Amt.

The Glommen river traverses it from north to south, till it reaches Konsvinger, when it takes a turn to the west. The Örkla river runs through its north-western parts, and the Trysil, or Klar Elv, its eastern **part**. This latter river runs out of Færmund Söen, **and** empties itself into the Wenern lake.

This province abounds in immense forest tracts, the principal of which are in the southern and eastern districts.

The Hedemarken Bönder are a very superior class to those found in other parts of the country; many of them are exceedingly wealthy. They are extremely hospitable; and, as a class, are much more lively in their manners than their brethren from other parts of the country, insomuch that they are called "the Frenchmen of Norway."

The accommodation to be met with throughout Österdalen is very superior to that found in the western parts of the country, both as regards general cleanliness and fare.

The same may also be said of the sæters, which in many districts are so extremely dirty, and so thickly inhabited by lively creatures of all sorts, as to render a stay in them extremely precarious.

The general scenery in this province is not imposing: there are no fosses or picturesque valleys to charm the traveller, though the interminable forest tracts present to the eye a majestic appearance not to be found elsewhere. It is probably owing to this circumstance that Hedemarken has, comparatively, been but little visited; travellers to the north generally selecting the more picturesque route of the Dovre Fjeld.

But in point of trout-fishing and general shooting combined, I should decidedly give the palm to this Amt before any other in the whole of Norway.

It would, in my opinion, be quite worth the traveller's while to select this route either on going to or returning from the north. Neither need the scenery of the Dovre Fjeld be missed, as a cross road from Neby in Tönsæt runs through Foldalen to Jerkin.

I do not think much of the **Glommen as a fishing** river, noble stream though it be. At all events I **have** never had, **neither have** I heard of others having, much sport in it.

Its tributary, the RENA' ELV, however, which **rises** in Övre Rendalen, and flows through Storsöen, **and** falls into the Glommen near Aamot, **is a splendid** trout-stream. It may be fished all **the way up from** the Glommen, but is best from Disæt **upwards. At** this place there is a very clean and comfortable station, close to the river, and capital sport **may** be had here. Above this is Lönsæt, at the southern end of the lake. The station here is kept by a wealthy Bönde, and is all, barring musquitoes, that the sportsman can desire. The **charges,** moreover, as is almost universally the case in Österdalen, are very moderate. **Trout and** grayling of a large size may be taken. In 1861, **two** Englishmen bagged in one day, fair fishing, rather over 120 lbs. of trout and grayling at this place.

The lake is about thirty miles in length, and a small steamer plies up and down daily. At the northern end **at** Akre the fishing is also excellent; but the accommodation, unless one can get quarters at a Bönde's Gaard, **is not** nearly as good **as at** Lönsæt. There is no fishing to be had higher up in Rendalen than this.

The fishing at Lönsæt is to my mind superior to that at Akre, not only because there is a much larger extent of water, but because there are not so many boys constantly flogging the water as is the case at the northern end.

At the very time that the large bag above named was made at Lönsat, I was at the northern end of the lake, and had but poor sport in comparison. The water was too high. But I discovered, and the experience of the natives confirmed me in my inference, that the fishing at Akre is best when the river is low, and at Lönsæt when it is high, and *vice versâ*. Attention to this may possibly prevent disappointment.

The MISTA ELV, a brawling and impetuous mountain stream, flows into the Rena at Akre. It abounds in splendid fish; but owing to its steep sides and general inaccessibility, is rather a difficult river to fish.

Capital fishing may be had in the Storsöen by rowing backwards and forwards across the mouth of the Rena. I have taken several fine trout and large pike here, spinning.

The TRYSIL, or KLAR ELV, running out of Fæmund Söen, is a magnificent river, and has been rarely visited by Englishmen. When I was there about three years ago, I was told that I was the second Englishman who had ever fished in it. It can be best reached from Akre or Lönsæt across the mountains. A guide and a pony are indispensable. The **journey takes about ten hours, and is as lonely and rugged as mountain fjelds covered with nothing but reindeer moss can make it.** On a clear **day the Dovre** may be distinctly seen in the **distance**; and the snow-capped top of Snehætten **stands out** in bold relief when the atmosphere **is clear. The** guide will require three dollars, including the pony; at least I had to pay that sum.

A short distance below Fæmund **Söen the fishing is** of a **most** superior class; **and though a good deal of netting** is done, yet it is a **district so thinly** inhabited that there are but **few** to interrupt **the angler. A** tent, though desirable, is not absolutely requisite. Very fair quarters, and a boarded bedroom, with a bedstead and clean sheets all to yourself (!), are to be had at Sundeth Gaard—a luxury not always to be **had in** outlying districts. Trout of a very large size may **be taken. The fishing is** best from boats, **as the river** is broad.

These two rivers, **the Klar and** the Rena, are decidedly the best rivers **in** the whole province. The Osen Elv, falling into the Rena a short distance **before this** latter empties itself into the Glommen, is a nice trout-stream; and the Aasta Elv, falling into the Glommen near Björnstad, is a very likely-looking stream, and has some remarkably fishy-looking pools.

Of the other rivers in this Amt I know nothing, and will not, therefore, hazard any information.

The general shooting in this Amt is first-rate. For elk deer, Österdalen, Rendalen, and Solör are the best districts in the whole of Norway, and will be more especially alluded to in the chapter on elk-hunting. The mountain plateau between Rendalen and Trysil frequently abounds with reindeer. The lofty Sölen Fjeld, midway between the two, is seldom, if ever, without them. A short distance from here there is a most comfortable and convenient sæter. Capercalzie are numerous in all the forests, and hjerper are extremely abundant. Good ryper-shooting may be had near Roraas, Tolgen and Trysil. Stor Elvedalen will be found an exceedingly good place for the sportsman, and comfortable quarters may be had.

Shot guns are never used by the peasants in Österdalen or Rendalen, so that for this reason better shooting may be had. Kongsvinger and its neighbourhood will afford good sport, and is within easy distance on the new branch of railway from the capital.

"In the autumn of 1859," a friend writes me word, "I made an exploring expedition through the forest country between the valleys of the Glommen and the Klar, and then into Sweden towards Dal Elv. This country lies to the north of that mentioned by Lloyd, and the greater portion of it had never before, I believe, been explored by any traveller. It is a wild and thinly-inhabited district, and the game is consequently but little disturbed. Bears seem to be pretty numerous in parts, and elks also. I think Gammel Lördalen, on the Lören Elv, a tributary of the Swedish Vestre Dal Elv, would be the best head-quarters. Tolerable accommodation is to be had at Eric Lördalens, and a capital bear-hunter, Johann Persen, lives close by. There were a great many wild ducks on the Lören Elv, between Gammel and Ny Lördalen. I was greatly pleased with the boats on the Lören, and the admirable way in which they are managed. The boats are very similar in form to some of the North American canoes; and I thought that Eric and his nephew handled their poles almost as cleverly in the rapids as my old friends in New Brunswick used to do among those of the Nessissiquit. In some parts of this eastern forest district I found black game very abundant, particularly on the eastern side of the Ösen Sö; it was, however, no easy matter to get shots at them."

Bears are tolerably numerous. In 1861, an officer in the Norwegian army, and an ardent sportsman, had the unprecedented good luck of shooting three bears in one day in Österdalen. The average number killed is $12\frac{3}{13}$ per annum.

Agershuus Amt.

This province, the capital of which is Christiania, situate at the head of the Christiania Fjord, is bounded on the north-east by Hedemarken Amt; on the north-west by Christians Amt; and on the south-west by Buskeruds Amt, and the Christiania Fjord.

It contains $40\frac{1}{8}$ square miles, and is divided into three Fogderies. Its scenery, though not grand, has a pleasing interchange of hill, dale, and plain, with extensive forest ranges.

The principal rivers are the Vormen, running from the Miösen at Minde into the Glommen at Næs, and flowing into the Öyeren lake.

The fishing in this Amt is very insignificant. To say that salmon are not found in it would be, strictly speaking, incorrect; but for all practical purposes there is no place worth trying. And though trout may be found in every stream and little "bæk," yet no sport is to be had, I may say, in any river in the whole of this province.

The Nordmarken lakes, about fourteen or fifteen miles from Christiania, in the middle of an extensive range of forest, contain many fine trout. Leave must, however, first be got from the proprietor, Baron Wedel, who preserves the fishing very strictly. Being, however, within such easy distance, it is much fished by the "cockaigne" of the capital; and as the accommodation in the forest cabins is as bad as well can be, it is scarcely worth while visiting, especially when much better places can be reached in as short a time. The fishing is entirely from boats, though many hundreds of small trout may be taken in the rivers. The northernmost of these lakes, Sandungen, the baron reserves for his own and his friends' fishing.

At Eidsvold, the terminus of the railway, and about forty-two miles from town, capital grayling-fishing may be had in the Vormen in the month of August; and good quarters may be found at Olsen's hotel, in the same building as the station.

Eidsvold is a convenient and central situation, as it is only three hours from town by rail, and about six by steamer from Lillehammer, the north end of the lake. It is a rarity to catch a trout here, but the grayling-fishing is really superior.

In the Öyeren Lake the *Perca luscio perca*, pike perch (gjörs, norsk) may be taken. This rare and peculiar fish attains a large size, and is frequently taken up to thirty pounds in weight. It is a quick-growing fish, and is excellent for the table. For further and fuller accounts, the reader is referred to Lloyd's 'Scandinavian Adventures,' vol. i. p. 27.

Reindeer are not found in this Amt. Elk may

occasionally be met with in the forests in the neighbourhood of Eidsvold. The Nordmarken forests used formerly to be great strongholds for feathered game; but proximity to the capital, in a country too where the game-laws cannot be strictly enforced, has of late years considerably deteriorated them. Ryper are not found in this Amt.

Fair woodcock-shooting may be had in the spring near Eidsvold, and in the autumn the Vormen swarms with ducks.

Excellent snipe-shooting may be had on some small islands at the northern end of the Öyeren lake. They are mostly the solitary snipe. I have heard of as many as forty couple being killed in the day. Of late the peasants have become rather tenacious, and the stranger may get warned off. They shoot themselves now-a-days (a few years back and they would never have dreamed of letting fly at a bird on the wing), and have rather a good plan for beating the ground. Two persons take hold of a long and heavy rope, one at either end, and let it drag on the ground. The shooter walks in the middle.

The end of July and beginning of August is the best time, just before they commence mowing. The route to the Öyeren is by rail to Lille Strömmen, and thence by boat for about ten miles down the river. It is easy to get back to Christiania the same evening.

Bears are rarely met with in this amt, $1\frac{2}{3}$ of a bear being the average per annum. In severe winters, lynxes have been killed near Christiania.

SMAALEHNENES AMT.

This Amt is bounded on the north by Agershuus Amt; on the east by Sweden; and on the west and south by the sea and Sweden.

It is very flat, and has extensive tracts of plain. In an agricultural point of view it is very important, as it contains more tillable land than any province in Norway. Its superficial area is $33\frac{3}{4}$ square miles.

The Glommen river intersects it from north to south, and in its course through the northern part forms eighteen falls of no great height, and then flows tranquilly till it reaches Sarpsborg, where it forms the grand Sarpfoss, 320 feet above the sea. Salmon go up to this foss, but I have never heard of their taking the fly.

In the neighbourhood of Frederickshald, memorable for the death of Charles XII., some fair salmon-fishing may be had in the ENNINGDALS ELV, flowing into Ide Fjord near Berby. Berby Gaard owns the fishing, where leave may probably be obtained.

The shooting in this Amt is insignificant, neither rein, elk, nor ryper being found. Bears are seldom met with, and form an almost inappreciable average.

CHAPTER II.

THE WILD REINDEER AND ELK OF NORWAY, THEIR HISTORY, HAUNTS, AND HABITS.*

PERHAPS of all sport (let us exclude lion and tiger hunting—bear-shooting is comparatively tame), that of hunting the wild reindeer is the most inspiriting, and possesses the greatest attractions. Glorious sport as salmon-fishing may be and is, yet, to come up on the fjelds after having been pent up in the valleys for six weeks, and to breathe the pure, fresh mountain air, affords a relief to body and mind which experience alone can fully appreciate. Grouse are generally abundant (not the red grouse of Scotland, though I believe they are exactly the same species, the difference in plumage being only caused by climatic influences), and ptarmigan may be found everywhere on the high fjelds. But reindeer-hunting is the peculiar charm of the mountains of Norway. I am not going to indulge

* This account of the reindeer has lately appeared in the 'Field.'

in any hypothesis as to the orthographical way of spelling the word, therefore, **reader, free your** minds from any alarm on that score.

First, let me tell you something of the history of the reindeer in **Norway,** which, thanks to Mr. Asbjörnsen (with whose writings **Mr.** Dasent has made the reading **public** well acquainted), I am able to do.

Like **all** other ruminant animals **in Europe, the** reindeer was formerly much more numerous than at the present day. It was plentiful in Germany in the **days** of Julius Cæsar. **That** distinguished **individual, great** general **as** he undoubtedly **was, was not much of a** sportsman, **for** he **seems to have had a very** confused idea **of what** the reindeer was, **and to** have confounded it **with the** elk and **the** wild ox, all **of** which animals he speaks **of** having found in the Hercynian forest. In **the Louvre at** Paris there is a mosaic which represents a reindeer feeding **by** the side of a **river,** the **banks** of which are thickly covered with fir. **It is supposed to** have been executed **to** commemorate **some victory of the** Romans in Germany. Cæsar also mentions that **the** Germans used reindeer **skins for** clothing. They must, therefore, have been very abundant; **a fact** which is most satisfactorily confirmed by the fossil remains of horns **and** bones which are found in the old peat-bogs up **to** the Baltic Sea.

From the northern parts **of the continent of** Germany—but long before Cæsar's time—the reindeer had wandered northwards as far, indeed, as the province of Scania, which was at that time connected with Germany; for not only in that province, but in Bornholm, Zealand, and in other places of Denmark, bones and horns have been discovered similar in all respects to those of the animal which is now to be found on the mountains of Norway.

But it is tolerably clear that the fossil remains just alluded to did not proceed from the Norwegian family. Neither did the German stock extend further north than Scania; for no traces or fossil remains are found in all the intervening terrain between Scania and the province of Nordland, whilst they are numerous in those districts immediately south of Scania.

The reindeer, then, must have first invaded Norway by a different route, and at a later period. Indeed, it was not till after the land between the Gulf of Bothnia and the White Sea had appeared above the surface of the water.

In remote ages, when the Siberian plains which now border on the Arctic Ocean were still immersed, the reindeer's original home was in the high alps of Central Asia. Simultaneously with the appearance of land above the surface, it is assumed that they began to migrate westwards, keeping to the high lands of Finland, which traverse that country, and which are, in fact, a collateral branch of the mountain ranges of Norway. By this same route, too, the Lapps unquestionably made their first appearance into Norway. Indeed, the very existence of this extraordinary people seems to have been mysteriously connected with that of the reindeer; and it is more than probable that the reindeer served as their pilots from the remote parts of Asia to the mountain ranges of Norway, while at a later period, again, the paths made by deer and Lapps from the fjords to the fjelds served as tracks for the Gothic race on their wandering up from the coast into the interior.

This seems to be the only reasonable solution of the fact that, in the alluvial deposits of Scania, fossil remains of reindeer are found bearing incontestable signs of being the remains of animals exactly similar to those now existing on the fjelds of Lapland and Norway, whilst in the intermediate parts not a single fossil remain has ever been discovered.

The wild reindeer may be found on the high fjelds of Norway as far south as lat. 60°, wherever the altitude is above the limit of the willow and the birch, viz., about 3,400 feet. They are more numerous in the west and south-west of the mountain plateaux than in the north-east, probably owing to the absence of Lapps in those parts, who hunt them *whenever* and *wherever* they can. Neither is the wolf, the Lapp's constant companion, so numerous as in the north-eastern districts, where the mountains are skirted by interminable masses of forest, and where the wolves have their regular home.

On the fjelds between Christiania and the province of Bergen, and in the Sætersdal fjeld, in the province of Christiansand, reindeer are more numerous than in any other part of the country. Incredible numbers of them are occasionally to be seen about Röldal and Voxli. Professor Nilsson, in his 'Scandinavian Fauna,' says "that in the beginning of June, 1826, he was told that the fjelds for the breadth of about three and a half miles were so thickly covered with these animals that they resembled an immense flock of sheep. The does had just calved, and the young ones were following their dams. The herd extended so far that the eye could distinguish neither beginning nor end. Ultimately they divided into three parts," &c. This account recalls to mind the statements of the countless herds of antelopes in Africa, or of the buffalo in America, so often dwelt on by travellers.

That branch of the Langfjeld which is bounded on the north by the Hallingjokul, and on the south by Nubseggen, is one of their favourite resorts. Some years ago it was by no means rare to meet with herds consisting of several hundreds here; and I have been only recently informed by a gentleman (now Professor of Mineralogy at the Christiania University) who spent his youth in these parts, and had been, moreover, a very skilful hunter, that he once saw a herd numbering between 5,000 and 10,000! Such sights are of course rare, and perhaps less common now than ever.

In that extensive mountain tract which includes the highest fjelds of Norway, between Gudbrandsdal, Valders, and Bergen Stift, by the Bygdin and Gjendin Lakes, and on Læsjo and the Romsdal Fjeld, large herds of reindeer may be found the whole year round; and it is no uncommon sight in the autumn to see herds numbering several thousands, whilst on the Rundene and on the Dovre Fjeld, between Hallingdal and Leerdal, herds of from 300 to 1,000 deer are frequently seen.

It often happens that, owing to wind and weather, the too-frequent attention of hunters, and the incessant persecutions of their old enemies the wolves, the reindeer entirely disappear from one district and appear in preponderating numbers in another.

Although, as above stated, they are to be found on all the high lands from the North Cape to Sætersdal (*i.e.*, through 10° of latitude), yet it is especially in the great continuous mountain ranges or plateaux, where the snow lies the summer through on the fjeld sides, that the reindeer properly have their home.

But, from the causes I have referred to above, they seldom remain on any one spot for a long time; indeed, they are constantly on the move, so that it by no means follows that they will be found in the same parts two consecutive years. The Dovre Fjeld, with its branches to the east, west, and south, is one of their favourite haunts. The Jotun Fjeld is probably the central point of that family, the divisions of which roam through the north-western parts of Gudbrandsdal, Valders, Nordfjord, Söndfjord, and Sogn. The immense plateau lying south of the road from Hallingdal to the Sogne Fjord, and containing numerous snow-capped mountains, the western declivities of which are covered with Hardanger glaciers or Folgefond, is not so sharply separated from the Jotun Fjeld, as to prevent the tribes which properly belong to each range at times intermingling with each other. On the extensive ranges between Hallingdal, Nummedal, and Thelemarken in the east, and Voss, Hardanger, and Ryfylke in the west, large quantities of reindeer are to be met with.

From the interior arms of the Hardanger Fjord the sportsman will perhaps reach the best terrain for hunting more readily than by any other route; but the want of anything like decent accommodation must prove a serious drawback to the amateur, unless he comes provided with a tent and canteen all complete.

At Lien and Argehoved, near the Mjös lake, in

Övre Thelemarken, between Langfjeld and Nubseggen, there are fine tracts for reindeer. Indeed, the inhabitants of these districts are "mighty hunters," and subsist principally on venison. Also from Lerdal, Lyster, Jostedal—branches of the Sogne Fjord—good opportunities for sport may be had; but here, too, the accommodation is extremely deficient. Maristuen, above Lerdal, one station short of Nystuen, the highest part of the Fille Fjeld, will, however, afford good **accommodation,** and is an excellent place to put up at **for those** who purpose hunting in **the Sulitind** Fjeld; and Fortun, the highest point in **Lyster, is** a good station for those who wish to hunt on the Hurrung Fjeld. Nystuen (not to be confounded with the one above), at the head of Valders, will also be **found** to afford decent **accommodation.**

Laurdal, in Gudbrandsdal, is a favourite resort for Englishmen (excellent general shooting is to be had in the vicinity); but it has been so much shot over during the last two or three years that it may be questionable whether good sport is to be relied on there.

The fjeld round Vaage parish will afford good sport, and especially Lomseggen, at the western extremity of the lake.

The **plateau** between Rendalen and Trysil, on the borders of **Sweden, is** occasionally good for reindeer. The accommodation **in** the **sæters of** this district is excellent; indeed, no other part of the country can vie with Österdal for the comfort, cleanliness, and good fare to be met with.*

Though wild reindeer are certainly to be met with in Finmark and in Nordland, yet they are comparatively few in number. Most of the deer in these provinces are tame, and belong to the Lapps. It has been computed that they amount to over 28,000 head. To the Lapp the reindeer is his sole possession, so that it is needless to say how jealously they are guarded. Indeed, there is a heavy penalty for shooting one of them purposely; and I would recommend no Englishman to indulge in eccentricities, for the Lapps occasionally take the law into their own hands, as the following history will show:—

"Some years ago a number of convicts escaped from the fortress at Vardohuus. In order to obtain food they had recourse to killing tame reindeer. . This exasperated the Lapps beyond measure. They tracked these unfortunate poachers from place to place, slowly, but as surely as the bloodhound follows on the track of a runaway slave. For years nothing was heard of them, till at last their blanched skeletons were found, bearing evident signs that their former inmates had fallen into the hands of their remorseless and avenging pursuers." Therefore, I repeat (*verb. sap.*), be careful

* *Vide* Appendix.

how you meddle with reindeer in Finmark. The Lapps are good shots, and very handy with their rifles.

I shall now, after having given the principal habitats (and I may state that my information has been derived *directly* from several of the best and most experienced Norwegian hunters), allude to the habits of the wild reindeer, together with some occasional remarks as to the manner of hunting them, which will, I think, prove of general use; but, before doing so, I would venture to caution any Englishman against going up the fjelds too lightly clad. We are not as a nation given to muffle up, and are rather apt to run into the opposite extreme. But for reindeer hunting it is quite necessary to have *thick* and *warm* clothing; for it often happens that the sportsman will have to lie concealed for hours behind a rock after having got into a tremendous perspiration, and the sharp mountain air, and now and then a snow-storm (by no means a rarity at high altitudes in August), not to speak of a drenching rain, rapidly reduce the temperature of the body, and a severe cold may be the result. Prudence is absolutely necessary; for to be laid up with a rheumatic fever, with no better accommodation than a sæter can afford, and the attendance of a sæter pige (girl), whatever be her charms (and I confess I never could detect them), out of reach of a doctor, and 1,000 miles from home, is not the most pleasing predicament to find oneself in.

The reindeer is unquestionably the most numerous of the large game of Norway, the red deer and elk being comparatively few in number. Yet, in proportion to their number, the quantity which falls a prey to the hunter's rifle is very unimportant; for they frequent the most inaccessible parts of the country, and nature has, moreover, provided them with extremely sensitive organs of smell.* It is of course a matter of extreme difficulty, and in fact only approximately possible, to ascertain with any degree of precision the numbers of wild reindeer which are annually slaughtered. But when one takes into consideration the quantity of venison which is to be found in almost every house in those districts which are frequented by these animals, bearing in mind that nearly every farmer is a hunter, some of whom kill as many as fifty head per annum (not unfrequently ten on a single excursion), it cannot be computed at less than between 2,000 and 3,000 yearly. Such being the case, there must *at least* be from 20,000 to 30,000 wild reindeer in Norway, in order to admit of such a yearly diminution. Perhaps it would be nearer the mark to estimate it at nearly double this number; for it is hard to suppose that one in every ten is annually killed; and this is the more

---

* An old Norwegian hunter told a friend of mine that he believed great numbers perished annually by falling into the crevices of the glaciers, and that these, added to what the wolves killed, far outnumbered those which fell a prey to the hunter's rifle.

probable when it is borne in mind that the flocks of tame deer in Finland and Nordland amount to 28,000 head, as above stated.*

During the winter months the reindeer keep to the high fjelds. Their food at this time consists almost entirely of reindeer moss and other lichens. Occasionally they descend into the regions of the birch and willow to eat the bark from the trees; but in spring they commence to migrate downwards from their lofty altitudes to visit the grassy dales in the vicinity of the sæters, while further on in the **summer they may often be seen grazing in the valleys between the high fjelds.** Occasionally **they may be seen in early summer** grazing

* Mr. **Asbjörnsen is** my authority here; but I must confess the **number reputed to be** killed annually seems exaggerated. Mr. A. speaks of one Hans Mo, " who annually killed from 40 to 50 head;" and of a hunter on the Dovre, " who annually sells reindeer hides to the value of 70 dollars, which must have been supplied by at least 40 deer." (N.B. May not some of these have been purchased?) On this point a friend writes me word, who has had much practical experience on the fjelds of Norway: "I was told a few years **ago of** one of the Gudbrandsdal hunters, who had been out six weeks, having killed six deer, as a wonderful instance of luck. B. tells me of a first-rate Vaage hunter, who once killed 13 in a year, and he says that the great man of all, 'Old Joe,' who is I suppose, *par excellence*, the 'mighty hunter' of Norway, who has been at it without cessation for fifty years, living almost all his life up in the high fjelds amongst the deer, has slain in his half-century between 500 and 600. I think one may judge also from the success of our English sportsmen. I have three or four in my eye now, first-rate stalkers and capital shots, who have spent several seasons on the fjelds, with sport varying from zero to, I think, nine head as the *maximum* ever reached, and I am sure any one of them would consider five deer in a season as ample recompense for all his toil."

H

quietly amongst the cattle. Should the musquitoes prove very troublesome the does betake themselves again to the regions of snow; but the old bucks, whose hides are not usually of such a delicate texture, find the sweet grass in the lowlands too attractive to be relinquished for the sake of a few troublesome gnats, and get uncommonly plump and fat. If the summer is an uncommonly rainy one, as has been the case for the last three years, the numerous fungi which the moisture draws forth seduces them into the Scotch and spruce fir forests, where they grow in abundance.

They begin to shed their coats about the latter part of July, previously to which they are of a greyish-white colour; whilst the operation is going on, dappled; and afterwards a dark greyish-brown.

A full-grown buck measures about six to seven feet in length, and about four feet in height. A very large buck might, perhaps, reach four feet six inches. The head is rather elongated, the nozzle thick, the eyes large and prominent (expressively beautiful, I always think), the ears about six inches in length, and oval. There are two beautiful specimens in the Zoological Museum at the University of Christiania. One of these, which is a very fine one, was shot by a friend of mine on the fjelds, a few miles south of Elstad station in Gudbrandsdal. It was the year of the coronation; and consequently the station-masters were often put to their wits' ends to provide something better than "fladbröd," thick milk, and boiled trout for the royal personages and their suites.

One day (it was a Saturday) my friend, who was, as his custom every year is, bivouacking on the fjelds in the neighbourhood, received an urgent and pressing message from the station-master, praying him to send by the following Monday at the latest ten brace of grouse. Now, the message did not arrive till late on the Saturday evening. What was to be done? Either he and his companion must go out on the Sunday, which they were not in the habit of doing, or else her Majesty would not get much of a dinner, that was certain. "Necessitas non habet leges;" and so off they started early on the following morning. Blush not, reader, if you happen to be a strict Sabbatarian! for the nonce, loyalty seemed to have been the predominant feeling in their minds; and if it will at all add to your satisfaction, let me hasten to tell you that they determined as soon as ever they had each shot five brace (for they were to go in different directions) to return home and atone for their misdeeds by a little penance. I don't feel at liberty to tell you what this penance was to consist in, but will leave it to your imagination to find out. Well, off they started. The elder of the two had soon accomplished his task; and not tempted by the tameness of the birds to follow them up, returned, according to agreement, to headquarters. No sooner had he got back than he began to look about for his companion, who had not yet appeared. After waiting a little time, and offering up a cloud of incense, he espied his friend walking slowly, and apparently as if he had been unsuccessful, homewards. "What! not got anything? Well, we *must* go out again. It will not do to let her Majesty go without her dinner," &c., &c. But while he thus held forth a sly leer came over his younger companion's face, and his frequent glances behind made him also look in that direction. "Halloa! what is that? why, 'Gud bevar mig!'" It was a magnificent reindeer, a buck with royal antlers! Like Jacob of old, he had found his quarry close to hand, within a mile of their quarters, and was fortunate enough to get near him and bring him down. There was no need to go after ryper then—a venison haunch would be more appreciated than grouse. And so there was rejoicing in the camp. The animal was flayed; the haunch and the five brace of grouse at once sent off to the station; and so it came to pass that the queen had a better dinner that day than on any other on her route up to Throndhjem. As it was such a noble animal, and the circumstances under which it was shot so interesting, the skin was sent to the University; and there you may see it for yourself, and if you ask for the history of it you will find my statement corroborated.

On the under side of the neck the **hair** is long and hangs down in a peculiar manner. **It has a short** tail, covered sparsely with **short stiff hairs.** Generally, **the** reindeer **is** somewhat smaller than the **red deer,** and its legs are shorter and appear to be more **nimble.** While **the tame reindeer seldom** attains a greater weight than 130 to **140 pounds, the wild** bucks are often found the double of this. I have heard of two bucks being shot on the Læsjö Fjeld weighing about 324 pounds **each.** The outer layer of fat on one of them weighed **forty-eight pounds!**

The antlers are smooth, rounded off, and flat on the inside; those **of the doe are of the same form** as the bucks, only smaller. The periods at which they shed their horns differ greatly. The old bucks usually shed theirs before Christmas, whilst the does and young bucks do not shed them till the spring. In **the** former, **they** begin to grow again in the summer, and **are then** covered with **a** soft hairy coating of skin. **By the** middle of September they are perfectly developed, and have now become hard and firm. At this time they may often be seen rubbing their antlers against sandbanks, **in** order to get rid of **the** coating of skin, which hangs down in long strips, and stamping with their **hoofs on** them till their horns **are** quite bare. **During this** operation they frequently lose a great deal of blood. Should the weather be sunny their antlers assume a blood-red appearance; but if rainy they are quite white. But towards the rutting season the horns of the bucks are often of a darkish-brown hue, owing to the does "staling" upon them. In the case of the young bucks the above operation takes place later on in the season, and of the does last of all.

Hjorthöis, in his description of Gudbrandsdal, speaks of "a smaller deer, which he considers to be the roe, and which, he says, is sometimes to be met with in large flocks." With all due deference to the distinguished naturalist, this statement is, I am inclined to think, incorrect; for the roe deer cannot live under the same conditions of climate as the reindeer, *and has, moreover, never been found in Norway.* Still, several of the peasants believe in their existence, though their testimony is no more to be relied on than that of Hjorthöis or the worthy Pontoppidan.

The phenomenon of the appearance of these smaller animals has been a sore puzzle to Scandinavian naturalists; but it is now generally supposed that they have been reindeer which have haunted the loftiest and most inaccessible regions, where a severe climate and scanty nourishment have been ill calculated to produce physical development; or else, that they have been stragglers from tame herds, and have subsequently relapsed into their original wildness. Either of the above suppositions is certainly a far more reasonable conclusion to arrive at than to have to believe in the existence of the roe in Norway.

As has been above remarked, the tame reindeer are considerably smaller than the wild. Moreover, the reindeer found in Spitzbergen are much smaller than the wild reindeer in Norway, though belonging to one and the same species. It is a well-known fact that a difference of 500 feet in altitude brings one to a temperature and vegetable growth corresponding to those existing under a latitude 200 miles further north. Now, according to this computation, the reindeer which frequent the highest parts of the Jotun Fjeld (which is two, three, or perhaps four thousand feet above the plateaux in the east and south-eastern parts) should correspond in size with those found 850 to 1,700 miles further to the north, which brings one to about to Spitzbergen.* Indeed, in the valleys of the Jotun Fjeld, whose peaks rear their summit up through endless masses of ice and snow which never melts, a Polar climate and a vegetation similar to that in Spitzbergen is found to exist.

But to come back to our subject. In the summer the food of the reindeer consists mainly of grass, leaves, buds of birch, &c., and moss. It seems especially to have a predilection for acid and bitter plants. The

* And yet some large bucks have been killed in the Jotun Fjeld.

Ranunculus glacialis, called by the peasants "rein flower," is a great favourite with it. This beautiful and delicate little plant seems to be the advanced guard of the flower world towards the regions of perpetual snow. It is found on the very edge of the glaciers, and is as pale as the melting snow itself. Its bud has a reddish tinge, like to that which the rays of the setting sun cast over a boundless waste of snow. It is a lovely flower to be placed so high up out of ken of the civilised world. No insect seeks for honey within its corolla; no butterfly ventures up to these ice-bound regions. It is peculiarly the reindeer's flower. They will even scrape the snow away with their hoofs to find it; and wherever the hunter sees the "rein flower" is untouched, he may take it as a sign that there are no deer in the neighbourhood.

Besides this, the bitter *Gentiana lutea*, called in Thelemarken "rein sorrel;" *Dryas octopetala*, or "rein grass;" the *Cerastium*, the *Rumex digynus*, and the buds and leaves of the dwarf birch, *Betula nana*, are eagerly devoured by them. But in winter the reindeer moss is almost their sole food, and of this nature has bestowed a plentiful and inexhaustible supply.

During the winter the herds usually graze only where there is snow. The largest and strongest bucks go in front, and scrape away the snow with their hoofs; for, being deprived of their only natural means of defence, they are unable to withstand the vicious pokes in the ribs which they receive from the does. This is the reason why the old bucks, after having shed their horns, separate from the main herd.

The reindeer is an uncommonly sure-footed animal; it runs with as great ease over the steepest slopes as on the level plain. Its broad hoofs keep it from sinking deep into the snow, and thus it does not so frequently fall a prey to the wolf as the long-legged elk, who gets completely bogged directly he attempts to make a run for it. Its general hardiness, and the smallness of its requirements, render it admirably adapted to the rugged and inhospitable regions it inhabits.

Some twenty years ago the experiment was made of keeping tame reindeer herds in several parts of Hallingdal, the Fille Fjeld, Hardanger, &c. At first the plan was found to answer, but gradually the animals diminished and died away from various causes, so that they have now quite disappeared.

The causes alluded to were as follows:—The tame herds attracted large flocks of wolves, which found the animal in a domesticated state a comparatively easy prey; many also got enticed away by their wild brethren; and, lastly, the Bönder complained that they spoiled the grass for their cattle in the neighbourhood of the sæters: for it is a known fact that cows, sheep, &c., will not graze where a herd of reindeer has been feeding. Thus, in about fifteen years from their firs introduction into those parts, they were entirely eradicated.

I shall now speak of the manner in which the Norwegians hunt them. It should, however, first be remarked that reindeer always travel against the wind, their sensitive organs of smell enabling them to detect an enemy at a long distance. Whenever, therefore, a westerly wind, for instance, has prevailed for any length of time, the hunter may expect to find them on the westward side of their favourite haunts, and so on. The sportsman will find these remarks of general use.

The regular Norwegian hunter, whose principal subsistence depends on venison, builds himself a hut of stone and earth in the tract he intends to hunt, always selecting a place where there is sufficient pasture for his horse. From this hut he sallies forth in the morning, returning at night if the chase has not led him too far away, when either he must bivouac under the lee of some rocky ledge, or seek, if possible, the friendly shelter of a neighbouring sæter. He is usually provided with a telescope, and takes his dog with him, a little wiry terrier sort of a dog, with long pointed nose, short ears, and curly tail. Unless it is a prodigy it is held in a leash. These dogs have a remarkably keen scent, and when well trained are a very valuable acquisition. I have known as much as 10*l*., and even more, given for one, which, though perhaps a small sum in an English sportsman's eyes, is a little fortune to a Norwegian hunter. They can scent a deer a surprisingly long way off, when they give unmistakeable signs to their master that they are on trail. I have known them scent deer three miles distant when the wind has been blowing fresh. They seldom or never give tongue, but should one ever transgress in this way, besides sundry pokes and kicks, accompanied by such a volley of oaths* as only a Norwegian, I think, is capable of evolving, it has to submit to the indignity of a muzzle.

To insure sport an Englishman should always have an experienced hunter and dog with him; for otherwise he may come plump into the very middle of a herd, but out of shooting distance. Moreover, if a deer be wounded, the dog is then of inestimable service, for he will follow it and rarely fail to bring it to bay.

When a hunter has succeeded in killing a deer, he immediately proceeds to flay it, takes the entrails out,

* I think the following specimens, which require a tolerable acquaintance with the language to be able to understand, will confirm this opinion. The Bönder seem to have an ascending scale, beginning with a simple "—— take you" to "May the —— boil your heart's blood;" "May he play a game of five-card loo in your sinful bowels;" "May he cut up your liver and lights into such small pieces that the lice may have to go on their knees to eat them up;" with many intermediate ones, but *this* is the climax!

and quarters it. He then wraps the skin round the venison, and buries it in a hole in the ground, care being taken to prevent the gluttons and foxes from paying it a visit, by heaping heavy stones upon it. He then hurries home for his horse, and carries it away the following morning.

Reindeer principally rely on their keen sense of smell to guard against surprise. The sight of a human being does not seem to cause them much alarm. I once shot at a reindeer which was a long distance off, and missed. Directly I had fired the animal stopped and quietly scrutinised me, then trotted off for a hundred yards or so, and stopped again. It was monstrously tantalising, for I had plenty of time to reload, only I was far out of shooting distance. Sir J. Franklin remarks this peculiarity in the North American reindeer. "Their curiosity," he writes, "often causes them to come close up and wheel round the hunter."

In the rutting time the Lapps frequently tie up a couple of tame does to serve as decoys, while they themselves lie in ambush.

In the middle of the day the reindeer take their siesta, always selecting for this purpose as inaccessible a place as possible. It is then almost an impossibility to get within shot of a herd, as some of their number always do duty as sentinels.

When a herd is on the move it is worse than useless to lie in their road, as their sharp noses readily detect danger, and they will start off in wild flight; and it is of little avail to endeavour to follow them in their rear. Should **the** herd disappear over a hill, the enthusiastic and inexperienced hunter will think " now is the time to push on ;" but not so the cool old hand, for he knows well, from dearly-bought experience, that after having disappeared as above said, they *universally* throw out three or four of their rear guard, which retrace their steps till **they come back to the top of the** hill down which the main body has only just gone. These remain there for some minutes, carefully **examining the** whole country in their rear; and not until they have satisfied themselves that there is no cause for apprehension will they quit the spot. They then scamper back and rejoin their companions, **who** are awaiting them out of shot of the summit of the **said** hill. Many and many a chance has been **lost by** incautiously appearing too soon from behind one's hiding place. The best and only safe way of coming within shot of a herd **that is on the move is** to approach them *on the flank*. But great caution is necessary lest a straggler gets wind of you.

The above remarks I have been favoured with by a friend of mine, a very experienced hunter, and they will, **I hope, prove useful.**

To the mountaineer the wild reindeer is of inestimable value, its flesh, hide, antlers, marrow, fat, &c., all being employed in several branches of domestic economy. When dried in the wind, the flesh is often used as a substitute for bread. The learned but not very trustworthy bishop, Pontoppidan, speaks of a use to which the antlers are put:—" When the reindeer shed their antlers, and the new ones begin to appear, they are covered with a sort of skin, and are so soft that they can be cut with a knife like a sausage, and are considered a great delicacy. Hunters eat them raw for lack of provision when on the high fjelds." This is not very improbable (as at this period the antlers consist of a web of small blood-vessels and stringy fibres), especially when it is borne in mind that hunters will not unfrequently take a draught of the blood from the fresh killed animal in lack of better nourishment. But the following remark of the worthy prelate is not quite so easily to be swallowed. He says: "There is a worm generated under the outer skin of the antlers, which it eats off when they have attained their full size;" and that " they have a peculiar hole in the eyelid to peep out of when they cannot hold their eyes open on account of the drifting snow; a proof," adds his reverence, " of the wise providence of the Creator."

Reindeer venison is an extremely wholesome and nutritious food. In flavour it very much resembles that of the red deer, but is somewhat darker in colour; it should be soaked for twelve hours previously to being roasted or baked, in vinegar and water. Unless it is well larded it will eat somewhat dry, and it should be served up with a sauce made of sour cream.

I have never eaten better sauces than those made by Norwegian cooks. Our English game would, in my opinion, be much improved by them. The following is the receipt of the sauce with which they serve up all sorts of game, and it cannot be too strongly recommended :—

RECEIPT FOR SAUCE USED WITH GAME, &c.—Game in Norway is always baked in an iron saucepan over a hot plate; a lump of butter is put in with it, and, when this has melted, about a tablespoon of water is added. It must be constantly stirred, and more water added as required. When the bird, or whatever it be, is done, the gravy is poured into a clean frying-pan, then one or two tablespoonfuls of *sour* cream are added, and the whole stirred about till it boils; it is seasoned with pepper and salt to taste. Sour cream is preferable to sweet cream. Game, &c., should always be well larded.

When the rutting season approaches (about the middle of September), the flesh of the bucks begins to have a strong and unpleasant flavour. That of the does is, however, eatable till over Christmas. Young venison is best in August. I would recommend any one who has a fancy to try what rein venison is like to write word to Mr. Bennett, of Christiania, who I am sure would, with his usual affability, execute any commission. There are few things better than a venison steak before it has been frozen; but this is only to be had up the country, as the Bönder wait till the frost has set in before sending it to the Christiania market.

One word of advice to novices, and I have done. Do not shoot a deer before the 1st of August, and don't take pot-shots at fabulous distances!

THE ELK IN NORWAY.

In olden times, when the population of Europe was considerably less than at the present day, and when the climate withal was much colder, and but little land, comparatively, under cultivation, the elk-deer was common in Central Europe. Julius Cæsar speaks of it as being found in the Hercynian forest; and, indeed, the Romans knew of its existence in Scandinavia, with which country they had commercial relations, and where they also had regular agents established. The Greeks, however, do not seem to have been acquainted with it, if we may take the absence of any allusion to it in the works of Aristotle or Herodotus as a negative proof.

The elk has long since disappeared from Germany. I believe 1746 is the date when the last elk was shot in Saxony.

In company with the reindeer, the elk made its appearance in the peninsula of Scandinavia at a time when the province of Scania was connected with the continent of Germany. Judging from the numerous fossil remains that have been found in the peat-bogs and morasses of Scania, it may be inferred that elk-deer were formerly very numerous here, and also of a larger size than the animals now existing. And even in the mediæval ages they must have been tolerably plentiful in these parts, for among the remains of slaughtered animals which a few years ago were discovered in the vicinity of the convents in that province, elk bones and horns were found in abundance, bearing evident marks of the knife or saw of the cook.

But gradually, as the land was reclaimed and put under cultivation, and, in consequence, became more thickly inhabited, the elk-deer seem to have shifted their quarters more towards the north, where the immense ranges of forest and wild mountain tracts afforded an insuperable (in those days) hindrance to the advance of civilization.

It appears from some very old documents that the elk-deer is mentioned as one of the "noxious animals" in one of the provinces of Sweden; it may therefore be assumed that it was numerous in those days. At the present day it is found in Sweden, south of the province of East Gothland, and is more numerous in Jemteland, Herjedal, and Dalarne, than in any other parts of the country. Angermannland is its northernmost boundary. It is not found, I believe, above the limit of Scotch fir, or about 3,000 feet above the sea.

Before proceeding to speak of its former and present habitats in Norway, it may be mentioned that elk-deer may be found in Finland, Lithuania, and Russia from the White Sea to the Caucasus. It is also found in the forests of Siberia to the river Lena, and in the neighbourhood of the Altai Mountains. In parts of North America it is found in comparatively large numbers.

The elk was formerly found much **further north in Norway** than **is the case at the present** day, and was **also much more numerous.** But towards the middle and latter **part of the** eighteenth century its numbers were considerably reduced. It was hunted remorselessly; and as its flesh, hide, &c., were extremely **valuable,** especially in a cold climate, where **provisions were** scarce, and warm clothing at **a** premium, **it is not very** surprising that "everybody's **hand was against**" the **poor creature.** At that time it could not look to the **law for protection, and had therefore to** trust only to the compassion and better feelings of the Norwegian Bönde.

Of course there were some few cases where attempts **at protection were** made, but these were few and **far** between; and even the marvellous tales which were current and were firmly believed by the Norwegian peasantry (who are even now-a-days far more ready **to** trust in the supernatural than the natural), *e. g.*, "that **elks,** when wounded, have been known to make for the nearest farm-house, and have then **sprung** on **to** the **roof, where they** have knelt down and begged for their life," did not prove a sufficient safeguard.

By the beginning of the present century it was tolerably evident **that the** elk-deer would soon take its rank among the animals of bygone days. In fact, between the years 1810 and 1830 there were only about three places where they were to be found, namely, in some parts of the province of Throndhjem and in Österdalen.

Fortunately, government now stepped in, and in 1818 passed a law that not a single elk should be killed for the next twenty years. In 1845 this stringent but necessary enactment was again modified, and now the law stands as follows:—that "elks can only be killed between August 1st and November 1st, and then only one on each separate property, under a penalty of forty dollars." This law is, however, frequently broken. For the penalty is so laid that half goes to the informer, half to the poor-box of the district in which the elk is shot. Thus if A. shoots an elk at an unlawful time, his brother B. has nothing to do but cut off to the nearest Foged, or magistrate, and lay an information against him, and recover half the fine; and as the flesh and hide, &c. are quite worth that sum, the poacher is not a loser, and has the fun into the bargain. The penalty is to be raised shortly, and several alterations, in fact, are to be made in the game laws * of Norway.

As may be imagined, it could be no very difficult thing to eradicate animals of such size from the face

* These will be found at the end of the chapter.

of any country. Mr. Asbjörnsen **instances** a case in point, where the elk was formerly numerous, and is now *non inventus*. And that is **in the Aland** Isles, **where**, " during the Finnish **war, they were so** plentiful **that the army was** provisioned **with elk** venison instead **of beef."**

During **the** last twenty years, however, elk-deer have been steadily on the increase, not only owing to the protection afforded them by the law, but because they have abandoned the more northerly and **easterly districts** for quarters where the wolf **has not been in such** large numbers. **And though many have been,** especially **during the last few winters, shot** at unlawful **times, yet the indignation that was** then evinced, and **the publicity that** was given to the cases, have done **a good deal** towards stopping this poaching.

A few years ago, elk were numerous in the Trysil forests, which adjoin Sweden. But so were the wolves; and these committed such havoc amongst them **as to** drive them more **to the** westward.

Besides Namdal, and some other places in Throndhjem Stift (diocese), elk-deer may almost always be found throughout Österdal, in Solörs, on the borders **of Sweden,** in the valley of the Glommen, Odal, Vingers, **and in some of the forests of Romerige and** Smaalenene.

They are not unfrequently seen in the forests near

Eidsvold, about forty-two miles from Christiania, and in many parts of Hedemarken. The engineer of the new railway from from Stor-Hamar (half-way up the Miösen lake) to Grundsæt, told me that one of the first trains they ran on that line nearly proved the death of a magnificent elk. Somehow or other it had got on the line as the train was coming up, and being unused to the strange appearance "of a great long thing with a green and red head puffing and *skreeking* like anythink," as the Yorkshireman said, it stood as if entranced to gaze on the strange phenomenon; and had not the engine-driver pulled up in time, it would in all probability have been run over.

Last autumn, 1862, two elk-deer astonished us in Christiania by making their appearance in the suburbs of the town. They had swum over a branch of the fjord, and had found their way into a man's kitchen-garden, much to the alarm of sundry old women and several little children. One of them ultimately got killed, I regretted to hear.

Before proceeding to speak of their habits, manner of living, &c., I would strongly recommend any English sportsman who feels desirous of having an elk-hunt to make a note of the following hints. By bearing them in mind he may stand a good chance of success. Let him then go by train from Christiania to Lille Strom, half an hour's trip, and from thence take the branch line to Kongsvinger, getting out at Skarnæs. Next, he must find his way by carriole to Stormoen, and inquire at the post-office for one "Frederik Olsen Knauserud, in Nordre Odal under Tannæs." He is an old and experienced hunter, and has shot not only numbers of elk, but more bears have fallen to his rifle, I have been told, than is the case with any other Norwegian. He is well up to the craft; has a good dog; and as "Nordre Odal" is, perhaps, the very best place for elk in the whole country, it is not unlikely that some good sport may be had. Some friends of mine hunted there last autumn, and saw three or four elk, if not more, killing two.

The principal food of the elk consists of the leaves of young birch shoots, the bark of different kinds of trees, grass, and young twigs. The birch, mountain ash, and willow tribe seem to constitute their favourite food. Of grasses, they like those the best which grow in marshy places; and the *Caltha palustris* is perhaps above everything else their most delicate morsel. In the rutting season they are said to devour eagerly the *Ledum palustre*, which plant is supposed to excite their amatory propensities. When hard pressed, and when their favourite food is scarce, they will eat the berries and shoots of the juniper, Scotch, and occasionally the spruce fir, fungi, and lichens.

Unripe corn proves an attraction which they cannot

resist; and then their visits undoubtedly cause a great deal of damage to the farmer, almost as much perhaps as the depredations of an elephant in a rice-field in India. But as soon as ever the corn begins to ripen, and the halm to harden, they discontinue their incursions.

While grazing, they place their fore feet far back, and bend the body over.

During the winter time they eat the twigs of birch, willow, and ash; and in lieu of these, reindeer moss.

Two contrary opinions have been held in Norway as to whether the elk committed injuries among the forest trees or not. Some asserted that it did an incalculable amount of harm to the young trees; others, that it was quite harmless. As is usually the case with extreme opinions, both are wrong.

In comparison with its large body, the elk requires but little food. For with increasing years it becomes idle and lazy in its habits. It rests during the night, never feeding in the dark, except when the moon is shining very brightly. Moreover, like the cow and the sheep, a considerable time is occupied in chewing the cud.

During the rutting season, the males are very savage, and dire are the conflicts that take place between them to gain the affections of the female.

From their great length of leg they are enabled

to lash out tremendously with their hind feet; but they usually defend themselves against **wolves, dogs, &c.,** with their fore feet, aiming their **blows with the** rapidity of lightning, **and so turning** the hoof as **to** strike the enemy with the sharp point.

The pairing season lasts about three weeks. At this time the male and female always select the loneliest and most inaccessible spot possible in the middle of the thickest part of the forest—not more than fifty or **sixty** feet square—and never leave it on **any account, except** when frightened away; and even **then they are sure to** return thither after **the lapse of a few hours.** During this season, the male may frequently be heard to emit a curious sound with its long lips, resembling a sharp crack, accompanied by a snorting like that of a frightened **horse, only** much louder and stronger.

As the calving time draws near, the female retires into the loneliest spot she can find, always selecting one which is thickly overgrown with bushes. Half an **hour** or so after its birth, **the** calf attempts **to stand up,** being usually helped **to** get **on** its legs **by** its mother's nose.

The young ones suck the dam till after the following rutting season; in fact, as long as there is any milk to **be had.** When they get a good size, they kneel down like lambs **in** performing this **operation;** and when they have grown **too** big even to suck comfortably in this posture, they will lie flat down on their backs. They continue to follow the mother till the third year.

The females evince great affection for their young, and have even been known to attack human beings when an attempt has been made to deprive them of them. But it seldom happens that the young calves are captured, for they are tolerably fleet of foot. If hunted they will turn, and run in a ring like a hare; and if brought to bay by a dog will lash out vigorously with their fore feet.

The female goes with young about nine months, and brings forth towards the middle of June.

The first time she has only one calf, but subsequently two, and occasionally three, but very rarely. The calves are not spotted at their birth, but are of a light-brown colour.

The elk is a first-rate swimmer, and goes ahead through the water with great velocity, making the water hiss and foam again. It is also able to traverse swamps without sinking into the mire. If the ground be very soft, it has recourse to an artful expedient. As soon as it begins to feel itself sinking, it sits down on its hams, stretches out its fore legs, and regularly "punts" itself along; but should it happen that the swamp is too soft even to admit of this, it adopts the same plan as the mountain ponies do under similar emergencies. It throws itself over on one side, draws its feet together, and kicks them out simultaneously with great violence, and thus manages to jerk itself along. In this way it is enabled to cross places where even the wolf gets completely nonplussed. **But on the** smooth ice it is perfectly helpless. **No cat on** walnut-shells, or donkey on stilts, ever looked half so ridiculous as does an elk on the ice. It falls down directly it begins to move, and owing to its length of leg is unable to rise again. The specimen that may be seen stuffed **in** the Zoological Museum **at** the Christiania University was shot when **on the ice on the** river **Glommen,** in Odalen, **a few winters back.**

The **elk can run very quickly;** but their powers of endurance **are not nearly so** great **as those** of the reindeer. They very seldom break into a gallop, except when **suddenly alarmed,** but usually maintain a long swinging, lurching kind of trot. The neck is then stretched out, so that the nose is carried parallel with the ground, by which the horns are **brought backwards** on each side of the **neck. In trotting, the hind feet** strike against the soles of the fore feet, and produce a clicking sound similar to that often heard in horses. When suddenly startled **they go off in** a straight direction, trampling down everything that comes in their way; **and their** course may be tracked for a long distance by **the** breaking of twigs and the snapping of branches. A full-grown elk will weigh from 700 to

900 pounds, so that it may be readily imagined that the momentum generated cannot be trifling.

Reader, when first you went out covert-shooting as a youth, can you not recall to mind how your heart went "pit-pat" as a beater shouted, "Look out; hare!" or "Mark cock!" Can you not remember how the whirring sound of the first pheasant, as it came down quickly with the wind across the ride where you were stationed, raised your excitement to the most frantic pitch? If you can still recall these feelings, you have a faint, but a *very* faint idea of what it is to hear the sound of breaking boughs coming straight towards you in the middle of a dense Norwegian forest. Now is the time to be steady, and keep that heart of yours from throbbing and bumping as if it would jump clean out of your breast. Ten to one you will miss if it be the first time you have been out elk-hunting. I did (though that is no reason why you should). I could no more have fired than have done—I don't know what impossibility. I stood like the cockney who had never fired a shot before in his life, when invited down to the country to shoot pheasants. Admiration of the pretty "long-tailed" creatures quite got the better of him, to the intense disgust of the gamekeeper.

The Swedes have a very apt term for the feeling which such sights produce in the tyro's breast, viz., "skogs-frossa." And I believe no *young* sportsman, at all events, will be able **to see a majestic elk for** the first time in his life, in its native wilds, **without** being attacked with this fever in a greater or less degree.

When a **flock of elks is** proceeding **through a** forest, and no danger is anticipated, they usually go one after the **other,** like a flock of sheep. Probably this *modus eundi* is common to all ruminant animals. Strict order is preserved in the line of march; the oldest **goes** in front, then the female, **while the young calves bring** up the rear. So closely do they follow **on each other's** heels, that **each one rests its nose on its predecessor's loins.**

When trotting, their footmarks **are** nearly in a right line, **and when they** gallop all four feet come down nearly together. Those of the male are **shorter and** thicker at the end than those of the female. This **is** caused by the former spreading the foot out, and by the **latter** compressing it.

I know nothing more interesting **than to watch an** experienced hunter **with his dog on elk trail. No** backwoodsman of North America, such as Cooper loved **to** dwell upon, went more cautiously to work than does **the regular** Norwegian hunter. If **you want** to see **a man's soul in his** work, just study his method of proceeding the first time you get an opportunity. See how carefully he examines the leaves and young shoots of that birch, and judges by the nibbled leaves how long it is since the elk was there; watch him turning up the dead leaves and scrutinizing a footmark; look at him crawling along cat-like on all fours to get a peep over yonder knoll. Neither is his dog idle; he enters into the sport heartily. Those deep-drawn sniffs, which would make you think the animal would suddenly collapse, indicate plainly that an elk is not far off. Now he stands up on his hind legs, and sniffs away among the birch leaves, where an elk's nose has been, not so very long before. Now he tugs away against the collar as if he would pull you along fifty miles an hour. You are close to your game. Tread very softly; a crackling twig or a rolling stone may mar the labour of a whole day, ay, of two or three.

It is intensely exciting work—much more so than in reindeer-hunting, because your horizon of vision is so limited, and you may be close on an elk before you know it.

The dung of the elk is soft in summer, resembling that of a cow; in winter it is hard, and looks more like a bunch of large nuts than anything else.

They are possessed of very acute senses, but their powers of smell are not nearly so delicate or so great as those of the reindeer. Judging from the widely-distended nostril one would think the contrary to be the case. On the other hand, their eyesight is extremely quick; and this again is remarkable, for in comparison to the size of the body the eye is very small. But lest this should not prove a sufficient compensation for their defective organs of smell, Nature has granted them a most extraordinarily keen sense of hearing. And it is principally for this reason that they are so difficult of approach.

When resting, they select rising grounds, where eyes, nose, and ears will be most likely to give them timely notice of approaching danger. When the weather is thick and foggy they will keep to the densest part of the forest, but resort to more open spots on clear and frosty days.

The Norwegian hunters use large-bored rifles in elk, reindeer, and bear hunting: these are usually made up in the country, and are not, therefore, remarkable for external beauty and finish. Still many of them carry well. Within the last two or three years, however, the Kongsberg rifle is getting gradually dispersed over the whole country. It is a breech-loader; and doubtless many of my readers will have noticed specimens at the late Exhibition. The barrel is on the Whitworth principle; and the breech-loading part is after their own invention, and is to my mind a most clumsy and unpractical contrivance. However, they are very cheap, costing only about three pounds.

The infection of rifle-shooting has reached Norway

and Sweden; there is scarcely a village that has not its shooting club. Little wonder if the number of native hunters increase!

Some of the old hunters will tell marvellous tales. Up in the country the peasants are extremely superstitious, and would, I verily believe, sooner give credence to anything very unlikely than to a plain matter-of-fact history. For instance, Mr. Asbjörnsen relates: " I have been told that it is worse than useless to aim at an elk's forehead unless at very close quarters; and in exemplification of this interesting assertion was informed that a man once shot seven times at an elk. All seven balls struck the animal in the forehead, and all seven glanced off in different directions. The suggestion that it was not owing to any extraordinary thickness of skull, but to weak powder, was, I need scarcely add, pooh-poohed."

According to an old saying, the elk-hunter must not only have a firm and steady hand, a sure eye, and a trusty rifle, but he must also be possessed of a hard heart. A dying elk, they say, looks at his murderer in a most reproachful and pitiful manner. I have read of a man who had killed several elks in his time. One day, when out hunting, he came upon a couple, and took aim at the largest one. The ball struck the animal in a mortal part, but it did not immediately fall to the ground. Meanwhile, it kept getting weaker and weaker from loss of blood, which gushed forth from the wound, but still kept its eyes steadily fixed on the man, looking at him in a most reproachful manner. Moved with compassion, he stepped forward to put an end to the poor beast's sufferings with his "tolle-kniv," when just as he was going to give the *coup de grâce,* the animal cast such a look at him that he was obliged to turn aside till it was dead. Meanwhile, the second elk, as is often the case, had returned to look after its companion. Here was a chance! Two elks in one day is not such a despicable bag to one gun. But the ordeal through which his nerves had recently passed had completely upset him, so that he could not find in his heart to shoot it. Then and there he made a solemn vow that as long as he lived he would never raise gun any more against an elk, for it seemed to him as if he had for all the world been guilty of murder. The memory of the scene haunted him, I suppose, like the killing of the albatross did the "ancient mariner."

Now-a-days in Norway the elk is, I believe, universally hunted with a single dog, trained for the purpose, held in hand. Last autumn, however, two were shot in Odalen by a party of hunters who adopted the plan of "*driving,*" *i. e.*, of stationing themselves in a line at suitable distances from each other, and employing a number of beaters and dogs to drive them in their direction. One of these animals weighed

K

from 80 to 90 'bismerpund,' the 'bismerpund' being 13⅓ pounds English. But in Sweden they have many different methods; for an account of which the reader is referred to Lloyd's interesting work on sport.

Many elks are killed, mostly at unlawful times, on "skie"—of which, for the benefit of those of the uninitiated, I will give a brief description. They consist of two long pieces of wood—those made of seasoned ash are best—about ten feet long, and four to five inches wide in the middle. They taper in front, and ultimately terminate in a point, being slightly turned up towards the toe, after the manner of a Chinese shoe. I believe they are peculiar to Norway, Sweden, Finland, and Russia. It is the *universal* method of getting about during the winter: in fact, the tremendous depth of the snow in many places would render any other mode of going on foot impracticable. It requires long experience to be able to manage them properly; and to be able to hunt on skie is an art that can only be acquired after years of practice. I believe Mr. Lloyd was one of the few Englishmen who was ever perfectly at home on them. To see a practised "skie-löber" (runner) is really a very fine sight. He will go down the steepest places with the rapidity of an arrow, his body slightly bent forward, holding in both hands a staff about six feet in length, the bottom end pointed to the ground behind him at an **angle of 45° (about). And though going at such a tremendous velocity, he** can steer clear of stumps or **trees with marvellous** nicety, often jumping as **much as eighteen feet when occasion requires it.**

On Sunday the peasants may often be seen in off-lying districts, for instance, in parts of Thelemarken, where there are no roads, coming to church, **men,** women, and boys; the women frequently carrying babies on their backs, gipsy **fashion. In the north,** the Lapps, I have been **told, leave the babies outside** the **church to keep them warm. They dig a** hole in the **snow, and pop them in,** leaving a **dog** to keep guard against any wolves. A friend of mine told me **that he has** often passed a comfortable night under the snow **in** preference to going into the filthy huts in parts **of Finland.** But it is of course dangerous to **do** so unless well wrapped up, or if the clothes be wet.

The practised "skie-löber" binds his skie to his foot so as to prevent their slipping; but for **a tyro this would** be highly dangerous, as a broken leg or sprained ankle may, and does, frequently, result from travelling with the "skie" fastened.

It **is a** most exhilarating exercise; the rapidity with which **one** rushes through the clear frosty air has a most wonderful effect on the system. The great danger to guard against is **catching** cold, which from the violent perspiration it educes may easily be the case. In Christiania it is usually the custom for parties of cadets, students, &c., to go out long excursions on Sunday, and have steeple-chases. The accompanying sketch, taken from the illustrated newspaper of the Norwegian capital, may suffice to give an idea of it. I should add that even on level ground seven or eight miles an hour, and even more, can readily be accomplished by a good runner.

But I must pull up. Let me see, I was saying many elk are killed on "skie." Their long legs stick in the snow, so that it is not difficult to come up with them. Many, too, fall victims to the wolves at this season, which are able to run over the snow without sinking very deep, though even these are easily overtaken by the hunter when equipped with his snow "skie."

In the winter of 1848-49 there were killed, unlawfully, in Vaaler, no less than 140 elks.

Though many elks are still shot unlawfully, yet instances (exceptional, undoubtedly) do occasionally occur where the most extraordinary scrupulousness has been evinced by the parties concerned, to the advantage of the elk. I remember reading in the "Morgenblad," a winter or two ago, about the capture of an elk which was enjoying a swim in a small lake some miles from Christiania. It had been seen from shore,

RUNNING ON SKIE.   To face p. 132.

and at once every boat was put in requisition. A whale chase could scarcely have been more exciting. In the bows of each boat a man was stationed, with a long rope like a lasso, ready to fling it round the animal's horns the first opportunity. After much dodging and doubling, one of the boats eventually succeeded in getting fast, and at once proceeded to tow the poor beast to land, *nolens volens*. "In the multitude of counsellors the city is safe," says an old proverb; it proved so at all events with the elk. Had there been fewer participators, the odds would, I think, have been decidedly against its getting off so easily. But as it was, the general feeling prevailed that it would be highly imprudent to resort to extreme measures in the presence of so many witnesses, unless the fortunate crew could first succeed in gaining the ear of the nearest functionary of the law. A council was held. "What shall we do with it, now we have got it?" "Ask the Foged, of course," said some one, brimming over with admiration for the laws of his country, especially for those relating to the preservation of game. So a message was sent to the Foged. "Elk captured; what shall we do with it?" "Let him go," was the brief reply; and thus the elk luckily escaped this time.

I heard of another instance which amused me not a little. An old woman had occasion one fine morning to row across a river to a place where a man had bought a small piece of ground. She had scarcely got half way over when she perceived an elk on the opposite side, standing at about the distance of eighty paces from the door of the man's cabin. It seemed as if meditating on a swim. Thinking it a pleasant sight, she "easied all," and sat looking at the noble beast. But soon other feelings than those of admiration began to be awakened within her breast. Winter would soon be coming on, and a good supply of elk's meat would be no bad thing, leaving the uses to which hide, horns, fat, &c., &c., could be put out of the question. By dint of signs and gesticulations she managed to make the owner of the house acquainted with the proximity of the animal. The man, who was himself an ardent hunter, but at the same time rather nervous about incurring a penalty of forty dollars, deemed it, however, prudent in the first place to consult his book and ascertain whether it was all right. Whether it was or not the story does not relate. But at all events his consultation ended in his bringing out his rifle; and he was just proceeding to stalk the elk after the most approved fashion when another difficulty occurred to him, *the animal was not on his property*. So in he went to have another look at the law. Meanwhile the elk, becoming aware that something was between "the wind and his nobility," and not relishing the appearance of the old woman in the boat, quietly trotted off into the forest. Awful was the wrath and excitement of the old lady, who saw all her fond hopes thwarted by the stupidity of Ole (somehow or other everybody seems to be called Ole), whom she declared she would bang well with her oars if she got within reach of him.

Amongst other plans to which poachers have recourse the following is perhaps the most general, and most successful:—

The whereabouts of an elk having been ascertained, one of the party, usually the one who is the best shot, conceals himself on the nearest hill. For the elk-deer when startled instinctively makes off to the first piece of rising ground in the immediate neighbourhood, whence it can have a good look out-on all sides. Meanwhile the rest of the party "ring" the animal, and if they are unable to get a shot, one of them makes a slight noise just sufficient to startle it, but not so as to terrify it. The elk at once makes off to the hill in question, where it in all probability meets with its end.

Some poachers, I am told, are able to entice the elk close to them during the pairing season by means of some peculiar call.

As above stated, the usual way of hunting elk in Norway is with a dog held in a leash. When the dog has got scent of an elk, which it frequently will do at long distances, the hunter gives himself up entirely to its guidance, still holding it in hand; for it is rarely that a dog arrives at such a pitch of "canine education" as to be allowed his liberty. When they have approached near to the place where the animals are supposed to be, the dog is tied up to a tree while his master proceeds alone to stalk them. In case one is killed the same method is observed in flaying, quartering, &c., as described before in the case of the reindeer. But so extremely quick of hearing are they, that it often happens that the labour of a whole, or even two or three days' hunting is rendered useless by the snapping of a twig or the rolling of a stone.

As may therefore be supposed, rough and stormy weather is more propitious to elk-hunting than calm and still weather.

I firmly believe, and several hunters with whom I have spoken have confirmed my opinion, that a double-barrelled smooth bore is much better adapted for this manner of hunting than a rifle; for it generally happens that you can only get a snap shot between an opening in the trees, and as a smooth bore will throw a bullet with tolerable accuracy for seventy or eighty paces, beyond which distance an elk, except when found in the open, is rarely shot, and is, moreover, much easier to take a snap shot with than a rifle, it appears only reasonable that preference should be given to it. Those who meditate elk-hunting will do well to practise snap shots both with rifle and gun (say at forty or fifty yards, and even more) at a target; and if they can only procure that extremely "rara avis in terris," a dead donkey, stuff him with straw, and put him on stilts, they will have the nearest approach I know of to the real thing.

The following account of moose-hunting in Nova Scotia, furnished me by a gentleman who has had practical experience both in that country and in Norway, will, I think, be found interesting:—

"There are three ways of hunting the moose in Nova Scotia, '*creeping*,' '*calling*,' and hunting on 'snow shoes.' I have had no experience of the last, not having remained in those parts late enough in the year; but I believe it is but poor sport, as the wretched moose sinking in the snow must sooner or later be run down, and you can get a shot at ten yards if you like.

"'Creeping' (*i.e.*, following in autumn with Indians by the track, or *stalking*) is the true sport, and I believe is only practised in Nova Scotia.

"The Micmacs are first-rate hunters. I had the best, I believe, in the province, though he was getting rather old. His instinct, for such it seemed, was marvellous. I was out for about three weeks in the woods in Nova Scotia in the latter part of September and beginning of October with two Micmac Indians. Captain H——, a most experienced sportsman, kindly came out with me for the first few days to 'set me going.' The following is an extract from my diary of our first day's hunting:—

"*September* 16*th*, 1857.—Up before daylight—a fine day with cool breeze—very good, they said, for 'creeping.' We set off in high hopes before sunrise, and in about an hour Joe found a fresh moose-track, which we followed through thick hardwood and over a 'barren.' It was marvellous to see the sagacity of the Indian. The moment he knew he was on game his countenance brightened, and every faculty of mind and body seemed brought into action, yet without displaying the least excitement or want of perfect self-possession. Where I could see no track (and sporting has sharpened my eye pretty well), he seemed scarcely for a moment at a loss. Where footprints failed, the turn of a leaf, the slightest scratch on a piece of bark, or a little twig, seemed signs enough. We worked our way rapidly but cautiously through the thick brush, carefully putting back every branch as we passed, feeling lightly with our mocassined feet the fallen moss-covered trees lest they might not bear our weight. H—— insisted that the young hunter should have the first chance, so I followed close behind Joe, who every now and then would turn and whisper,

'Moose passing through here **two** hours ago,' (the Indians are very partial to the 'present participle'). 'Here **moose** lying down,' 'Moose biting this only one half-hour since,' then very softly, 'Put on cap, we close **to** moose;' **and** accordingly in a few minutes (about **two** hours after we had commenced to follow the tracks) he stopped suddenly and pointed, but without saying a word. A fine bull moose was lying down within **thirty** yards of us. I was standing a little to **the right**, and unluckily some thick young spruce prevented **my** seeing him. H—, who was **to the left, had a** fine chance, **but** his rifle **missed fire, and away** went the moose, **crashing** through **the** forest without giving me **even a** second's sight of him. After a pipe of **consolation** for our ill-luck we got on the track again, and after following him for an hour more came up with him among some burnt wood. I got a shot at about sixty yards and hit him; he fell, but immediately rose and went off, and we still followed him perseveringly. This time, however, **he** seemed determined to wear us out, as he kept almost entirely in the burnt forest, so that we had perpetually to climb and scramble over the fallen and half-rotten timber for some two hours. Joe **said the** moose was evidently hard hit; but as he was leading us away from our camp, and the day was advancing, **we** judged it better **to give** him up, and to make the best of our way back.

"After this I had a long run of bad luck, hunting diligently day after day, and very seldom finding tracks fresh enough to be worth following, but in the last week I was fortunate enough to kill two moose. I was then encamped on a little island in the middle of St. Mary's Lake, in the heart of a wild and uninhabited part of the province. I roused my sleeping Indians before daybreak, and without waiting for breakfast 'Old Joe' and I set off for the opposite shore in the little leaky 'dug-out' with which we had contrived to navigate the lake. We trudged for some distance through thick forest, and before dawn had reached a 'barren,' where Joe intended to try the effect of a 'call.'* After some little time the call was answered from a great distance. Gradually the sounds became nearer and nearer. At last a fine bull moose emerged from the forest on the opposite side of the 'barren.' He soon disappeared again, however, and as Joe's most artistic 'calls' could elicit no further reply, our patience was at last exhausted, and we judged it best to go on and try whether we could not track him. To our intense disgust we very soon saw him coming out of a hollow in the 'barren' (very much nearer than we had supposed him to be), and then trotting off to the woods again. I was on the point of firing, but Joe wisely

---

* The "call" is made of a long roll of birch-bark. They are much used in Norway for calling the cattle home in the evenings.

prevented me as it was too **far**. As the moose had seen us there was of course **no use in** following him further then, so we went off to see about our breakfast. **As** we were re-crossing the barren Joe lingered on a rising ground to have another 'last fond look' towards **the** forest. Turning round, I saw him lying down and beckoning to me, so I immediately crept up to him and observed, in the direction he pointed, another bull moose standing at the edge of the forest some 500 or 600 yards off. He also, no doubt, **had been attracted** by the 'call.' **We lay and watched** him anxiously, **as gradually and very slowly he came** nearer and nearer to **us.** At last he was within a hundred **yards, and** standing still, **but he** was facing me, and a tree was somewhat in **the way too, so** I dared not fire. What a noble fellow he was, **as he** stood there with his long black hair glistening in **the** morning sun! At last he **moved** slightly to the left, and I fired, **aiming** immediately behind the shoulder. He wheeled about and **trotted** off as if nothing was the matter. The second barrel **of** my rifle missed fire. I then rushed **over to** where Joe was lying and seized my smooth bore, and gave him both barrels as he was making rapidly for the wood **at about 200** yards. This brought him **too.** In a few minutes **more** Joe's knife was in his throat. It turned out that **the ball of** my Lancaster rifle had entered where I intended it should, **and had** passed through the body, almost touching the heart, and that one ball of the smooth bore had gone through the neck, while another had broken one of the hind legs.

"The day I killed my other moose (and indeed, had I been fortunate, might have secured two right and left) I had a great chance of a bear. One does not put the cap on the nipple until the moose is supposed to be near. Whilst we were looking for tracks a bear crossed us, and sat down to look at us, within fifty yards of me. But of course, whilst I was fumbling in my waistcoat pocket for a cap he was off.

"One night a bear came and prowled round my 'camp' for a long time, attracted, no doubt, by the smell of my pork. Unluckily it was a pitch-dark night, and I could not see him; so at last, getting tired of listening to him, I rolled myself up in my blanket again and went to sleep.

"For moose-hunting in Nova Scotia you must 'go in for it' in a much more business-like way than the Norwegians do. There is no use trying it unless you regularly take to the woods for a fortnight or so, and it is pretty hard work, for you have to carry everything you want for the expedition on your back, sharing the labour of this equally with the Indians. Your '*impedimenta*' consist of a camp (under which high-sounding title is signified a piece of oiled calico about six feet long by five feet wide, intended to be tied in a slanting position to shelter your head and part of your bodies from the wind and rain at night), blankets, two or three tin kettles, tea, sugar, ship biscuit, and salt pork, and last, but most important of all, an axe. It is no easy work sometimes in 'changing country' after a hard morning's hunting to have to shoulder your heavy bundle in the afternoon and trudge some ten miles more through the dense forest, often through swamps and over 'windfalls,' with only the left hand free to climb over the latter. Happy is one if encamping that night one can feel out a 'var,' or Balsam fir, to make one's bed. But it is a glorious life!"

"I think," adds my informant, "that the moose of North America is larger than the European elk. Certainly the heads are much finer in America. I have seen a great number of heads in Österdalen and elsewhere, and none are to be compared to mine, or to many others I have seen in Nova Scotia." But to return.

Amongst the wild animals of Norway the bear, the wolf, the lynx, and the glutton are the elk's deadliest foes. Probably fewer fall a victim to the "paw of the bear" than to either of the animals above mentioned. Indeed, Mr. Asbjörnsen mentions that in Österdal it was looked upon as an improbability, almost amounting to an impossibility, that a bear would kill an elk, and that when such was reported to have been the case it was ten to one the fabrication of some poacher who sought to cast the blame of "elk-murder" on Bruin's broad shoulders in order to avoid getting into trouble himself. There is reason in this, and little doubt but that poor Bruin has had to bear the blame of countless infringements of the game laws innocently.

But that a bear will kill an elk when he gets an opportunity I should be slow to disbelieve, even if the following well-authenticated account did not solve the question. In the autumn of 1850 two hunters in the woods near Aamot in Österdal, suddenly came across a bear which had just brought down an elk, and which was so busy in sucking the blood that it was not aware of the approach of danger, and accordingly paid dear for its presumption. As it occurred in the proper shooting season there was obviously no reason for deception being practised on the part of the hunters.

Wangenheim avers that in the forests of Lithuania many elks are killed by the bears.

"Bruin never ventures," he writes, "to approach a herd of elk, but only looks out for an outlying deer, approaching it stealthily till sufficiently near to give the fatal spring. When once he has got the animal tightly hugged he commences to suck the blood from the throat. His thirst being slaked, and the elk quite dead, he then covers up the remains with leaves, boughs, and moss, and pays daily visits to his larder till there is **none of** it left.

"Should the elk, however, discover the approach **of its** adversary, instead of seeking to save itself by flight it prepares for the battle. Fear is probably the cause of this, and not pugnacity. With its long legs it is capable of lashing out tremendous blows, which require all the activity and dodging Bruin is capable of to avoid. It not unfrequently happens that the bear gets such a '**oner**' over the **ear as** to make him cry 'peccavi,' and to 'ficher le camp;' for at the best Bruin in Norway is a **cowardly beast.** I have **been credibly** informed that **a herd** of cows, in a part of Sætersdal, gave a bear which had approached their pasture ground on the mountains such a tremendous drubbing, charging at him simultaneously on all sides with their horns, as to make him change his offensive intentions, and execute a '*strategic movement*' on the shortest possible notice. But should it happen that the bear is able to avoid the deadly kicks and get alongside his prey, he deals the poor elk such a tremendous blow on the head with his powerful forearm, as to knock him out of time altogether. Sometimes he will even spring on his back, when the affrighted animal at once dashes off, wondering who the ―— is on his back, through the midst of the forest, to the great discomfiture of the rider, who slips igno-

L

miniously off, and goes growling off to lick himself. It must be a strange sight to see."

Such is a sketch of the account Wangeheim gives; but I should be sorry to vouch for its correctness.

If a herd of elk discover a bear in their immediate neighbourhood, they are the challengers, and at once boldly advance to give battle. Lucky then for Bruin if he has time to clamber up a tree, from whence he can safely and calmly "look out upon his pursuers."

The wolf is by far a more dangerous enemy to the elk than the bear. For Bruin is safely stowed away in winter quarters, sleeping and sucking his thumb, at a time when the elk is less able to defend itself than at any other, viz., when the snow lies deep on the ground. But a single wolf never ventures to attack an elk alone; and even supposing that one were to succeed in getting firm hold of it by the loins, its weight would not be sufficient to prevent the animal from rushing off through the forest, and giving him a rougher ride than he had bargained for. It is principally the young calves that fall victims to these ravenous animals.

In hard and severe winters, when the wolves congregate in packs, the elk suffer most from their depredations. But even then, so greatly do they stand in fear of the awful kicks, that it is only when reduced to the last extremity that they will venture to attack a herd. In such cases they endeavour to separate a deer from the main body; and if they succeed in so doing they set after it like a pack of foxhounds after Reynard, following it unceasingly till they bring it down. Doubtless, many elk fall a prey to the wolf at this season, when the snow lies deep on the ground, as their long legs sink too deep in the snow to be of much service to them either in showing their heels or in using them as a means of offence.

The lynx and the glutton have never been known to attack a full-grown elk. The attentions of these animals are confined to the young calves, or to any that have been wounded or are sick.

Like the reindeer, the elk is much tormented during the summer with musquitoes and all kinds of abominable flies, with which the forests and swamps of Norway abound.

It has been computed that an elk seldom attains a greater age than sixteen or seventeen years.

Wangenheim mentions that it is a common occurrence to light upon dead elks in the forests of Lithuania. The diseases to which they are peculiarly liable are "splenitis" and "dysentery," owing, probably, to their making use of stagnant water in very hot summers. This can, however, scarcely be applicable to the elk-deer in Norway, where it is scarcely possible, either in forest or on fjeld, to go a mile without meeting with a mountain stream of the clearest and most delicious water.

The uses to which the dead elk-deer can be applied are as manifold as in the case of the reindeer; the flesh, hide, hair, knuckles, marrow, fat, sinews, hoofs, &c., being all and each employed in various branches of domestic economy.

At the proper season elk venison is considered to be a wholesome and nutritious food, though coarser and less palatable than reindeer venison. The flesh is of a darker colour. As may be supposed, the calves prove the best eating.

From the middle towards the end of the month of September, the flesh of the bucks is uneatable, having a rank and nauseous taste, on account of the approaching rutting season. Still, I think, the stomach of a Norwegian Bönde is capable of digesting almost anything;* an assertion which those who have travelled much in the country will doubtless corroborate. The best time for eating elk venison is undoubtedly in the beginning of August, though that of the does may be eaten till towards the end of September.

Mr. Asbjörnsen says that he has been informed by an experienced housewife in Solöer, who used to keep

---

* On seeing them eat, I have often thought of those lines of Horace, beginning—
"Dura messorum ilia," &c.

a large establishment, and had to **feed** as many **as** twenty people daily, the year round, that she **con**sidered "one elk was about equivalent to two cows with regard to quantity of meat."

I mentioned above that nearly every portion of the animal **is** used up some way or other in household economy. Thus, the hide is tanned and serves for straps, sole leather; the part under the belly is made into wash-leather, and is used for gloves, **lining for** coats and cloaks, and **formerly was generally used** for breeches. The **knuckle joints, which are firm** and of a remarkably white **hue, are used in** turner's work; while the horns **form handles for knives,** or are boiled **down into glue. From the hoofs** finger-rings are **made,** which are considered to **possess** some inherent **and** potent charm. The hair is used **in** stuffing pillows, cushions, &c. In fine, with **the** exception of the "in'ards," every part is used up.

Elks can be very readily tamed and domesticated. According to Professor Nilsson, successful attempts have been made to bring up young calves and tame them. **At the** Veterinary Institute in Stockholm a **cross between a** tame elk and **a** cow has been obtained. But, **according** to Wangenheim, similar attempts in Lithuania **have proved** to be failures. The experiments made there **with** rearing and taming elk partially succeeded; for a time **the** animals thrived remarkably well, and **became extremely plump** and fat; but they never arrived at such a pitch of domestication as to be used as draught animals.* They all of them died, however, before completing the third year, of diarrhœa or dysentery.

The average number of elks that are shot in Norway has been computed to amount to about 200 head per annum; many, perhaps the greater part, unlawfully. And Mr. Asbjörnsen considers that the total number of elk-deer in Norway may be put down at about 5000 head.

The value of an elk-deer ranges from 20 to 30 **dollars**, or from £4 10s. to £6 15s., though they are often worth more. The flesh of a full-grown elk seldom weighs less than 40 bismer-pund, though they have been known to attain double this weight.

Of late years the number of elk that have been shot unlawfully during the winter, both in Norway and Sweden, has attracted the attention of government; and I was informed that a bill would be laid before the Storthing which is at present sitting,† the object

---

* An officer at Halifax, Nova **Scotia, kept** a young bull moose for a considerable time in the **barrack-yard.** Its great delight was to lie with its head on a **soldier's** lap, **and** have tobacco-smoke puffed up its nostrils! It got its master into numberless scrapes **by** its love for cabbages. No paling was high enough to prevent **its** invading the neighbouring kitchen gardens. It died at last from an over-feed of turnips. I have **been** told that moose have been trained to draw in America.

† March, 1863.

of which is, as far as elk are concerned, to raise the penalty for shooting these animals at unlawful periods so considerably as to render it less easy for the poacher to escape with a mulct, which evidently did not meet the requirements of the case.

Every true sportsman will, I think, feel interested in this matter, and will be glad to hear that these noble and majestic animals, the pride of Norway's forests, as the reindeer are the ornament of her mountain wilds, will be better protected against the attacks of the poacher.

It has often occurred to me whether it might not be possible to introduce these animals into the extensive deer forests in many parts of Scotland. If the climate would suit them—and there is not such a wonderful difference after all—there can be little doubt, I think, that they would thrive, especially when it is borne in mind that the absence of their great enemy, the wolf, would tell not a little in their favour. At all events, would it not be worth the trial? I do not apprehend it would be a matter of great difficulty to procure a few calves, and if once got, the passage from Norway is a trifling consideration. It has long been my wish to see both the elk, the reindeer, and the hjerpe (*Tetrao bonasia*) introduced into Scotland; and, at the risk of being considered presumptuous, I cannot but think it might answer. With reindeer it would probably be more questionable; but in my humble opinion I think both elk and hjerpe would thrive admirably in company. Indeed, some twenty or thirty years ago, perhaps more, a herd of tame reindeer was sent over to Scotland. A Norwegian friend of mine told me he remembered seeing them being driven through the streets of Christiania previous to embarkation. The experiment did not succeed.*

I have more than once alluded to the superstitions that are so prevalent amongst the Norwegian peasantry. In Mr. Asbjörnsen's celebrated "Huldre Eventyr," a fair idea may be formed of the queer tales and odd things they believe in. I was asked by the talented author of this book to translate it into English, but a glance over its contents and style at once showed me that it was beyond my capabilities to render the slang expressions into anything like idiomatic English; and at the same time to preserve the character of the work. And even by the very best translation possible, this

---

* Lately, through the exertions of Professor Rasch and of other gentlemen interested in the acclimatization of animals, &c., a few young chamois from the alps of Bavaria have been introduced into the country. They are to be kept in an enclosed space for the first winter, and will be turned out in the neighbourhood of Gausta Fjeld, Thelemarken, next spring. This locality, which, though much colder than many other parts, yet being remote from the sea, the air from which is said to have an injurious effect upon these animals, has been selected as the scene of operations. I hear that they are doing well, and that there is every prospect of the ultimate success of the project.

admirable sketch of peasant superstition would lose more than half its value.

Countries abounding in immense **forest** tracts and lofty mountains, lakes, and cataracts, always have **been** a stronghold for superstitious beliefs. And this is **doubly the case in a** country like Norway, which **is** thinly populated, and where in the off-lying districts the means of communication are bad. Moreover, the long winter nights engender a love for story-telling; and added to this, that during some months of the **year new** faces are seldom seen, it is no wonder **if the "traditions of the elders"** are held **in esteem.** Further, in **the** valleys especially, the peasants are exclusive to a degree : they mix but little with the natives of other valleys ; and it is rare that a marriage takes place between a couple who have not been born and bred in the same neighbourhood. **The** consequence of these united circumstances is, that **the love of** the marvellous is kept alive, and that tales and stories are handed down from father to son as precious heirlooms for belief. Any one (could not Mr. Borrow try his hand?) who was sufficiently at home in the different dialects of the country, might make a most entertaining collection of tales and strange stories from the valleys of Norway.

There **is** scarcely a lake, I may say, in Norway concerning **which** the peasant has not some strange tale to relate ; either that it is of unfathomable depth more questionable; but in my humble opinion I think both elk and hjerpe would thrive admirably in company. Indeed, some twenty or thirty years ago, perhaps more, a herd of tame reindeer was sent over to Scotland. A Norwegian friend of mine told me he remembered seeing them being driven through the streets of Christiania previous to embarkation. The experiment did not succeed.*

I have more than once alluded to the superstitions that are so prevalent amongst the Norwegian peasantry. In Mr. Asbjörnsen's celebrated "Huldre Eventyr," a fair idea may be formed of the queer tales and odd things they believe in. I was asked by the talented author of this book to translate it into English, but a glance over its contents and style at once showed me that it was beyond my capabilities to render the slang expressions into anything like idiomatic English; and at the same time to preserve the character of the work. And even by the very best translation possible, this

* Lately, through the exertions of Professor Rasch and of other gentlemen interested in the acclimatization of animals, &c., a few young chamois from the alps of Bavaria have been introduced into the country. They are to be kept in an enclosed space for the first winter, and will be turned out in the neighbourhood of Gausta Fjeld, Thelemarken, next spring. This locality, which, though much colder than many other parts, yet being remote from the sea, the air from which is said to have an injurious effect upon these animals, has been selected as the scene of operations. I hear that they are doing well, and that there is every prospect of the ultimate success of the project.

admirable sketch of peasant superstition would lose more than half its value.

Countries abounding in immense forest tracts and lofty mountains, lakes, and cataracts, always have been a stronghold for superstitious beliefs. And this is doubly the case in a country like Norway, which is thinly populated, and where in the off-lying districts the means of communication are bad. Moreover, the long winter nights engender a love for story-telling; and added to this, that during some months of the year new faces are seldom seen, it is no wonder if the "traditions of the elders" are held in esteem. Further, in the valleys especially, the peasants are exclusive to a degree: they mix but little with the natives of other valleys; and it is rare that a marriage takes place between a couple who have not been born and bred in the same neighbourhood. The consequence of these united circumstances is, that the love of the marvellous is kept alive, and that tales and stories are handed down from father to son as precious heirlooms for belief. Any one (could not Mr. Borrow try his hand?) who was sufficiently at home in the different dialects of the country, might make a most entertaining collection of tales and strange stories from the valleys of Norway.

There is scarcely a lake, I may say, in Norway concerning which the peasant has not some strange tale to relate; either that it is of unfathomable depth see; but on application found that, as it was not considered worthy of a place amongst the archives, it had been destroyed. I would have given a great deal to have seen it, and have made a verbatim translation of it.

From what I could ascertain as to the result—for I was at the lake in question last summer, and made a point of gathering what information I could—it appeared that some inquiry was made into the matter.

I should think it more than probable that an elk may partly have been the cause of this too. Somebody very likely, as in the first story, had seen one swimming about, and had at once put it down for a monster; while the remains of fish on the bank, probably the work of an otter, served to confirm the reports that had been spread of its devastations.

While going up the Bandag's Vand on a steamer, the captain drew my attention to a narrow part of the lake, through which we were passing—perhaps eighty yards wide—which the peasantry firmly believed to have been caused by a sea-serpent which, tired of remaining in the upper part of the lake, had forced its way through the narrow channel connecting them, and made it larger and deeper.

THE GAME LAWS AT PRESENT IN **VOGUE IN** NORWAY.

REINDEER HUNTING begins August 1st, and ends April 1st. Penalty for shooting one at other times, 10 dollars.

ELK SHOOTING begins August 1st, and ends October 31st. Penalty, 60 **dollars.** Only one may be shot yearly on one property.

RED DEER. Same as elk. Two may be shot annually on the same property. Penalty, 30 dollars.

HARES may be killed from August 15th to June 1st. Penalty, 2 dollars.

GREY HENS AND FEMALE CAPERCALZIE may be shot **or snared** from August 15th to March 15th.

BLACK COCK, MALE CAPERCALZIE, HJERPER, and EIDER DUCKS, from August 15th to June 1st.

PARTRIDGES from Sept. 1st to Jan. 1st.

The penalty in the above cases is 1 dollar.

CHAPTER III.

THE FEATHERED GAME OF NORWAY.

From the casual remarks interspersed here and there in my description of each Amt, I am induced to think that I may have given too bright a colour to, and raised too high expectations of the general shooting to be had in Norway. I therefore hasten to soften it down a little, and to impart a more sober tone to the picture I have drawn.

If a man be a true lover of nature, and a true sportsman into the bargain (and how often do the two go together!), the pleasure and gratification he will experience from rambling through the wild and glorious scenery of "gamle Norge" will prove a compensation to any disappointment he may undergo in the matter of sport. If the free life, the grandeur of the forests, and the desolate, nay savage, wildness of the fjelds, the noble cascades, and, not the least, the pure atmosphere of the mountains, possess charms for him, I may say the principal charms, so that whatever **sport** comes in his way is looked on as subordinate **to the** former, and **will prevent** him growling **and grumbling** when he returns **to** his night quarters, that "he has come all **the way to** Norway merely to shoot this wretched brace of **ryper**;" or **that** "he **has** gone *bear-slaying* through **the** forest days together and seen nothing but a capercalzie rising a hundred yards out of shot;" then a visit to Norway will amply repay him, both as regards **body** and mind. But if, **on the** other hand, **he expects to** make a large bag of **grouse, and will be** disappointed if he cannot kill, **at least, his twenty brace a** day, and fall in **with a** bear **or two, and kill** sundry reindeer, and perhaps **an** elk, then **by** all means **let him** stay at home. Norway **is** essentially a country for *sportsmen*, and not at all a place for shooters.

It is, indeed, **a rare** occurrence to be able to bag **as** much as fifteen brace a day; and even that will require a great deal of very hard work. No doubt on some of the islands off the north-western coast large bags may be made, but I am now speaking of Norway Proper.

A Norwegian friend of mine, and an excellent shot, told me that he did not know any place where "he could **feel** confident of killing ten brace in the day."

The **fact is,** the shooting has considerably deteriorated, principally because the introduction of railways and steam communication have rendered it a profitable employment to the Bönder to snare and trap the game for the markets; for it is seldom that they shoot them.

In 1859, a friend of mine was shooting in the neighbourhood of Maristuen on the Fille Fjeld, than which no better grouse-ground can well be imagined, and though he had two good dogs with him, yet never a feather did he see.

In the above remarks I am of course only alluding to the feathered game. As regards reindeer hunting, which is *par excellence* as far as shooting is concerned, *the* sport of the country, the matter is totally different. But even on this I would remark that whoever wishes to have good sport it must be made his whole and sole object; everything else must give way to it, and the sportsman must not be led here and there by tempting offers of a bear, or an elk-deer, &c. And further, whether reindeer hunting will repay the time and labour devoted to it depends principally on a man's powers of endurance, physical and moral. And I would strenuously advise no one to set out on a reindeer expedition who cannot undergo a large amount of bodily fatigue, and endure a still larger amount of disappointment.

Fortified, however, with strength of body and strength of mind, determined not to be put out of tune by poor accommodation, and still poorer fare, he will, in all likelihood, be more than repaid for all the toil to which he has had to submit.

To insure sport amongst the feathered tribes, it will, I think, be most desirable to engage the services of a regular hunter, or at least of one who is well acquainted with the ground, otherwise much valuable time will be thrown away. A good hunter will expect his dollar a day; but in ordinary cases half of this sum ought to be sufficient.

In my humble opinion, of all the feathered game of Norway, the HJERPE (*Tetrao bonasia*, Gelinotte, Hasel-huhn) is the best for the table, and affords the worst sport.

These birds are abundant in parts of Norway and Sweden. In size they are about as large as the French partridge, and resemble that bird much in the shape of the head and neck. Their meat also is white, as is the case with that bird. The plumage is speckled, grey and brown, and the male bird has a black patch on the throat. The legs are feathered.

The Norwegians hold the hjerpe in great esteem as an article of food, prizing it before ryper, black game, or capercalzie; and I have over and over again (in fact, it is a universal custom) seen woodcocks offered for sale in the market, with their bills cut short off, so as to palm them more readily off upon the uninitiated for this favourite bird.

Unlike the black game and capercalzie, hjerper are monogamous. They lay about the middle or end of June from six to eight eggs. Their food consists of the young shoots of spruce fir, seeds, &c. Indeed there appears to be a most intimate connection between their very existence and the appearance of this tree; it being only in those districts where there are large forests of spruce fir that they are found in any quantity.

Thus, on the western coast south of Throndhjem, they are not to be met with, but in the neighbourhood of that city they are exceedingly plentiful; and while this latter district abounds in forests of spruce fir the former parts are almost destitute of them. In Nordland again, at least in its northern parts, they are not known; and it is a significant fact that the limit of the spruce fir has been placed under lat. 67°. But in Österdalen, Rendalen, Trysil, &c., they are numerous; and here there are more extensive forests of spruce fir than in any other parts of Norway.

The peasants frequently shoot them by enticing them with a *call* made to imitate their peculiar cry. They go into a part of the forest where they are known to be, and can thus allure them into their neighbourhood very readily. By remaining perfectly still these birds will perch on the trees close by. But even then it is often a difficult matter to discover their whereabouts; for they remain perfectly immovable, and as the colour of their plumage bears a great resemblance to the bark of the tree, it is only by scanning each bough in succession from one end to the other that they can be detected. A friend of mine has assured me that he has remained under a tree for a quarter of an hour in which he knew that a bird had perched, before he could distinguish it.

They are generally to be found in the thickest and most retired glades in the forest, where they are but little exposed to disturbance; for they appear to love quiet. If it were not for this propensity they would be exposed to countless enemies, as a more stupid bird, perhaps, does not exist.

From the above description it may, I think, be inferred that hjerpe shooting does not offer great attractions. In fact I should pronounce it to be extremely stupid and unprofitable work.

That these birds would thrive admirably in some of the largest of our Scotch forests, or even in parks in England *where they would not be exposed to disturbance*, I fully believe, and in this opinion Professor Rasch confirms me. The great difficulty, however, seems to be to get them there. In the first place, it is no easy thing to procure the eggs, or, if procured, to hatch them. The above-named gentleman told me that, when a young man, he has repeatedly made the experiment, but never succeeded in bringing them up.

The only feasible plan, I think, is to trap them late in the autumn; but as the Norwegian peasant has the most barbarous and primitive traps to be found anywhere in the world, and thinks only of the market and the *everlasting dollar*, it is almost useless to rely on any assistance from that quarter. When in Norway I was authorized by the Acclimatization Society to offer a large sum per head for any specimens brought alive to me, and in good order; but I never succeeded in my endeavours, though I used every means for making my wishes known. It is true one man near Dahl, about thirty miles from town, caught one; but fearful lest it would fret itself to death, if kept even for a short time in solitary confinement, he wrung its neck. Imagine my disgust when I heard of it! The certainty of a mark to the prospective contingency of a couple of dollars proved too strong an inducement to the Bönde's calculating mind.

The CAPERCALZIE (Tiur, Röy) are generally plentiful in large forest districts. It is an interesting sight to watch the male bird (tiur) when he is paying his addresses to the female (röy). It occurs in the month of April. At about one A.M. the male birds begin to "spille," or "lege," as it is termed, literally "play." They perch usually on the branch of a Scotch fir tree, and commence making a peculiar noise with the beak, emitting three sounds in succession, like the knocking together of two pieces of wood or bone, after which a hissing noise follows, caused **by sucking in** the breath, when the eyes are either closed or turned upwards like a person in a fit. Whilst this latter noise is going on the bird is, as it were, completely entranced, and totally insensible; but when the knocking sound begins again, great caution must be used in approaching him, as he is then on the *qui vive*. The **best** plan **is** to watch for an opportunity to run in when the hissing is going on, and **to stand stock** still, **or get behind** a tree, if possible, **as soon as** this is over. **By a careful** observation of these **rules they may be** approached at very close quarters, **and thus** an interesting phenomenon in natural history be witnessed.

Unfortunately numbers of them fall victims at this season to the poacher, who, like his brethren in all other parts of the world, is well acquainted with **the** habits and customs of birds.

It is even said that the hens, when they perceive any danger approaching, will keep flying round and round to try and warn the male bird; and if that does not succeed, will even knock their entranced lord off his perch to bring him to a sense of the peril he is exposed **to.**

The **sounds** emitted **by** the **cock** birds, as above described, **are partly** amatory, and partly serve **as** challenges to other males to the combat; **for** like all others of the grouse tribe, the male capercalzie is extremely pugnacious.

The best plan, perhaps, for securing sport either among these birds, hjerper, or black game, is the one adopted by the Bönder themselves. They use a little dog which ranges rather widely, and which commences to give tongue when on scent. The birds then invariably perch **close by, and** the dog remains barking at the foot of **the tree in** question till his master comes up.

A small-bored rifle is generally **used,** though as regards the calibre the peasants are not particular; for to get the bird is with them the main object. Shot **guns, in fact,** are but little known in the interior.

The capercalzie are tiresome birds, because they run so prodigiously, **and when** they do rise it is generally out of shot. I would warrant them to spoil any dog, however steady, in a very short time.

During the summer the tiur lives as an old bachelor, and will only be found in remote parts of the forest, high up **towards** the fjelds.

The BLACK GAME (Urhane) are very numerous in **parts** of Norway, and as the reader must be perfectly **familiar with** their habits it would be superfluous to say much about them here.

The cross between the black game and capercalzie is by no means uncommon. It takes place, probably, between the black cock and the röy. The characteristic marks of either species are readily distinguishable in the hybrid.

The GROUSE* (Skov-rype) is, according to Norwegian naturalists, the same bird as the red grouse of the British Isles, the difference of plumage being only occasioned by the climate. I believe that Mr. Gould entertains the same opinion.†

Whether this circumstance is of itself sufficient to constitute a separate species, I do not feel competent to discuss; but I believe that in the case of hummingbirds, species are frequently distinguished with reference to the colour of the plumage only.

The grouse in Norway commences to change colour in the spring, when the neck and half the breast assume a reddish hue. In winter the whole of the bird is white, and it may be remarked that the 'pinnæ' are always white. Low scrub on the mountain-sides is the usual sort of ground for finding them. On some of the islands off the north-western coast they are extremely abundant. As they are in every respect exactly similar to the red grouse, the colour of the plumage alone excepted, it is needless to speak further about them. I would, however, strongly recommend any one who takes

* It may be remarked that wherever ryper have been mentioned in the above pages, this species has been intended.

† I perceive, from a correspondent in the 'Field,' that the British grouse has been introduced into Sweden; so that in lapse of time a solution of the question may be expected.

an interest in natural history to pay attention to the different gradations and changes their plumage undergoes at various seasons of the year, as may be seen in the Zoological Museum at the University in Christiania.

The migrations of the skov-rype from one part of the country to another are very remarkable; that is to say, where one year the sportsman may find an abundance of these birds, the next he may scarcely see a feather, and *vice versâ*. As a case in point, a friend of mine in crossing the Vlo Fjeld in 1860 found the ryper very plentiful: in the autumn of the following year, happening to be in the same neighbourhood, he had every expectation of meeting with good sport; but, after beating a very considerable extent of the fjeld carefully with his two dogs, *he failed to discover a single bird*. The same thing happened to him elsewhere; and he tells me that some of his Anglo-Norwegian sporting friends have noticed the same to be the case in other parts of the country.

The cross between the black game and the rype is rare, much rarer than that between the black game and capercalzie. This may probably be accounted for by the fact that the rype is for the most part monogamous, while the capercalzie and black game being both of them gregarious, there is more chance of their coming in contact with each other.

The PTARMIGAN (Fjeld-rype) is found on all the high fjelds of Norway. It changes colour exactly in the same degree as is the case in **Scotland**. They are extremely plentiful in parts, and are often very tame; but that they are capable of affording sport I disbelieve.

A cross between this bird and the skov-rype has never been **found** in Norway. I can assign no other reason but that they occupy totally different terrains, the ptarmigan never, or rarely, descending into the regions of grouse.

The PARTRIDGE (Agerhöne, or Raphöns) has **of late** years been on the increase in the south and **south-western** parts of the country. In the neighbourhood of Christiania **a few coveys may occasionally be** seen, and on **the islands in the fjord I** have frequently seen a fair sprinkling. I do not know how far north they are to **be found. An** English gentleman who resided at Hamar, on the Miösen, had a covey on his grounds two or three years back. I am not aware that the "red legs" exist in the country. A friend **of** mine **writes** me word that when at Fleermoen, a little above lat. 61°, on the borders of Sweden, between the Klar and Dal rivers, he found a covey of partridges. "I stopped the night," he writes, "at Fleermoen in **a** house round which there was a 'clearing,' **and, as** usual, made inquiries about the game in the neighbourhood, both large **and small.** They did not give me a very promising account: but mentioned that a 'pair of birds,' they didn't know what they were, had come over from

Sweden the year before, and that now there was a flock of them near the house. I instantly started off to investigate the matter. My dogs very speedily got a point in the rye stubble, and up got a covey of eleven strong partridges. This was about the end of September, 1859, and as I only killed two and a half brace, I hope if a second Englishman, and a second couple of English dogs, should ever make their way to Fleermoen they will have the satisfaction of finding that the three remaining brace have meanwhile become the founders of a flourishing colony."

During the last winter, however, several coveys have been seen in the neighbourhood of Throndhjem, a little above lat. 63°, and hopes are entertained that they will increase.

The EIDER DUCK (Edder fugl), although not properly classed among the feathered game of Norway, is yet, I think, worthy of a place in this chapter.*

The principal breeding-places of the eider duck are the coasts of Greenland, Spitzbergen, Iceland, Norway, the Faröe Islands, and the Hebrides. They usually select small remote islands, called Aegge-Vær,† for their breeding-places. These Aegge-Vær very con-

---

* The greater part of the following description has already appeared in "Chambers' Edinburgh Journal;" and as I was the author, I do not feel guilty of plagiarism in making use of it.

† **Væer is** a reef of rocks above water.

siderably enhance the value of the **property** to which they are attached. **About** the **end of February or** beginning of March, the birds repair to the open **sea** along the coast in large **flocks.** The male bird seldom pairs **before the** third year—some naturalists say not before the fifth—but the female obtains a mate when she is one year old. The call of the male with which he woos his mate is exceedingly melodious. Bloody and severe are the battles fought amongst the male birds at this season; twenty may perhaps be seen **all at once** fighting desperately **for the possession of one hen, who** swims all the time quietly along behind the combatants, waiting **till the contest has been decided, when the** fortunate **bird** immediately claims her as his prize. When once his superiority has been thus publicly asserted, he suffers no further molestation. This important business of finding a husband being **at** length satisfactorily settled, the female selects a convenient place in **which** to build her nest, **choosing** generally the protection **of** an overhanging rock, or the shelter of a juniper-bush, which latter shrub is **found in** great abundance. The nest is formed on the outside, of birch twigs, next to which comes a layer of moss or soft grass; and the **inside is lined with** the down which she plucks from her breast, **mixed** with switch-grass.

She lays generally from five to eight eggs, according to her age. She sits on them very assiduously, plucking from time to time fresh down from her breast, which she heaps up so as to form a high embankment round them, and to hide her from view while on the nest. When she leaves the nest in search of food, she covers up the eggs with the loose down, as the male bird takes no share in the process of incubation. If the nest be robbed of its eggs, she will, in common with other birds of the duck tribe, lay more; but supposing that the first five are taken, she will lay only three the next time; and if these be again removed, she will only lay one egg. A traveller in Iceland says that he has been informed "that these birds lay quantities of eggs; and that it is usual to stick a short piece of wood, of about a foot and a half long, through the nest, and that the duck will keep on laying till the top of the stick is hidden by the eggs; and that then she mounts up on the top, and begins sitting." The author, however, seems inclined to doubt the veracity of this statement. It is usual amongst the Icelanders to take the down and the eggs twice, as a matter of course, before the bird is allowed to sit; but after making her nest for the third time, she is so nearly bare, that the male bird has now to contribute towards the stock from his own breast. Should the nest be robbed again, they quit the place, and never return to it. The process of incubation takes from four to five weeks. Their food consists principally of mussels, shrimps, slugs, and **crabs.** Pontoppidan asserts "that they are able to dive to a depth of ten to twelve fathoms." But **while** feeding, they are subject **to great** annoyance **from** the numerous **tribes** of **gulls, which, not** being able to dive, avail themselves of their labours, and the moment the duck reappears on the surface with a shrimp or slug in its mouth, pounce down, and carry it off. While sitting, their great enemies are the crows and ravens, which some of the country people declare will **pull the** female off the nest to get at the eggs.

Some **of** the **principal** Aegge-**Vær along the** Norwegian **coast belong to the** Lofoden group, and are also **to be found in the** Varanger Fjord, a little to the east of the North Cape. The last-mentioned places are the property of the Amtman of Finmark, who farms them out, receiving his rent in kind from the tenant— namely, five hundred pounds of half-cleaned down, and two barrels of cloud-berries (*Rubus chamæmorus*). About twenty-five years ago, the produce from **these** Aegge-Vær was about **two** hundred pounds of clean down; now it is little more than half that quantity, though every possible care and precaution is taken to protect the birds from injury. Not a gun is allowed to be fired off within three miles of the breeding-places, except **once a** year, when four reindeer out of a herd belonging to the British vice-consul at Hammerfest and the proprietor are shot; on which occasions, an experienced Lapp is brought off from the mainland, with whom to miss would be an indelible disgrace. Moreover, no one is allowed to land there without special leave from the proprietor.

When the time approaches for the eggs to be hatched, people are kept on the watch; for the down ought to be taken before twenty four hours have elapsed from the time when the young ones leave the shell, and should rain fall on it, it is spoiled.

On an average, each nest yields about one ounce of cleaned down. As soon as all the down has been taken from the nests, the grass and dirt are carefully picked out with the hand; but there are always so many broken pieces of birch twigs intermixed with it, that recourse is had to another expedient. The down is either spread out to the influence of the sun, the heat of which is great in those northern latitudes, or else slowly baked in ovens. The twigs thus become quite brittle. The down is next laid on smooth boards, and rolled with a heavy rolling-pin, which treatment effectually breaks up the brittle wood, and reduces it to dust. It is next placed on a frame in shape something resembling a French bedstead, across the bottom of which are arranged laterally pieces of packthread, at intervals of about one-quarter of an inch, and is stirred quickly backwards and forwards with two light wooden wands. The dust and dirt thus fall through on to a board which is placed underneath, and the process is repeated until no more is found to come away.

The down is now ready for use, and is stored up in bags for exportation or sale. The whole process is **very** tedious; and is the more felt to be so, as in the short northern summer there are so many other necessary things to be attended to.

The unclean down will not yield quite **one-sixth** clean, the value of which will be **about** twelve shillings on the spot. **Owing, however, to** the alarming diminution in **the numbers of** the birds, **no** dependence can be placed on obtaining any considerable quantity.

Formerly, a large quantity of eider-down used to be imported from Spitzbergen and Russia, but mostly of an inferior quality. To an inexperienced eye, it may be difficult to distinguish between the live and dead down; but there are one or two characteristic marks **which** infallibly test the quality of the article: not only is the live down much the lighter and more elastic of the two, but if a handful of it be thrown up into the air, even when a tolerably fresh breeze is blowing, it will adhere together in a compact mass, and not a particle of it be lost, whilst the other will be scattered in all directions, like so much thistle-seed; or if it be placed before a fire, it will be seen to rise and expand in bulk very rapidly, which is not the case with the other. The quantity of live down requisite for an average-sized quilt is from two and a half to three pounds, which may with ease be so compressed as to be contained in a common-sized hat. If more be used, the object is defeated, as the down then becomes lumpy, and collects in the middle. Twenty-five years ago, it was no uncommon thing for small vessels to bring from five thousand to six thousand pounds of eider-down from Spitzbergen to Hammerfest, in Lapland, chiefly, it is true, of an inferior quality, and that by no means improved by lying in the hold for a month or six weeks.

During the latter part of the last century, Iceland alone used to export to Denmark from two hundred to three hundred pounds of cleaned down, and from fifteen thousand to twenty thousand pounds uncleaned. The birds have, however, been exposed to such unfair treatment in that island, spite of the laudable endeavours that many individuals have made to propagate the species, and the protective measures adopted by the Danish government, that they have very considerably decreased in numbers; for not only have the nests been robbed of their eggs and down two or three times during the hatching season, but the birds themselves have been shot in a merciless manner, as well for the sake of their feathers as for the flesh. For instance, if

A. sees a duck, he shoots it, on the principle that B. should not get it; B. acts from similar motives with regard to C.; and so on till it comes to Z.'s turn, who does just the same as the others, for fear A. should return; and as the eider-duck is the easiest of all ducks to kill during the breeding-time—when they will, in fact, sit so close that they may be knocked on the head with a stick—it is not much to be wondered at that they have diminished very seriously on this island. In Norway, however, they have been jealously preserved; and not only has the Storthing recently passed a law rendering every one who shoots one of these birds, or robs a nest, amenable to a fine, but they are especial favourites with the peasants: indeed, along the whole coast of Norway, where they annually resort in great numbers, they are held as dear by the natives as the robin-redbreast is with us; and this principle proves a far more efficient means of protection than any fine or penalty. Generally speaking, they build their nests on the small islands with which the whole Norwegian coast is so plentifully sprinkled; but very frequently they will repair to the mainland, building close to the farmhouses and fishermen's cottages, even under the very doorsteps, as if they knew that they were among friends. In such cases, they become as tame as farmyard ducks, suffering the goodwife to lift them off the nest, and receiving food at her hand. And yet, notwithstanding all the care that has been taken of them, they have greatly diminished, and it is to be feared still continue to do so every year.

As above stated, a very large quantity of down used to be exported from Iceland, but entirely for the Danish market. In the year 1750, the company in that island sold as large a quantity as amounted to 3745 banco dollars. The relative value of clean and uncleaned down in those days may be ascertained from the following computation, that the former was valued at forty-five fish per one pound, and the latter at sixeen fish per one pound.

The earliest mention that I can find of eider-down in any English writings occurs in "The Description of Europe, and the Voyages of Othere and Wulfstan," by Alfred the Great. Otherus, who was a Norwegian nobleman, speaking of the Finns and Biarmians, says that the revenues of the nobles "chiefly consisted in skins of animals, down, and whalebone," and that "some of the richest proprietors had to pay as much as forty bushels of down."

The use of eider-down was believed, in the early part of the last century, to be excessively injurious to the health, producing epileptic seizures; which opinion is refuted by Bartholin, a Danish writer on medicine, who says: "Neither ought that idle report to frighten us, that epilepsy is brought on by the use of these feathers. No one that I have ever met with or heard of has ever incurred any risk thereby."—*Vide* 'In Med. Danorum Domesticâ,' p. 66. Still, all those who have travelled on the Continent know the oppressiveness which is caused by having to sleep with a feather bed thrown over one—a practice which cannot be conducive to health.

CHAPTER IV.

BEAR AND LYNX HUNTING, ETC.—REMARKS ON BIRDS OF PREY.

ENGLISH bear-hunters in Norway may be declined like adjective pronouns, *i. e.*, divided into three degrees—the *positively* unfortunate, the *comparatively* lucky, and the *superlatively* successful.

The first are those who have toiled and moiled at "bear-slaying," without ever catching even so much as a glimpse of his shaggy highness; the second those who have been fortunate enough either just to have seen him, or to have missed doing so by an inappreciable *punctum temporis;* and the third, those who have actually shot a bear, and perhaps brought home with them a pot of the genuine grease as a trophy, which in all probability proved so unpleasant to the olfactory nerves as to have been thrown away from not having been properly prepared.

That there are a good many bears in Norway, the remarks interspersed above, and the returns which have been extracted from official sources (a copy of which, for the last fifteen years, is subjoined), will prove beyond a doubt. And the only reason, and I think it is the true one, that I can assign for so much disappointment having been experienced, is simply owing to the fact that "would-be bear-hunters" do not come out early enough to Norway, or devote enough time to it.

That by far the greater number of bears are killed either in the winter, or early spring, I am fully convinced from the experiences of old hunters; and the way it is managed is as follows:—The peasants track them to their caves (*hie*) in the beginning of the winter, and either shoot them as they are lying asleep, looking for all the world like babies, with their fore-paw in their mouth; or if that be impracticable, get a comrade to stir Bruin up with a long pole, and shoot him as he attempts to bolt. But to be able to do this it is necessary to be expert in the use of the skie, or snow-shoe—an accomplishment not so readily learnt.

For the spring shooting a different method is adopted. During the winter the Bönder put out the carcase of a horse or cow in the neighbourhood of a bear's winter quarters, piling up heavy stones upon it. About the middle of April, when Bruin wakes up from his long sleep, the hunter frequently visits it; and as soon as ever he perceives that a bear has been attracted to it, he watches it carefully day and night, and seldom fails in making a bag. In bear districts most of the Bönder employ a hunter in their service, who gets a certain payment from them, together with the government reward.

It is toilsome and severe work; for it not only necessitates being early up in the country when it is still bitterly cold, but the fatigue that must necessarily be undergone, added to the wretched accommodation and poor fare to be met with in outlying districts, renders it a question whether the contingency of a bear will repay the trouble. On the other hand, it is more than probable that an ardent sportsman, capable of undergoing all the above disagreeables, would attain the object of his desires. And perhaps his best plan would be to make the acquaintance of some Bönde in the summer, and make arrangements beforehand with him to lay out Odde, *i.e.*, the carcase above spoken of, and then come out at the preconcerted time.

There is no doubt but that bears are shot in the summer, but it is only occasionally, I am inclined to think; and, at all events, the Englishman's chance of sport among them at this season is infinitely more remote. Still, if a man is capable of undergoing a great deal of hard work, and can digest an enormous amount of disappointment and vexation of spirit, giving himself entirely up to this one absorbing object, he may possibly (if he is fortunate enough to secure the services of an honest and clever hunter, and his beardog, why then he may), by great good luck, get a sight, at least, of a bear. I say an "honest" hunter, because there are many who, knowing the bear-loving propensities of "those mad English," profess to be able to find a bear for you on the shortest notice, without the slightest positive knowledge of their whereabouts. A stranger, therefore, who has had no previous acquaintance with the country and the habits of the peasants, stands an extremely good chance of being egregiously taken in, and of passing an uncommonly unprofitable summer.

To any one whose main object it is to kill a bear, the early spring is unquestionably the best time; but, then, as a friend has very justly asked me, "Would there be full satisfaction in the prize, lean and ragged as he then would be?"

I heard last year in Norway an amusing account of a bear-hunter, or rather two bear-hunters; and as it happens to be a true one I will give it.

Two men, who knew nothing at all about hunting or shooting, managed to find out a hie. Feeling diffident of their own success they imparted the secret to a regular hunter, but cautiously kept the whereabouts of the cave dark till they had struck a bargain. They offered the man five dollars as his share if he would kill the beast for them. Now, as a bear's skin is worth, if it be a good one, fourteen dollars in the market, and the government gives a reward of five dollars for every bear killed, and the flesh is worth twopence per pound, it was plain to the calculating "jæger" that he ought to have more, and therefore refused to do the job for them on these conditions. They refused, however, to listen to his demands for an advance; and fearing lest he should by chance find out the "hie" for himself, determined to attack the bear without him. Fortified, therefore, with an extra allowance of "Throndhjemske" (aquavit), and equipped with a couple of axes and a long stick, they sallied forth. Arriving at the place, it was arranged that one should do the "drawing out" part of the business, while the other should stand by with uplifted hatchet to test the toughness of Bruin's skull when he should "put out" an appearance. The pole was accordingly inserted and "braddled" about; presently a low growl was heard, and at last out came the brute's head. The party with the pole, however, no sooner had the bear's head shown itself, cut off as hard as his legs could carry him. His companion, more courageous, now brought down his axe with all his force right on the bear's skull Somewhat stunned at this unexpected reception, Bruin dropped down in his hole, but recovering after a short time again attempted to get out and see what it was all about. Again did the axe come down with more vigour than ever on his devoted head, and again Bruin disappeared to prepare for round number three. And so it went on for some time, till at last the man and the axe got the day, and Bruin lay dead at his feet.

The above story was told me in Norwegian, and loses not a little by being translated.

In the month of February, this year, 1863, an old she-bear and two cubs were shot in Östre Slidre, in Valders, in the following way:—Three men one day found a "hie," and one stuck a pole down it to see if Bruin were at home. He had not done so long ere he "got a bite," and called to his comrades to aim in the direction of the pole. They accordingly put the muzzles of their rifles as far in as they could in the required direction and fired. Supposing the bear must have got his "quietus," he now commenced crawling into the "hie" to see the result, but had not got far before the bear bolted right over him and escaped. She was killed, however, the following day, and it was found that her jaw had been already broken. The two cubs were lying quite dead at the bottom of the "hie." Lucky was it for them that the old bear made off, as their guns being unloaded they would probably have come off worst had she attacked them.

In the middle of March, this year, a man discovered a bear "hie" *in a hay barn*. In company with two others he had gone to fetch a load of hay home, when all at once he found himself attacked by a huge bear. They, however, gave Bruin such a drubbing between them with stout poles that he was glad to run off. On searching the barn they found a "hie" and two cubs, one of which they secured. The other got off. It was about as big as a yearling calf.

I think the best time, altogether, for hunting is the early autumn, though at the same time the chance of making a bag is not, as I have said, so great then as in the spring. At this season, when the berries are ripe, Bruin, who is uncommonly fond of fruit, and will devour and spoil large quantities, may not unfrequently be met with out in the open. "Or again, later on," my friend informs me, "when the snow begins to fall, and when the bears are thinking of retiring to their winter quarters. I did once make an expedition of some days in the snow in a part of the country where the bears had been committing considerable damage; but unluckily it was just too late—(what a common complaint this is among bear-hunters!)—they had 'put up' for the winter, and a heavy fall of snow had obliterated the tracks. In the course of my numerous expeditions in summer-time after bears in Hardanger, Nordland, and in other parts of the country, I have very frequently come upon and followed fresh tracks for very long distances; but I could plainly see that, owing to the density of the forests, the chances were at least 100 to 1 against me. At times, indeed, in the Hardanger mountains I have found fresh tracks on the open fjeld in June and July, and no doubt bears are seen occasionally during the summer. Still, as a rule, they generally keep to the thick forest at that time of the year; and, as I have said, the chances are enormously large against one's getting even a glimpse of them. No doubt, on the other hand, a good bear-dog would diminish these chances; but these are not so often to be found when wanted."

A large proportion of bears are annually killed by a sort of "infernal machine," *i. e.*, a trap formed by several gun barrels pointed towards the carcase of a cow, and so arranged that they will all go off when a wire is touched. A gentleman whom I know very nearly met with the fate intended for the bear he was in pursuit of, from one of these machines. It seems that, according to law, no trap can be set until public notice thereof has previously been given at the parish church. But unluckily on this occasion his guide had not been sufficiently attentive to his religious duties, and therefore knew nothing about it.

I am not aware whether the Swedes adopt a plan for trapping bears which is very common in North America. "Several trunks of trees are tied together (and made heavier by stones being laid on them), and set in a slanting position, so that when the bear pulls at the bait underneath the whole concern immediately falls and squashes him. The bait is usually a large piece of fish tied up in paper, and when it gets 'high,' if there be a bear within reach of the savour thereof, he is sure to come to it."

For bear-hunting generally, I think a double-barrelled smooth bore, carrying a large bullet, would be best. Added to this, a revolver and a "couteau de chasse" should be taken. It would be foolhardy to depend upon a single barrel alone, or to go on a bear expedition without an experienced hunter; for it is seldom that Bruin is so disabled at the first shot as to prevent his rushing in, which he will be pretty sure to do.

Many of the Norwegian bear-hunters have at times got fearfully mauled.

As a rule, a bear will not attack a person unless wounded or provoked, though instances have occurred where he has been the aggressor. One of these occurred a few years ago in Hardanger, where a bear, without provocation, attacked four people who were quietly at work, and severally injured them. Two of them, a man and a woman, subsequently died from the injuries they received.

I would strongly recommend any one "going in" regularly for bear-hunting to provide himself with a small tent. Edgington's patrol tents are well suited for this work. Thus the hunter can shift his quarters

TABULAR FORM SHOWING THE NUMBER OF BEARS KILLED IN EACH AMT FROM 1846 TO 1860.

Amts.	1846	1847	1848	1849	1850	1851	1852	1853	1854	1855	1856	1857	1858	1859	1860	Total.	Average.
Smaalehnenes	2	.	.	1	2	.	.	.	.	.	.	1	1	1	.	8	8/15
Agershuus	1	2	.	2	.	1	1	.	.	1	1	.	1	.	.	12	12/15
Hedemarken	15	10	10	22	15	19	10	5	10	15	12	8	9	7	16	183	12 3/15
Christians	7	12	5	6	5	18	3	3	9	8	23	9	7	5	9	129	8 9/15
Buskeruds	14	16	16	23	12	9	13	3	17	14	19	15	15	11	23	220	14 10/15
Jarslberg and Laurvig	4	1	3	8	6	5	2	2	3	.	.	5	2	.	.	41	2 11/15
Bratsberg	45	38	32	44	32	37	19	15	41	32	30	39	43	23	36	506	33 11/15
Nedenæs Robysgielag	13	17	25	32	20	30	31	11	19	22	13	36	18	23	18	328	21 13/15
Lister and Mandals	4	4	2	6	3	3	2	3	1	1	1	1	.	1	1	33	2 3/15
Stavanger	2	3	.	4	1	2	4	3	3	2	2	3	.	1	2	30	2
S. Bergenhuus	1	.	2	4	3	1	4	2	1	1	.	1	1	1	4	29	1 14/15
N. Bergenhuus	6	14	25	25	13	19	16	8	7	7	8	15	13	17	27	217	14 7/15
Romsdals	29	28	29	30	25	22	14	5	6	12	13	12	10	14	12	259	17 4/15
S. Throndhjems	7	16	16	17	10	14	5	11	.	11	15	6	5	9	13	161	10 11/15
N. Throndhjems	30	36	42	28	35	34	32	52	26	27	30	20	37	22	26	437	30 7/15
Nordlands	23	57	37	45	23	40	23	23	31	35	41	57	34	16	29	514	34 4/15
Finmarken	16	15	19	28	41	22	23	18	19	24	26	31	19	18	19	338	22 8/15
Total	219	270	264	325	246	276	202	142	198	212	234	259	215	169	225	3456	—

Total in 15 Years, 3456, or 230 6/15 per annum.

at pleasure. It would be the best plan, and the cheapest, to buy a couple of Norwegian ponies to carry the "impedimenta," &c. They can readily be sold again, and, perhaps, not at a loss.

I question much whether there are any Englishmen who have ever hunted lynxes in Norway. These animals are, however, tolerably abundant, much more so than one might suppose from the yearly returns. The average number killed annually is about 120. Hedemarken, Bratsberg, South and North Bergenhuus Amts are the best districts for them.

The manner of hunting them is as follows:—

In the early winter, after a light fall of snow, the hunter takes with him a couple of hounds, inferior specimens of our foxhound breed. Their bodies are protected with a coat of mail, or rather leathers, consisting of bands or straps to protect them from the lynx's terrific claws, without impeding the free action of their limbs. It is but seldom that a lynx escapes when once his tracks have been discovered.

I can well imagine it to be an exciting chase. When hard pressed the animal turns to bay, and if the dogs are experienced ones they take good care to keep at a respectful distance till the hunter comes up; but if they are young at the work they will often run in to close quarters—a piece of audacity, however, seldom tried twice, for the powerful claws of the lynx are capable of inflicting terrible wounds. Young lynxes will generally run up a tree when hotly pursued; and, I am told, that by taking off one's hat and placing it on a stick near the foot of the tree, they will remain there till it becomes quite dark. By far the greater number of these animals are trapped; for accounts of which the reader is referred to Mr. Lloyd's " Scandinavian Adventures."

I was struck one day on perceiving among the official returns of birds and beasts of prey slaughtered annually in Norway, the eagles figuring so largely.

For the fifteen years from 1846 to 1860, the marvellous quantity of 48,453 eagles are stated to have been killed, giving an average of about 3,230 per annum; and as government gives a premium of half a dollar for every eagle, no less sum than $24,226\frac{1}{2}$ dollars, or about £5,384, has been disbursed for eagles alone during that period. The law stands as follows:— "That every sea-eagle, eagle, whether young or old, shall be paid with half a dollar, and every mountain-owl or kestrel with one mark." But in order to insure that the mousing hawks should not be included, it was determined that only those hawks which were not shot should obtain the premium; for it is an established fact that nine-tenths of the preying hawks are caught in nets. But to a Lensmand (a civil officer, a sort of bailiff) not skilled in natural history, it is not difficult to palm off the young of the larger hawk tribes as eaglets.

Accordingly, Professor Rasch computes that out of the 64,129 præmia that have been paid for birds of prey during the fifteen years, 50,000 have been disbursed wrongly; and what is still worse, that the greater part of the alleged eagles have belonged to the useful kinds of mousing hawks. And he considers, therefore, that the law has not only been injurious to Norway, but also to Europe in general, and adds, in the report he has drawn up, "As all these birds are migratory, it is almost certain that the *immense* quantities which have been slaughtered here have been the main cause of the numerous complaints that have been made in parts of Germany at the diminution of the mousing hawks."

In Norway, as in other countries, the eagle and sea-eagle are not common birds.

CHAPTER V.

REMARKS ON THE ARTIFICIAL BREEDING OF SALMON IN NORWAY.

During the last ten years, the attention of the Norwegian government has been directed towards the propagation of salmon by artificial means. In a country like the Scandinavian peninsula, which has such an extent of sea-board, and which abounds in rivers large and small, running into fjords which intersect the coast, there are so many natural facilities afforded for the protection of the young fish, that it only requires some additional attention on the part of the inhabitants themselves, to make Norway stand at the head of the salmon-producing countries of Europe.

Fully alive to the disadvantages which many parts of the country labour under in an agricultural respect, owing to the rigour of winter and the unfertile nature* of the soil, the government, with a laudable generosity,

---

* The whole area of Norway is about 121,800 square miles, out of which not more than 1,060 are under cultivation.

has endeavoured to promote the propagation of fish by rendering pecuniary assistance, and by the appointment of officers to superintend in the management of the operation.

I should think the subject might well engross the attention of those English who lease rivers in Norway for a term. By getting the several proprietors to co-operate with them, they might find it worth their while to set on foot hatching apparatuses near their waters. Of late years there have been several complaints as to the falling off of salmon; and though bad seasons may have had a great deal to do with this, yet there is no doubt but that poaching at unlawful times is carried on to a very great extent. This can only be remedied by persuading the proprietors not to poach themselves, and to take more care in the preservation of the fishing, and in the propagation of the fish. No doubt a difficult matter!

It is somewhat remarkable that the artificial propagation of fish was first discovered in Norway by a simple labouring man in 1848.

One harvest-time he had been obliged to keep at home on account of a bad leg. To amuse himself he used to get down to the river-side, and watch the trout on their spawning-ground. Being of an observant nature, he was struck with the manner in which the operation was carried on. He remarked that the male fish placed itself alongside of the female in such a position that its head reached to about the middle of the body of the latter. He further noticed, that whilst the process of discharging the ova was going on, the female turned somewhat on her side with a quivering sort of motion, and that the male emitted his milt simultaneously. It therefore occurred to him that by pressing the spawn out of the female, and the milt from the male at the same time, in water, he would obtain a quantity of fructified eggs, which, by being placed in convenient places in brooks, would in due time bring forth fish. No sooner conceived than executed. He threw out his nets and caught a male and a female fish ready to spawn. His wife took the one and he the other, and they squeezed their contents out into a bowl of clean water. He then took the eggs and placed them in a sheltered place in a stream where there were previously no trout. The following summer he was rejoiced to see that it swarmed with fish. Convinced, therefore, of the success of his plan, he constructed for himself a breeding-box close to his house; and notwithstanding the jeers and scoffs of his neighbours, who thought it impious, to say the least, in interfering and meddling with things which belonged to Nature alone, continued to breed fish every autumn. Such was the first attempt at hatching ova in Norway!

I will now proceed to give a brief account of the

hatching apparatus generally in vogue in that country, as communicated to me by Professor Rasch.

The case in which the hatching-boxes are placed (and which is under shelter, so that the water does not freeze) is twelve feet long, thirty-four inches wide inside, and **five** inches deep. The bottom must be perfectly water-tight, **and** very evenly planed. The sides are formed of single smooth-planed boards, which fit tightly against the bottom, to prevent any leakage ensuing. The uppermost end of the case, and **into which** the water runs from the pipe, is of the same height as the sides. The whole is divided into five compartments, **the first** of which receives the water from the **pipe. This** compartment is eighteen inches wide, while the other four are each thirty inches wide. The partition boards are one inch lower than the sides of the case, and **have holes bored in** them at a distance of two inches from the bottom, by means of hot wire. They are bored **in two rows** (*vide* fig. 1.), four below, and three above. **The water can thus run** evenly throughout the length of the case.

The hatching-boxes (fig. 2), four of which are placed in **each** compartment, are constructed as follows:— The sides consist of smooth-planed board, two feet long, three inches high, and an inch and a half thick. The bottom is a glass plate, two feet long, and seven **inches** wide. The ends are of perforated zinc, or brass wire-work, the same height as the sides, which are strengthened by two transverse pieces of wood. All the wood-work should be of well-seasoned material,

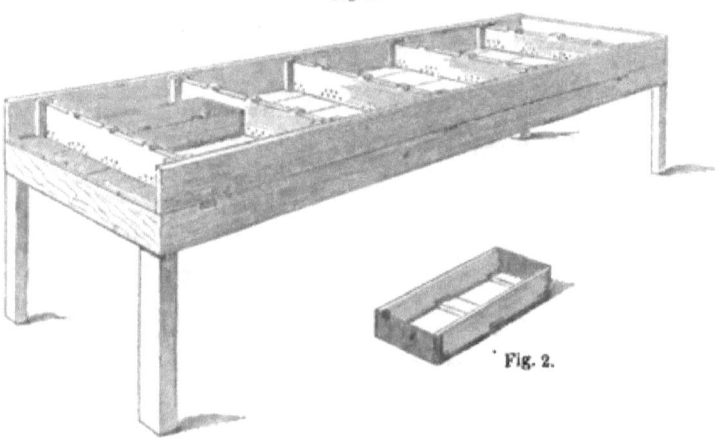

Fig 1.

Fig. 2.

and those parts which come in contact with the water should be glazed, as any resinous or pitchy substance in the wood would prove injurious to the ova. I should mention that the first compartment into which the water falls should be furnished with a network lid of zinc wire, which forms the bottom of a framework three or four inches high, so as to prevent the water running into the next compartment except through the holes in the zinc lid. Thus the larvæ of destructive insects, worms, &c., will be kept out. The upper end of the case should stand two inches higher than the lower end. The water which runs out from the last compartment is prevented running out the whole width of the case by means of two pieces of wood, which are fastened to the sides, and reach nearly to the middle, and is carried off by a pipe.

The slimy deposit which comes even from the purest water, and settles on the eggs (it is not detrimental unless there be too much of it), can easily be got rid of by gently moving the boxes, and allowing it to pass through the ends.

After the lapse of about four weeks it will be well to take the hatching-boxes out of the case to ascertain which eggs are good. The action of the air will render them all transparent; but on replacing them in the water, the unfruitful ones will assume a milky opaque colour. These can readily be removed with a pair of fine pincers or long tweezers. The exposure to the air does not hurt the eggs, but care must be taken that they do not become dry on the surface. After repeating this process three or four times, all the bad eggs can be removed. "I am convinced," is the remark of Professor Rasch, "that in a case of the above size I could hatch 10,000 salmon ova in each box, which would thus give a total of 160,000," there being four hatching-boxes in each of the four compartments. If the fry are to be kept any time in the boxes, care must be taken that they be not overstocked; but 3,000 may well be kept in them from two to three months."

ARTIFICIAL BREEDING OF SALMON. 199

Where water from a spring cannot be directly obtained the following plan is often adopted. The scale of operations is, however, necessarily more limited. A large tub, or other wooden vessel, is fitted with a tap. Care must be taken that it shall have previously lain a sufficiently long time in water, so that all the deleterious substances from the wood shall have been extracted. It is then placed on a stand at a sufficient height from the ground to allow the case containing the hatching-boxes to be placed beneath the tap; and they should have a gentle inclination, so that the upper end be about half an inch higher than the lower.

The water, having passed through the boxes, empties itself into another vessel, at least as large as the tub, and should be so regulated that it shall run out in twenty-four hours. The tub, therefore, only requires replenishing once in that time. If the water be at all muddy, it is well to place a layer of fine sand mixed with charcoal at the bottom of the tub.

Even in a common tea-saucer a great many ova may be hatched out.

The saucer is placed in a deep soup-plate, and a couple of moss-stalks laid over the edge in such a manner that they shall act as syphons. A constant flow of water thus takes place from the saucer into the plate. In about twelve hours half the water from the saucer will have run out, so that it will require filling again morning and evening. When necessary, fresh moss-stalks can be substituted.

It is of course best to procure the male and female fish to be operated upon direct from their breeding-ground, and as short a time as possible before the spawning commences. Where this is impossible, they should be kept in fish-boxes or reservoirs; care, however, being taken that they be not kept too long in confinement before being used, as this would have an injurious effect both on the ova and on the milt. One male fish is sufficient to fructify the ova of a great many females, and can be used from six to eight days in succession.

It is not difficult to ascertain when the female is ready to spawn. Her distended abdomen gives easily to a gentle pressure, and an undulating movement which is perceptible on touching it, shows that the spawn is already disconnected from the ovary. She should then be held by the head in a vertical position, so that the ova will of their own weight fall down towards the vent. When the fish are large, it is best to have three persons to assist. One takes the fish by the head, and the other by the tail, holding it horizontally over a dish, the vent downwards, whilst the third very gently presses along her stomach and sides. When the bottom of the dish has been covered with ova, in layers of two or three deep, the fish can be released into the tub of water from which she was taken. The dish, by the way, must previously have been nearly filled with water. Before operating on the male fish, the water from the dish had better be drained off, and fresh poured in. The male fish is then taken and handled in the same way. A small quantity of milt, just sufficient to discolour the water after being gently stirred with the fingers, is sufficient. It is then put back again into the tub, and while the **female is** again being brought out, the contents of the **dish** are to be emptied into another **tub half filled** with pure water. When all **the roe has been pressed** out and fructified as before with the milt, and again emptied into this tub, the water **is** allowed to run out through a hole previously bored in the side about an inch above the bottom. By the motion of the water running out, all the eggs will be brought into contact with the **milt**. In about five or ten minutes the ova can then **be** removed into the hatching-boxes.

If the eggs are in **a** fit state, the very smallest pressure is sufficient **to squeeze** them out; and it has been found that with **due** care the female suffers no injury from the manipulation, and will be as fruitful the following year as ever.

The unfruitful eggs after they have been some time in the hatching-boxes will be covered with a peculiar parasitical plant, "*Leptomitus clavatus*," which gives them the appearance of being wrapped in cotton. These should be removed, as, though the other eggs will not be immediately infected, yet the fibres of this vegetable growth will in time get around them, and prevent the water having free access to them, when they, too, will die. The unfruitful salmon eggs should be at once removed; but when the ova are very small, as is the case in trout, &c., it is better to wait till the parasitical plant has appeared before removing " the tares from the wheat," as the operation can then be performed more easily. It is therefore much better not to have a layer of small stones at the bottom of the case, as many of the ova will sink between them, and from remaining unperceived may in time cause great damage. It is true that the salmon instinctively makes a hole and covers her ova with small stones. But she, in all probability, only adopts this precaution in order *to protect them against their numerous foes*, and not that the development of the embryo may be thereby in any way accelerated.

On the Transport of Ova.

It might not unnaturally be supposed that it is best to transport the ova in the same element as that in which they are deposited in the ordinary course of things, viz., *in water*. But it must at the same time be remembered that every fertile egg contains a living being, which requires a constant supply of air for its preservation, and that the quantity of air contained in a confined vessel is more rapidly consumed by the ova than fresh air can be absorbed from the surface. The consequence will be that unless fresh water be constantly supplied, or the water in the vessel be by some means aërated, the embryo contained in the egg must die. But not only will the constant replenishing the vessel with fresh water be troublesome, and often impossible, but will also be attended with great risk to the safety of the ova.

If it is borne in mind that it is not the water, but the air which is therein contained that is essential to the preservation of the ova, it will be apparent that if they be kept moist, and have a constant supply of fresh air, the necessary conditions will be obtained. The readiest and easiest way is to pack them in damp moss (the marsh moss, *Sphagnum*, which absorbs moisture like a sponge, is the best), through which the air will readily circulate.*

In a common wooden box the moss will retain its dampness so as not to require wetting for several days. And indeed caution is requisite when it is so sprinkled that the temperature of the fresh water be not lower

---

* Professor Rasch told me that he has hatched ova in damp moss, without even immersing them in water at all!

than that of the moss. Moreover, it is only necessary to sprinkle the topmost layer of moss, as the moisture will gradually percolate through the contents of the box. Neither should too much water be sprinkled on at one time, lest the ova at the bottom of the box should be immersed. To obviate this contingency it is best to turn the box over once at least in the course of the day.

In packing the box the bottom should first be evenly covered with a thick layer of the moss, which should be previously washed quite clean. On this a layer of eggs should be evenly spread, then should come a thinner layer of moss than before, and so on, alternate layers of eggs and moss, till the box is nearly full. On the top of all a layer of moss of the same thickness as the first should be laid, so that when the lid is fastened down the whole shall form a compact mass, and all shifting of the contents be rendered impossible. The elasticity of the moss will prevent the slightest danger from pressure accruing to the ova. If the weather is extremely severe the box should be protected. It may be remarked that ova should not be transported till the eyes of the embryo are visible.

A few precautions are necessary on unpacking such a box containing ova. The temperature of the box, and of the water in the hatching-case, must be compared with a thermometer. Supposing that of the former to be the greater, the moss should be gradually sprinkled with water from the latter till **they are both** equal. Great care must be taken not to hurry this operation.

The contents of the box should then be emptied into a good-sized tub half filled with water of *the same temperature as that in the hatching-case.* By gently moving the hand about among the moss, the **ova will** sink to the bottom, and the moss remain floating on the surface. The water should now be drained off, and **the** ova at once deposited in the hatching-boxes.

Should the water in the hatching-boxes, however, be of a higher temperature than **the** moss in which the ova were conveyed, these **can be at** once removed into the hatching-cases after they have been detached from the moss as above described.

On the Enemies to the Ova and Young Fish.

The greatest **care** must be taken **to prevent the entrance** of insects and larvæ into the **hatching apparatus.**

The most dangerous **enemy** to the **ova and the young** fish is, perhaps, the water-newt (*Sorex fodiens*). If the apparatus cannot be raised to **a** sufficient **height above** the ground, it should be protected with **a perforated tin or zinc lid.**

A curious instance occurred at the hatching establishment **at Greffsen,** a water-cure 'establishment near Christiania, **a few** years ago. The apparatus was raised two feet above the ground, and was not, therefore, protected with such a lid. A large quantity of eggs had been hatched out, when, lo and behold, one fine morning the young fry had nearly all disappeared! A number of traps were accordingly set on the floor of the house, and the following morning the intruder was captured. It turned out to be a water-rail which had found ingress through the mouth of a drain.

The Dytisci, **Hydrophili, and their larvæ,** and the larvæ of the *Libellula* and ***Agrion* are also** very dangerous enemies. The *Libellula depressa* is especially **a deadly foe,** and will even devour the two to **three** months old fish. It is extremely tenacious of life; and has **been known** after having been kept a whole day in spirits to recover **when placed in water** where there were young fish, **and in** a very **short time to** commence attacking them as if nothing had **happened.**

CHAPTER VI.

SKETCHES FROM SÆTERSDAL.*

SCENERY.—THE MANNERS AND COSTUMES OF THE IN-
HABITANTS.—TRAITS OF CHARACTER.—ABDUCTIONS.—
ANECDOTES ABOUT BEARS.

SÆTERSDAL is certainly one of the most sequestered of the retired mountain valleys of Norway. Of all the crowd of tourists from Christiania who stream out over fjeld and valley, and traverse the far-famed Thelemarken, there is scarce one who ventures over the mountains into Sætersdal. To the English traveller it is a *terra incognita*, and indeed is but little known to Norwegians themselves; for the attractions it offers are few, unless the love of exploring unknown tracts makes up for other deficiencies. Moreover, it lies very much out of the way of our regular tourists. Still it is easy of access, for already, on coming from Thelemarken

* By the permission of the Editor of Cassell's 'Illustrated Family Paper' I am enabled to lay before my readers an account of these strange people. My information is principally gathered from a series of letters which appeared in a periodical published in Christiania.

through Bykle to Valle Præstegjeld * in Sætersdal, one may find a broad and well-kept-up road, winding its way for more than ninety miles through the whole extent of the valley along the Bygland Fjord, and the banks of the Otter to Christiansand.

Where it passes through wild and precipitous places, as in Bygland's Præstegjeld, there are now roads built at much expense, and with great skill, on the face of the cliff. In former times there used only to be a wretched bridle-road, from which horses used frequently to be precipitated, or, under the most favourable circumstances, only prevented from falling headlong into the depths below by means of a restraining power applied to their tails. And this but half a generation ago!

Not without reason did the peasants christen this place "Devil's Cliff." A yawning abyss opens on the right, while on the left the mountain rears its side, covered with birch and wild cherry growing between immense blocks of rocks. These huge boulders, which seem to have been hurled down in wild disorder by giant force into the valley below, along the foaming river or dreamy fjord, form a peculiarity of Sætersdal landscape, and give it a wonderful air of defiance and savage wildness, perhaps nowhere else to be found. Here the marks of "Thor's hammer" may be seen,

* Præstegjeld, or "parish."

giving evident signs of the hard contest he sustained! The Bygland's Fjord below seems still to preserve remembrances of it deep in its silent bosom; but the Otter rages and chafes as if at the bare thought. Alas, that none can interpret its noisy language! The voice of tradition is hushed.

In passing underneath these huge blocks, it is impossible to refrain from shuddering at seeing them suspended, as it were, overhead. They seem as if they had not entirely stopped after their violent course; as if they were lying there, lingering and reflecting whether they should venture a spring down into the abyss. Occasionally it happens that one or two of these loiterers at length finds a convenient moment for this last leap, of which it has been pondering for centuries; and then, as if actuated by some sudden idea, rushes with a crash like the roar of a cannon, down into the depth in a wild dance, dashing everything along with it in its passage. There are also points where the valley becomes wider, and where the road winds through a more smiling landscape; but still, Nature never quite loses her character of wild and exaggerated power.

Gazing on such a prospect, one cannot but acknowledge that such a picturesque bridle-road—now boldly rounding a projecting rock, now hidden to view in a thick coppice, or again creeping down into the valley below, made with no calculation, and devoid of art, graceful in its capriciousness—would form a suitable frame to this magnified picture. But when you now roll along at your ease in a comfortable carriole through the whole length of the valley, you swallow with a feeling akin to gratitude the dust which is the constant attendant of a prosaic high-road, if you can only first rightly appreciate the prosperity and civilizing influence which is mixed up in its particles. Formerly, there was only a miserable bridle-path along which the Sætersdal peasant had to lead his mountain pony, taking his produce to the town on its back, and bringing home in the same manner the purchases he made. The old folk in the valley look back (as old folk are wont) with unspeakable regret on these bygone days, which they regard as the age of contented simplicity, in comparison with the conceited depravity of the present time. It is true, they used to bring less from the town, and took fewer articles to market; but they were satisfied with less, and did not long for that which they neither knew of nor were used to. Now, however, luxuries and superfluities, *brændeviin* and coffee, frippery and foppery, are more easily conveyed on a broad road, and in a capacious cart, which formerly four horses could scarcely have dragged. At that time, too, the old-fashioned hats, with their national buckles, broad crowns, and narrow brims, did not vie with that pest of town civilization which, beginning at the head, will soon descend lower, **and exchange** the genuine Norwegian costume for **the tasteless "Dano-French"** tail coat. The old inhabitant sees them **disappear with** regret, **as** they give place **to** the broad-brimmed, **be-tasselled** caps, which the Norwegian peasant seems to receive with especial affection wherever the national dress is disappearing.

There was a time (and there are still **to be found** old men who wear this dress) when **the** Sætersdal peasant used to go about in **his long white frock,** short yellow leather **breeches, long white stockings,** and garters **with tassels;** but it is long ago, **and the** rising generation scarce remember it. Then the overwhelming power **of** civilization came from the north over the Fjeld, not as now, from the south through the valley. Then there was no regular road, and the **traffic with** Christiansand was but small; but therefore consequently greater with Thelemarken, whence came the fashion which swept away in its devastating current the knee-breeches and the long peasant frocks, introducing in their place the short jacket and the enormous trousers **peculiar to** that district. Now-a-days, the Sætersdal **peasant** is completely immersed in his breeches, while at the same time he is hung up in his jacket, thus quite putting **to shame the old** proverb—" He who is born to be hung cannot drown;" **for** here, as is so often the case elsewhere, the fashion is carried to the extreme without any regard to tastefulness.

These walking breeches, with long dangling sleeves and short clipped head, with an ear on either side sticking up as a handle, have scarcely anything human about them, but possess a remarkable bearish look; and the word "*Buxe-björn*" (or "Bear-breeches") can only be duly appreciated and understood on seeing a Sætersdal peasant. But there was good reason for abolishing the old costume, for the knee-breeches, which were held on the hips only by a single button, did not nearly come up to the short waistcoat, thus leaving a large part of the body uncovered, except by the thin shirt—a very insufficient protection against the severe climate of a Fjeld district; and the people maintain that colic and cramps in the stomach are much less frequent than formerly. It must, therefore, be allowed that in this case appearance has been sacrificed to health; a great deal more than can be said of many other fashions that have come into vogue in the world, in which a total disregard to health and good taste has been the distinguishing feature. The dress is set off by a lively array of buttons, an upright green collar, light green facings, cords, and cuffs, with yellow and red embroidery upon a grey ground. The *söljer* (silver brooches) and silver studs are not wanting.

The peasants' shoes have a peculiar turned-up peak,

which gives them a *kömmager** appearance. The trousers, which are as narrow below as they are wide above, and reach only to the small of the leg, are trimmed at the bottoms with broad green ribbons, and buttoned at the side, leaving the thick white stockings visible above the shoes. In the winter they wear a sort of white woollen gaiter reaching to the knee, stitched at the sides and tops with broad dark cords. In the summer, however, adapting himself to the heat, he lets down a part of his trousers from under the arms, thus exposing on either side a triangular patch of not over clean linen. In this way, in the most practical manner possible, he adapts his huge trousers to the different seasons of the year.

 The national costume of the women has, however, undergone no such changes. Unlike their sisters in other parts of Europe, they pride themselves on adhering to antiquated customs; and, it must be owned, the dress of the Sætersdal woman, which remains quite unchanged since the days of Axild, is both characteristic and pretty. The short skirts, which reach only as far as the knee, with closely-sewn folds, have a peculiar crinoline appearance about them; while the red silk kerchief which is gracefully thrown over the head, the

---

* *Kömmager*, a shoe peculiar to Iceland, with a turned-up peaked toe, something like a Chinese slipper. It is made of reindeer skin, the head being only used. It is, I believe, universally worn by the Lapps and Finns in winter.

glittering studs of silver on the snow-white linen, and especially the woollen shawl, with its broad red stripes woven in with yellow on the white ground, thrown as a plaid jauntily over the shoulders, give their costume a picturesque and captivating appearance. The Sætersdalians are readily distinguished from the inhabitants of surrounding **districts by their** tall stature, broad muscular backs, **and a regular, frequently** antique cast of features. The *tout ensemble*, **even to the** oval form of the face, and the small **coquettish whiskers which** every Sætersdal peasant wears, as well as his **short** jacket and **low** broad-crowned hat, gives him a peculiar **foreign look, and has** contributed to the opinion which circulates **as a dark tradition, that** he **is not of** the genuine Norwegian race, and that foreign blood runs in his veins. **It is said** that ages ago, in the remote past, some Scotch families **found** their way into Sætersdal, and especially into **Bykle, and** settled there; **and that in** time they became so intermixed with the Sætersdal peasants, that all indications **of their foreign** extraction became obliterated, **except from this dim** tradition and their outlandish features. **This** subject, however, we will not discuss, but will rather describe their character, manner of living, the secluded position of their district, and **their** disinclination to enter into connection with those **who do not** dwell among them; for the Sætersdal peasant is **not** generally well received out of his own parts, owing to his national peculiarities and independence of bearing.

He wears his hair cropped close, stiff, like the bristles of a pig; but in front, bordering on the forehead, he allows it to grow into a pigtail (or *spör*), which he takes a pride in plaiting and twisting behind the ear. He is as proud of his pigtail as the Oriental of his beard, and would not part with this ornament at any price; and the principal cause of his dislike to soldiering is a fear of the brutal military scissors, which would clip off his pride, his joy, his darling pigtail, the moment he is enrolled. He differs from the Indian only in this, that the one wears his pigtail in front—the other farther back. With both people it has a sort of challenging air about it; but in the one case it refers to a scalp, in the other to an eye. In a fight, for instance, the Sætersdal peasant, with that precision and certainty which only long habit can give, seizes with his forefinger the pigtail of his enemy, and with his thumb endeavours, and often succeeds, in gouging out his eye. Many a living testimony now wanders about with one eye, as Odin, a victim to the conservative predilections of his opponent for eye-squeezing. Not unfrequently, too, the nose and ear bear marks of the contest. To bite off and swallow his opponent's nose or ear is thought just as little of as squeezing out his eye, and is not considered as any disgrace in a Sætersdal fight.

But should he have a fight in the town, he acts as a man of taste and good breeding, and only uses his knife; but amongst his own people his sharp teeth come into play, and he seldom disdains to seize the defiant pigtail of his enemy, which, on such occasions, falls over the forehead in a most inviting manner.

But unless excited by brandy or ale, the Sætersdal peasant is not usually pugnacious or obtrusive in manner. He is superstitious to a degree, owing to the wild solitude of the district, and the traditions from olden time. "Aasgardsreien" still goes about and jests, and many are the tarred crosses which the peasant marks over his door at Christmas-time, to keep the powers of evil away. He firmly believes, too, in spirits; and there are few of them who at least once in their lives have not seen and heard the wild, ringing gait of "Aasgardsreien." After sunset he will hardly ever venture out of doors, and even threats or promises will not induce him to go a single step after darkness has fallen. He is very sluggish in his movements, more so than is usually the case among the Norwegian peasantry; excessively egotistic, and of a calculating turn of mind.

He will not readily do any service to a stranger; and when any request or demand is made, and he thinks the party able to pay, he never forgets to weigh, as far as possible, the favour asked of him against the money expected. "How much will you give?" is a question which he will ask at every step; and before this important point is decided, not an inch will he budge from his place.

This is a sad trait in his character, but, unfortunately, too true, as every stranger who has come in contact with a Sætersdal peasant will allow. The cause of this disobliging and calculating spirit, which is so uncommon generally speaking in the country, is difficult to explain. It must arise from his isolated and secluded position, which has given his feelings, thoughts, and interests, a sort of spiral form, constantly converging towards a point, which point is himself. Intercourse and contact with others will probably considerably ameliorate this failing.

It were to be wished that it would also be instrumental in checking and restraining another peculiarity, which obtains certainly more amongst the Sætersdal peasants than any others in the country. It is their abominable filthiness! In this they certainly gain the palm—at all events, there are very few who approach them.

The Sætersdal peasant has an innate horror of water, and washes himself (properly) only every Christmas time! On his cottage floor, which has not undergone any cleansing process ever since it was laid down, his pig jumps cheerfully about; the hens sit on the shelf, between milkpans and cheeses; while the cock majestically struts about on the tester-bed. In the same room which serves as dairy the Sætersdal peasant sleeps with his family and servants, amongst pigs and goats, and other smaller and still more lively animals.*

The peasant of a higher rank has an especial shelf under the roof for his cheese and milk, and, as is usually the case, this is on the tester-bed, which does not contribute to make the one more dainty, or the surface of the other more white and pure. When a milk-bowl is produced, especially in summer, it seldom fails to be covered with a thick coating of dust and smuts, which leaves the spectator in doubt as to what it really is. But the native Sætersdalian eats it without even blowing the dust off, so little does it disturb his equanimity; for in the great vessels where he keeps his sour milk for a whole year, one can see worms, and other such trifles, running about as merrily as possible. It all goes down, in enviable combination!

It were easy to relate many a striking incident in corroboration of the dirtiness of the Sætersdal peasant; but no description could possibly give a correct idea of it. To appreciate it properly you must go and visit

---

* A friend of mine had, some years ago, to pass the night in a Sætersdal cottage—at least, a part of it; for he was so tormented by the "lively animals," that he had to make a bolt of it, stark naked, into the river close by, before he could get rid of his company. Next morning he looked as if he had got the measles!

him in his home, see him roaming about amongst pigs, goats, **fowls,** cats, and ducks, on **a floor** beyond all description, **the** coating of which would be amply sufficient to manure a moderate-sized field, **and** in an in**credible atmosphere,** composed of the thickest impurities, arising from the human and animal world which this novel Noah has collected in his ark. No Irish **cabin** ever came up to it! In the next place, you should **see** him in his hideous leather breeches, **in his** nameless shirt sleeves, that have no more of their **original colour** than had the milk **above mentioned,** with his wife and daughters, in their summer dress **and** home costume, the **short white woollen blouse** which they wear underneath **their** dark, short-skirted, corded over-dress, and whose whiteness is replaced by a yellow-brown gray, which forms the ground colour, in which are a multitude of marks and spots of all shades and colours like a rain**bow;** though the greasy and dark spots *are* the **most** numerous. One can hardly believe that they are **the** same beings which so short a time ago might have been seen in the churchyard so clean and picturesque-looking in their best Sunday attire ; but that, reader, was the poetical and bright side, this the prosaic and real—for **the** fundamental element is dirt! The white shining shirt sleeves, and silver studs, and cleanly appearance **are laid** aside as soon as service is over. It does not **last even** to the close of the day, but **is** put by **after** a few hours' ostentatious parading for the boundless filth of the ensuing week.

But how can it be otherwise? For where hard and heavy labour bows down the delicate and effeminate, these at least must give way.

It will strike the traveller painfully, not only in Sætersdal Proper, but in the more southern districts, and the whole western coast, on seeing the hardest and severest work imposed on the weaker sex. Whilst the husband, with a clay pipe in the corner of his mouth, is stretching himself at full length in true Oriental indolence, you may see the former weighed down under the roughest field work.

The women hoe, thrash, plough, cut wood, and carry water; whilst the men, just for once in a way, drive a load into the town. The laziness of the Sætersdal peasant is so great, that he almost looks on it as something derogatory to put his hand to any farm work. He often lets out his whole property on lease to one less opulent, who farms it for him, assuring him a certain rent, on which he lives; whilst he shamefully wastes his time in slothful indolence. There are peasants who, as far as regards the softness and fineness of their hands, can compete with any "*Forening*"[*] *habitué*, or lion of the metropolis. Ask such a Sætersdal gentleman why he does not manage his own farm

---

[*] *Forening*—The Almack's of Christiania.

himself, and you will get a *naïve* and astonished reply. "He needn't work, he is rich; he isn't compelled to do it." They cannot understand why a person works, unless from the greatest necessity. Amongst a people of such idle tendencies, it is very common to find along with this letting out of farms an arrangement made by which the owner secures a maintenance for himself, so as to be able to pursue an idle, slothful, lounging existence; and it is easy to understand what a depressing influence such a proceeding must have on the value of property, and the progress of agriculture. It has, moreover, a destructive influence on the whole family life, and often by the side of affection for parents, there creeps in an element of calculative speculation on the probable event of their death, so as to set the estate at liberty.

The Sætersdal peasant (as with all uncivilized people), is greatly addicted to strong drink, and on particular occasions—at all events at marriages and Christmas feasts —there is nothing more common than to see men and women, like the Samoïedes, drinking together, till at last they roll down in a state of unconscious helplessness.

And still by the side of this barbarity, there are to be found traits of a romantic chivalry in their nature, at which one cannot help marvelling.

In Sætersdal abductions are not uncommon. It is an old custom, and seems to have taken its origin from the desire of forming alliances and connections not between their children, but **between their farms**; indeed, it prevails to a great **extent** amongst all the peasantry of Norway. In some of the valleys, **the inhabitants** would on no account marry out of their district. Hence, as may be supposed, in a thinly-inhabited **neighbourhood, where the choice is not great, frequent** intermarriages **occur; and the** effects resulting **therefrom are extremely injurious.** This, combined with other causes, such **as the solitary and sedentary** life they lead, the poor and **insufficient food they have to put up with,** is in all probability the **reason why there are, in** proportion to its population, more **lunatics, idiots, deaf** and dumb, &c., to be found in Norway **than in any** other European country, Switzerland, I **believe, alone excepted.** It is a constant occurrence for uncles to marry **their nieces—a practice** not confined to the uneducated and " quasi-barbarous " peasant, but adopted also by **the higher** and educated classes of towns, the metropolis not excepted.

As regards family connections, a **stiff-necked, aristocratic tendency prevails** among **them,** not surpassed by any nobility; and the peasant in Sætersdal, as elsewhere, is in this point decidedly an aristocrat; and one often, therefore, hears speak of unhappy alliances, but **still** oftener that the will of **the parents** has been set at nought, and that the **affair has** been decided by the heart, and not by the understanding. There is frequently **an instance of a labourer's son** marrying a farmer's daughter, and the calculating prudence of the old folk being **set at nought. And** then abductions come in, with all their romantic episodes. How old La Fontaine would rejoice in his grave if he had **any idea that, amid the** stern reality of this " steam-age," and in the very heart of one of Europe's enlightened countries, his theories were turned to practical **purposes by shepherds** and shepherdesses!

Let me draw a **picture.** " The **moon is shining**—a lonely field valley—a cottage in the **valley's bosom. . .** A shepherdess appears—she **is stealing** out of the paternal **abode with a bundle** under her arm, in which are her few treasures, her ornaments, and the necessary articles **of apparel. . .** The herdsman waits by appointment. One last tearful look at the home **of her** fathers—and **she is** lifted up by his strong arm, **and is** carried off at the saddle-bow!"

Now all this sounds excessively romantic, and **yet** nothing can be truer. Nothing is wanting to complete the picture, even to the tragical despair and fury of the father, and the final pardon. Unfortunately, as far **as** regards effect, the despair and **the fury evinced** are completely damped by the stoical resignation **(a national** trait among Norwegian peasantry!) with which he gives way **when he** finds it cannot be helped. It has never been heard that an abduction has caused any hostilities between families. When once the thing is done, and the abducted bride has reached her new home, he submits with patience to what cannot be avoided. Exasperation would only make him ridiculous, for the bold lover has the precedent of long-established custom, and the laugh on his own side.

It certainly has occurred that the parents or relations have kept guard over a too amatory maiden, and, for further precaution, have even kept her under lock and key, or bolted her in the cellar; but almost always the loving couple have found means to obviate all impediments—"for if a man's stratagems are deep laid, we know well that a woman's are unfathomable." When a girl has had two or more suitors, and she gets at last weary of such an existence, it often happens that, in order to put an end to it, she allows herself to be carried off by the one who has been the secret object of her heart's affections. The rejected rivals have then nothing else left than to find another sweetheart as quickly as possible. Such is the prescribed custom. They are to be then seeing going from door to door, and making proposals to the first girl they meet with; for if the rejected rival can only feel inclined, and can get married before the favoured lover, *then—and then only*—has he wiped out the disgrace which the refusal and the being jilted has cast on his good name and reputation; a custom which, if generally followed, would contribute not a little to the promotion of wedlock, and the preservation of morals, and to the destruction and discomfiture of all bachelors and convents. More than one has obtained his bride in this way, "*par droit de conquête;*" and the custom prevails to this day.

But, on the whole, one cannot deny that there is a noble pride, a deep feeling of independence, and love of liberty that hates constraint beyond everything, belonging to their good qualities, and shining brightly through all their slothful habits and dirtiness.

The Sætersdal peasant is bold, openhearted, straightforward, and hospitable. With a brimming beaker he meets the guest who passes over his threshold, and drinks to him, and offers him the strong, foaming ale, which, however, it is not the mark of good breeding to quaff off till after repeated and pressing invitations on the side of the host, and continued protests on the part of the guest, in order that the former may have ample opportunities for displaying his persuasive powers.

As regards enlightenment, the Sætersdal peasantry stand remarkably low. Very few of them can read, and still fewer write. Their ideas are, naturally, primitive to a degree. The rotundity of the earth they still look on as a most doubtful matter.

Like our venerable forefathers, they believe the world to be flat, like a pancake, in the middle of which the Almighty has placed Norway, and Sætersdal again in the

Q

middle of this; and that America, the sea, *Jötunheim*,* are on its extreme limits. The theories of Galileo do not seem to have made much progress here. That the earth remains still, and that the sun, moon, and stars revolve round her at a respectful distance, is considered to be an incontestable fact. Like the old man in the fable, the Sætersdal peasant has a confused idea that an emperor is superior to a king, and an empire to a kingdom, and the Pope—of whom he has mysterious and uncomfortable conceptions—over them all.

It is still to be hoped that better means of intercourse and growing enlightenment will tend to remove such ideas; and in time even to obtain the mastery over that filth which has justly made the Sætersdal peasant so renowned, and which is so prevalent even where his circumstances are comparatively affluent, lying like a heavy weight on soul and body, and blunting all perception for the beautiful, and for real prosperity.

Sætersdal and the neighbouring districts are excellent hunting quarters. On the high grounds are to be found reindeer; on the mountain side, ptarmigan; while black-cock, foxes, hares, wolves, and bears abound in the forests. As the peasants never keep dogs, and hares therefore are only hunted in the winter when the snow is on the ground, it frequently happens that they lose their instinctive shyness, and it is no unusual thing in

* Home of the giants.

the summer to see them sitting by the roadside, so seldom are **they scared** by the chase!

Bears are very numerous. In Sætersdal Bruin lives as a private gentleman in undisturbed possession of his estate, respected if not **beloved by** his neighbours; but like other "Majesties by the grace of God," he **cares** little about affection, so long as he is respected, and this he certainly is in Sætersdal; for the genuine Sætersdalian is too indolent and lazy, and **perhaps also too** cowardly, to meddle with a bear, even **when** it is the attacker, and, by way of amusement **or** pastime, sticks its claws into a cow or cow-boy.

On the whole, the bear is a remarkably good-tempered **animal. One day** a few summers ago, Bruin took it into his head, by way of a little change, to have a short walk along the high road. Now, the Lensmand (sheriff's officer) was also out in the discharge of his duties, and meeting his highness in Fandsklev (Devil's Cliff), endeavoured to inform him in the politest **way** possible—by a gentle shower of small stones—that he should at least give half the road to the official authorities. Bruin, however, without allowing himself to be imposed on by a display of gold cord, gave him to understand by a majestic and significant growl that he **had a desire** to **remain** quiet, and that he did not particularly approve of small stones. The Lensmand, therefore, was compelled to turn back, and leave his majesty to continue his solitary promenade undisturbed. Such encounters are by no means rare.

Some *Fossekarle** once met with a bear taking a bath in Bygland's Fjord, on a hot summer's day, and forthwith attacked him, armed only with their boathooks. They had a very narrow escape, however; for the bear wishing to make their personal acquaintance, had succeeded in clambering up into the boat, when it fell dead from loss of blood.

It is not, however, in Sætersdal Proper, but rather in the contiguous districts, that most bears are to be found. It is here, too, that the regular bear-hunters live. They have a real passion for the chase, and make quite a profession of it.

One of the most renowned bear-hunters in this district is Niels Knudsen Breistöl, a famous blacksmith, who not only manufactures his own rifle, but also provides his countrymen with weapons of his own make. His rifles are well known, and are much sought after. In Evje, too, there lives a well-known bear-hunter; and on a farm called Moy there is a man who is said to have shot about a hundred bears; but it would be tedious to reckon all the bear-shooters in a district where there is scarcely a peasant who does not go out in pursuit of

---

* *Fossekarle* (literally "waterfall fellows"), are those who are employed in conveying timber into the river or lake, for floating it down.

them, and where there are to be found those who have shot scores of bears, and but few who have not at least twice in their lives obtained head-money. It is quite remarkable with what indifference the peasants speak about the dangers encountered in this sort of chase. One would think that they looked upon it almost as a common hare-hunt, as some of them have indeed said. The bear, they say, is not dangerous; for it only attacks when it has been wounded, or as one of them significantly remarked, "*when he is insulted.*" The object, therefore, is to insult him effectually with the first shot; for the peasants always use single-barrelled rifles. One very seldom hears of mishaps, although instances are not wanting. When an accident does occur, they often manage to escape in a most wonderful manner. A story is told of a man who had wounded a bear, but not mortally. The enraged animal immediately attacked him, and dashed him to the ground, falling on him; fortunately, he was scarcely injured. The man, who thus was lying underneath the bear with his face against its stomach, carefully watched his opportunity to move just as the bear moved, so that it could not seize him with its fearful paws. Meanwhile he succeeded in getting hold of his knife, and while thus crawling about under the bear, accompanied this sort of "backward galop" with repeated enlivening stabs in the shaggy stomach of Mr. Bruin, who at last becoming tired of this sort of pastime, sneaked away growling from his unpleasant companion. But it is not everybody who gets off so easily. One sometimes meets with people who have been frightfully wounded; and it is only astonishing that this is not more frequently the case, owing to the reckless courage, almost amounting to carelessness, which they display in this chase, which is generally carried on single-handed. With the utmost coolness does the peasant repair to the den where Bruin is enjoying his winter slumbers, and crawl in unarmed; then when he sees two eyes sparkling through the gloomy darkness, and has ascertained that the place is occupied, and that "the governor" is at home, he crawls out again backwards, fetches his rifle, which he politely left outside the door, and creeping in again, takes aim at the eyes, and slaughters the bear.

A cow-boy once shot at a bear which he met by chance with small stones, for want of better ammunition. On being asked how he dared to fire only with a charge of small stones, "I never gave it a thought," said the boy. And this is quite characteristic, for so it is with the peasants; they do many such things, which might presuppose a lion courage wanting that mature deliberation, without which true courage cannot exist. They don't think about it. This is not deliberate courage. Occurrences as those just mentioned happen so naturally that they are but seldom known out of the immediate district; and the hero of the adventure would be excessively astonished if he noticed that any one attached peculiar importance to it, and would perhaps deliberate the next time, and so, in all probability, not succeed so **easily**.

One more incident. Some little time ago a bear used to prowl about a particular part. He was called the "horse bear," because he had despatched so many horses in his time. His fame had extended **far and** wide, and he had often been hunted. He **had had, more**over, to submit to a regular "**Klapjagt,**"* something quite uncommon in these parts, **but had** always contrived, though often wounded, to escape.

In one of these encounters he got severely wounded in one of the hind legs, causing the foot ever since to be quite awry, so that he could easily be recognized wherever he went. Wild and savage to the extreme from all the persecution to which he had had to submit, **he** would attack people whenever he saw them, even if they had not "insulted" him. Some time elapsed when the slaughter of various cows, and the breaking down of cowsheds, gave convincing proofs that he was again in the neighbourhood, and great was the panic caused by the advent **of** this terrible "horse bear." Therefore, one of the most renowned bear-shooters in the valley, **who had** often had an encounter with these

* When the whole country is called out to beat the woods.

princes of the forest, determined to go out in quest of him. One fine day, then, throwing his single-barrelled rifle over his shoulder, he started out. He had been gone but a short time, and had snuffed about in the wood, when suddenly, on emerging from a moderately thick copse, he perceived the "horse bear" making straight for him. Taking aim, he fired, but whether the unexpected meeting had made his hand shake a little, or whether there was any other reason, it is certain that the shot did not take effect where it was intended. The bear was wounded, but not mortally. Furious, it raised itself upon its hind legs, and attacked the man. As he was only armed with his single-barrelled rifle, there was no possibility of reloading. His position, therefore, was critical; for if he attempted to fly he was irretrievably lost, and if he remained standing the prospect was not much better. He did not take long to reflect. With a determined look, and grasping the barrel of his rifle firmly in the right hand, he awaited the approach of his terrible opponent, determined to sell his life as dearly as possible. But the furious brute, perplexed, and undoubtedly awed by the steady gaze and firm mien of the hunter, after having advanced a few steps towards him, suddenly disappeared in the thicket. Thus the "horse bear" escaped again, but was shot not long after.

A short time back a bear had taken his annual trip

from Sætersdal into Bygdelag, in order to visit his old haunts. He had been seen one day in the spring in Evje parish on the eastern side of the river Otter, sitting in a most philosophical manner on its bank, and probably cogitating whether he should venture an expedition across or not. After having gazed at the water in this manner for a considerable period, he seemed at last to have come to the conclusion that it was not quite convenient, for presently, with a "right-about-face," he disappeared. A short time after, a bear was noticed wandering about in Iveland, near the river Otter. It had been seen about there in several places, and seemed especially to keep about the neighbourhood of the farms Kless and Ivedt. It was in one of the outlying fields of this last-mentioned farm that it attacked a cow-boy, who endeavoured to keep it away from the mash-tub by shouting and throwing stones at it. Getting, probably, tired of this racket, or being struck by some of the stones, he at last flew upon the cow-boy, and tore his clothes to pieces. Matters seemed becoming serious for the poor lad, who was far away from any human assistance, and quite unarmed. The bear would soon have made short work of him had not a courageous heifer, who had hitherto prudently kept neutral, now that matters were going beyond a joke, thought it high time to interfere. Without long reflection, and only waiting for a favourable opportunity, it attacked the unbidden stranger so courageously and ably, **that at last, either** by a well-directed butt, or either that the bear thought it silly to be beaten by such an ignoble animal as a **cow**, it sneaked off quite crestfallen. Meanwhile the cow-boy, who had had such an unexpected opportunity for studying Bruin's expressive physiognomy, got off, thanks **to the noble assistance of his** horned ally, with torn breeches and **some few** trifling scratches—a cheap price for such an honour! After this rencontre his growling highness repaired to other places, **and** they heard no more of him that year. Knud Breistöl, **and one or two of the** shooters in the valley, were naturally **out** after him, when one morning when it was dusk he sneaked by **them** unawares. Knud fired, as did the **others**; but it was still dark, and there was no time to take steady aim, so the bear probably saved his skin whole and sound for **another time.** If it is actually the case that the renowned **Count Raben is** as clever in shooting **bears as he is said to be** in shooting pigs from his travelling carriage, it is strange that Sætersdal has not witnessed his exploits, for here he would have an opportunity of acquiring both honour and bear-skins; probably, however, this "terror of the bears" has laid aside his weapons.

But cultivation and civilization **will** soon drive the **bears away** from this mountainous valley, as they have **from so many** others, and it is easy to see that their **lot** will be like that of the aborigines in America and Australia: their race will in time disappear from the country, and one will have to take a journey to Siberia in order to get a bear-skin.

Once, but it is longer ago than in the memory of man, there were beavers to be found in the valley—a fact which the names of certain farms clearly indicate; but these too have long since disappeared; the law was too late in protecting them against destruction. It is said, however, that even yet in one remote mountain-lake remains of their clever building operations are yet to be seen. But the otter at least does not bear its name in vain, for otters are found here in plenty, and there are few to look after them and hunt them.

English travellers who are desirous of studying the habits of a strange people, and who do not mind putting up with such inconveniences as dirt, and poor accommodation, will probably find a visit to Sætersdal both interesting and remunerative.

CHAPTER VII.

THE VEGETABLE PRODUCTIONS OF NORWAY.

If Norway offers peculiar advantages to the sportsman, so also does it present many interesting phenomena well worthy of attention as regards its vegetable products.

Before, however, discussing these, I purpose to lay before the reader a brief geographical description of this part of the Scandinavian Peninsula.

Norway lies between lat. 58° and lat. 71°, and its greatest length from Cape Lindesnæs to the North Cape is about 900 miles, a distance equivalent to that between London and Gibraltar.

Its superficial area may be estimated at about 121,800 square miles, half of which lies at an altitude of more than 2,000 feet above the sea-level, while about 3,200 square miles are within the limit of perpetual snow.*

---

* The snow limit under the following latitudes may be thus placed :—

Under latitude 61°	.. Sulutind	..	5,500 feet.
,,	62½° .. Dovre ..	..	5,400 ,,
,,	70° .. N. Cape	..	2,400 ,,

VEGETABLE PRODUCTIONS OF NORWAY.

Norway is essentially a mountainous **country**, in which the mountains form the most **prominent** feature, whilst the **valleys or lowlands occupy** but a subordinate part.

The **loftiest ranges are** to be found between lat. 60° and lat. 62°, **in** which there are peaks from 8,000 **to** 9,000 **feet above** the level of the sea.

Nothing can exceed the desolate wildness **of these** regions, the native home of the wild reindeer, **to which the** *Cladonia rangiferina* and other **lichens** impart a sombre and yellowish **tint, adding not a little** to the depressing uniformity of the landscape. It is in this part that **most of the glaciers are found.**

In the south-eastern parts of **the** country the direction of **the valleys** is from north to south; but on the western coast the sea makes deep indentations into the interior from west to east, forming the fjords or firths.

They are often of considerable length; *e.g.*, **the Sogne Fjord** is not less than twenty-two geographical miles from its mouth to the extremity of its innermost arm.

Sometimes they are, so to speak, narrow fissures in the rocky mass, the sides of which rise perpendicularly from the sea, and never permit the full light of day to penetrate to their bottom, as in Lyse Fjord in Ryfylke, **and** Sör Fjord **in** Hardanger; and sometimes, though less frequently, they form capacious basins as the Throndhjem Fjord, the sloping and even sides of which dotted here and there with pasture and arable land, afford a pleasing contrast to the dull monotony of the pine forests.

The principal geological formations of the mountains are granite, gneiss, mica-slate, and quartzite. These exercise a great and appreciable influence not only on the external configuration of the country, but also upon its fertility. In some places, indeed, towards the south-east various kinds of limestone are met with, and here the vegetation is found to differ in a very marked degree.

The greatest part, therefore, of the country may be said to consist of immense mountainous tracts intersected in different directions by deep valleys. The bottoms and sloping sides of these are adapted for the abode of man; but it is not usual to find habitations of a stationary character at higher altitudes than 2,000 feet above the sea; and even the sæters, or chalets, where the peasants usually reside a couple of months in the summer with their cattle, are seldom above 3,000 feet.

Although the valleys occupy but a subordinate proportion of the whole area of the country, yet are they more than any other part deserving of attention, as they comprise all the habitable and tillable terrain of Norway.

In their lowest part runs a sinuous stream. The intervening portion between the river and the foot of the fjelds is covered with small patches of grass and corn land, which surround the low log-built houses of the peasants; while the mountain slopes on either side are clothed with luxuriant forest tracts, in which the white stems of the birch trees form a pleasing relief to the sombre uniformity of the Scotch and spruce fir.

The observing traveller, who for the first time visits one of the valleys in the south-western, and more especially the western, parts of the country, cannot fail to have his attention arrested by the immense quantities of water which he meets with. He sees it trickling down in silvery stripes from the fjeld tops, hundreds of feet above his head on both sides of him, and, where it has a perpendicular fall of any distance, assuming beautiful feathery wreaths, till it at last finds its way into the watercourse below. Well may he think, "Where on earth can all this water come from?" A little consideration will, however, explain the phenomenon.

The warm south-westerly winds blowing over the sea, the temperature of which is considerably increased owing to the Gulf Stream, are laden with moisture. But when they come in contact with the lofty, snow-clad mountain ranges on the western coast, a continuous condensation is the result. Thus, when these winds have prevailed for any time, the upper regions are constantly enveloped in clouds and fog. The rounded form which the mountains assume, moreover, prevents the moisture from being so rapidly dispersed as would be the case were they pointed or peaked. In the winter months, therefore, the snow is heaped up in immense masses on the high plateaux, which in the summer are again deluged with rain. Consequently, when, after the long winter, the mild winds and rains of the early summer ensue, an enormous mass of water is collected above, which naturally seeks an outlet. But owing to the flat and uniform formation of these plateaux, an outlet is not so easy to find, and the valleys, moreover, are narrow, and situated at long distances from each other. The result, therefore, may be readily imagined that each valley receives enormous quantities of water from these immense fjeld tracts above.

This circumstance naturally exercises a great influence on the mass of water in the rivers, causing them to rise rapidly and overflow their banks about the beginning of June.

Before dismissing this subject, it may be well to mention another phenomenon which is not unfrequent in Norway, *i. e.*, the green colour of the water in some of the rivers. An instance of this is especially noticeable in Gudbrandsdal, where the Otta Elv joins the Laagen. The water of the former is of a peculiar sea-green colour, and it is very easy to distinguish the water of either river from the other, even for some tolerable distance after their junction. The whole mass eventually assumes the same green appearance, and thus continues till it enters the Miösen at Lillehammer, in fact, colouring the water of the lake for some little distance below its debouchure. The Otta Elv rises in the glaciers on the Lang Fjeld, and is at first of a milky appearance, and is opaque; but when the silicious matter with which it is laden is deposited, it assumes a bright sea-green colour, and becomes transparent.

The ultimate transparency of the water is even more remarkable than is its assuming a green colour.

In the upper parts of the Orinoco a similar phenomenon was observed by Humboldt, where the water in several of the small tributary streams was transparent and bright yellow when examined in a glass, whilst in the bed of the river it assumed a dark coffee-brown colour, and appeared quite black in the shade.

Something similar to this has also been observed in parts of the Amoor, and of the Jumna.

Norway abounds, too, in lakes, mostly of an inconsiderable size, and often lying at great altitudes. As is usually the case with mountain lakes, they are of great depth, and their waters are intensely cold and very transparent. Generally speaking, their width is inconsiderable.

The Miösen, which is the largest, and is about 70 miles long, is 400 feet above the sea. From several of these, rivers take their rise, and run in opposite directions. The most remarkable instance of this sort is to be found in Læsjöværks Vand, which is 2,050 feet above the sea, and is the source of the Rauma running through the valley of Romsdal, and the Laagen which flows through Gudbrandsdal and enters the Miösen at Lillehammer (*vide* p. 40). From a large fjeld morass, called the Kol, in the highlands of Hardanger eight rivers take their rise, running in different directions.

The whole country abounds in morasses, many of which are capable of being reclaimed for agricultural purposes, but which in their present state exercise an injurious effect upon cultivation. For instance, in the "stift," or diocese of Christiania, which comprises about one-fourth of the whole superficial area of the country, there are not less than 1,156 square miles of marshy ground below, and 764 square miles above the limit of corn. And although of late years the forests have been much reduced, yet they still occupy a very considerable proportion of the superficial area of the country.

Hence, it may readily be seen that the extent of tillable land in Norway is proportionately insignificant; in fact, not exceeding 1,060 square miles, or less than $\frac{4}{113}$th part of the whole superficial area.* But still,

* The population by the last census amounted to nearly 1,500,000 souls. Of grain of different sorts, 656,993 imperial quarters were imported; 15,378,535 lbs. rye meal; 2,776,086 lbs. flour; 71,726 lbs. flour; and 205,537 lbs. grits.

though the Norwegian **Bönde is far** behind the rest of the civilized world in an agricultural point of view, and does not half turn the natural resources of the soil to their proper advantages, yet of late years a marked improvement **may** be noticed in this respect. Several morasses have been drained and rendered fit **for** cultivation, and waste places have been redeemed.

The traveller will also, I think, have been struck with the way in which every little fertile spot on **the** fjeld side, if even only **a few** yards **square, is** turned to account. And he may have noticed, **as** he has been driving in his carriole through some **of the** valleys, the peasant busily employed in cutting the handful of grass that grows up there hundreds of feet above his head, and laying it over hurdles to dry in the wind.

The system of irrigation which obtains in some parts, **too,** may have attracted his attention. It **is** extremely curious and ingenious. Troughs of wood or of birch bark are placed to catch the water from **some mountain** rill, which is thus conveyed, frequently to very long distances, and often crossing the road fifteen to twenty feet above it to the farmer's field.

The *modus operandi* **is as** follows:—**A hole is dug in a part of** the field into which the trough **conveys the water.** A man, armed with a broad wooden **spade,** then sprinkles **it** as far around him on all sides as he can reach. At **a short** distance from this **is another** and similar hole, connected by a drain with the former, and in this manner by a network of drains and holes dug at convenient distances, the whole field can be irrigated in a comparatively short space of time. The farmer thus renders himself in a great measure independent of rain; and indeed in those parts where this system of irrigation is carried on, he views with great concern the approach of wet weather. "The rain I can make for myself, but I can't manufacture hot weather," he says.*

As might be supposed, in the neighbourhood of Christiania, and of other important towns, farming is carried on after a much more improved method than in the interior; and it is a common thing now-a-days for young men to study the science of agriculture in Scotland, a country which in so many respects resembles their own.

To the peasants who live far up in the interior, remote from the sea-coast, a good haytime and harvest is of inexpressible value. During the last two or three years, however, the rainy weather has been very adverse to good crops, and poor harvests have been the result.†

---

* When I first saw the operation, I was under the impression that the man was wilfully trampling and breaking down the standing corn.

† In the old heathen times, when unpropitious weather and bad harvests happened, the blame thereof was attached to the king; and if no other remedy was found of avail, his subjects would sacrifice him to the gods, in order to propitiate the Divine wrath. This fate happened to King Domalde in Upsala, who, after two bad years

The amount of suffering, nay, positive **starvation**, that accordingly ensued is perfectly inconceivable. I can only compare it to the Irish famine **of 1848**.

The high floods of 1860 caused an immense amount of damage, for they literally washed off the **top soil** from the fields, leaving nothing but a deposit of slime and grit behind. Many of the peasants thus became completely ruined, and had to sell their farms **for a** mere nothing, and emigrated to America **in numbers** truly surprising for so **small** a country.*

As above stated, **Norway extends** through 13° of latitude, **consequently one may expect** to meet with striking **climatic changes.** Other modifying circumstances must, however, be taken into consideration. A glance at the map will show what an extensive seaboard Norway possesses, and, as is well known, this fact **alone** prevents† extremes of heat and **cold** in

---

in succession, was in the following autumn sacrificed by his subjects. The same fate also happened to the ancestor of the Norwegian autocrat, Olaf Trætelgja, who lived at the end of the seventh century. On the other hand, there was a general belief that the corpse of a king under whose reign there had been prosperous harvests, possessed a charm, so as to insure a succession of good years. Thus in 860, when Halfdan Svarte died, his body was divided into four parts, one of which was sent to each of the four quarters of the country for **interment.** *Vide* Schübeler's 'Culturpflanzen Norwegens.'

* From 1851 to 1855 the numbers of emigrants amounted **to** 21,921. In 1861 I believe them to have amounted to 6,800!

† Thus, at Bergen, lat. 60° 23' 37", the mean temperature for the whole year is $+8\cdot21$ Centigrade; the mean temperature for the winter $+2\cdot21$, and for the summer $+14\cdot75$. At the North Cape for the whole year it is $+0$; for the winter, -5; for the summer, $-6\cdot25$. At Christiania, lat. 54° 54' 43", it is $+5\cdot37$; $-5\cdot0$;

the immediate neighbourhood of the coast. But on penetrating for a few miles into the interior, out of the influence of the sea air, the cold in winter is intense to a degree, while the heat in the summer is equally oppressive. To give but one instance. At Valle, in Sætersdal, in the south-west, lat. 59° 12′, lying at an altitude of 1,000 feet above the sea, the thermometer in summer may stand at $+42°$ Cent., and in winter fall to $-35°$!

In these northern latitudes the winters are of course very long, and the summers very short. And what makes the winters still longer is that for all practical purposes there is in fact really no spring.

Winter may be said to begin about the end of October, and to last till the middle of April. At this period an interregnum of about three weeks occurs; and though the sun's rays have great power at mid-day, and though the days are now longer than is the case in England, yet the melting snow, and the great depth to which the frost has penetrated into the ground, neutralize any effect that might have been produced, and every night there is a sharp frost. Thus, vegetation is retarded. About the beginning or first week in May, however, a change occurs. Suddenly, as if by magic,

---

$+15\cdot5$ for the corresponding periods. At Ullensvang, in Hardanger, lat. 60° 16′, the mean temperature for the whole year is $+7\cdot25$ Centigrade; for the winter $-$ months $1\cdot0$, and for the summer $+15\cdot16$.

everything springs into summer: the trees of one accord put on their mantle of green; the wagtail, swallow, cuckoo, and corncrake come in rapid succession; and by the **middle** of the month the weather begins to be very hot. Last year (1862), for instance, at Christiania we could sledge on the fjord till the end of April, and by the middle of May the trees were covered with their summer foliage!

A curious climatic phenomenon may be noticed towards the latter part of August. **For three or four** consecutive nights, called "iron nights," sharp frosts occur, which frequently do considerable damage to the unripe corn; but after this, warm weather again ensues, and lasts till the end of September, or even till the beginning of October.

This sudden transition from winter to summer, and the absence of the cold blighting winds so prevalent in England during the months of March and April, **has** a great and beneficial effect on the vegetation, and **it is** seldom that the currants and gooseberries get **cut** off by early frosts. When **once**, however, vegetable growth commences it **is** carried **on** with amazing rapidity. My observations have led me **to** conclude **that vegetation in the** neighbourhood of Christiania, lat. 57° 54' 43", at midsummer, is about a fortnight behind that in the midland parts of England.

As just **mentioned,** the corn often suffers great

damage from the frosty nights in the latter part of August; but the position of the locality exercises great influence, for it often happens that the corn is ripe for the sickle on the side of the fjeld facing the south, while that on the opposite side is still green. In Jemteland, in Sweden, the peasants heap up large masses of brushwood on the north side of their small patches of corn to protect them against the north-westerly winds which prevail usually during the night-time.*

As may be anticipated from the configuration of the country, the quantity of rain that falls in different localities varies exceedingly. Thus, while but little rain falls in the eastern districts, an immense quantity falls on the western coasts. At Bergen,† for instance, it may be estimated at 85 inches, while at Christiania, taking the average of twenty years, it is 20·7 inches. In 1859 it was at this latter place 21 inches, while in the disastrous year of 1860 it amounted to 30·5.

It is no exaggeration to say that Norway enjoys

---

* During the summer, when it is fine weather, a wind called the "Sol-gang" is prevalent; that is, the wind follows the sun, blowing in the morning from the east, and during the evening and night from the west.

† The rain at Bergen is quite proverbial. A native of that city informed me that he should say they did not have fifty fine days in the whole year. And though the skipper's logical (?) inference, that because it rained when he sailed out of the port, and rained when he returned, that it therefore always rained there, is no more to be relied on than that Calais is a very windy town, because the hat of the author of "A Sentimental Journey" was blown off as he turned the corner of a street; yet from the immense quantity of rain that falls there it will be evident that the wet days must far outnumber the fine ones.

a milder climate than any other country in the world lying between the same degrees of latitude; and though proximity to the sea does undoubtedly prevent extremes of heat and cold, yet the comparative mildness of the climate is due to another cause, which shall now be alluded to.

The Gulf Stream impinges on the western coast somewhere about lat. 62°. From this point of impact it takes a northerly direction, and follows the coast line to the Russian frontiers on the Arctic Ocean. In consequence of this the sea never freezes along the whole extent of the northern and western coasts;* and, further, it is owing to this that the mean temperature at the North Cape, and at Christiania, during the winter months, though these places are separated from each other by 12° of latitude, is the same.

Arriving at the Russian frontier, the Gulf Stream flows into the White Sea, and, afterwards, taking a bend towards Nova Zembla, touches the Spitzbergen coast under lat. 80°, about.

From observations made by Magister Torell in his expedition to Spitzbergen in 1861, it was proved beyond a doubt that this branch is a continuation of the one which impinges on Norway, for they discovered quanti-

* Even within 100 miles of the North Cape no ice is to be seen, so that the navigation along the whole coast of Norway is open the whole year round. In fact, the chief fishery, which affords employment to between 20,000 and 30,000 men, takes place during the severest portion of the winter, and between lat. 65° and lat. 70°.

ties of glass bottles drifting off the coast, which only the inhabitants of the Lofoden Isles, and of Finmarken use in their cod fisheries as floats for the nets.

Thus the northern parts of Norway are not only habitable, but are considered by many as agreeable places of residence.

But there is another cause, which, in connection with the above, exercises a great influence on the vegetation of the whole country—the more appreciable the higher the latitude,—and that is the long days, or, in other words, the continued light. Under lat. 70° the sun never sinks below the horizon from May 24th till July 19th. At Throndhjem, lat. 63° 25′ 45″, it rises at 1·50 A.M. on June 1st, and sets at 10·13 P.M.; and at Christiania, lat. 59° 54′ 43″, it rises on this date at 2·40 A.M., and sets at 9·23 P.M. Consequently, during this period, the earth does not become so cooled during the short nights as in more southern latitudes, and therefore vegetation continues without interruption. Thus, in Norway, a continuous degree of warmth produces the same effect that a higher temperature during the day, and colder nights do in countries further to the south.

It might not unnaturally be supposed that, owing to the greater distance from the equator, a longer time would be required for the development of a plant the further it is found to the north. Such, however, is not the case. Corn and other plants will ripen under a much lower temperature, and in a much shorter time,* in Norway than in any of the more southern countries; and even in the same country there is a marked difference in **this respect** between the southern and northern districts. Corn or other seeds brought from a southern to a northern climate require at first a **longer** time to ripen in than the same species which have been cultivated there for some time; and conversely, seeds brought from a higher **to a much lower latitude** will **in** the first and second years ripen earlier than those of the same species which **belong to that** lower latitude.

Again, **it may** be remarked that so long as a plant is not cultivated further north than is compatible with its attaining its full development, the seed increases both in size **and** weight for the first three years; but **it** diminishes in like manner if cultivated several degrees furthe rsouth. The greater the difference in the latitude the more marked is the disparity.

Again, the flowers of plants assume an intenser colour, and the foliage **of trees a** brighter green, the further they are found **to the north.**

Those plants **whose roots**, leaves, flowers, &c.,

---

* To give only one instance: six-rowed barley takes ninety days to ripen in from the date of sowing on the banks of the Nile. From an experiment made by Dr. Schübeler, with seed of the same variety obtained from Alten, only fifty-five days elapsed between the date of sowing and of ripening.

possess aromatic properties, develop this peculiarity to a surprising degree the further north they are found. Even an interval of 3° of latitude produces a marked difference in this respect. Thus, the bird cherry, lily of the valley, &c., &c., have a much stronger scent in the neighbourhood of Throndhjem than near Christiania.

Another curious fact may, moreover, be noticed, that in the case of fruits their sweetness diminishes in proportion as their aroma is more fully developed.

In average summers different varieties of plums will ripen as far north as lat. 64°, and wall grapes at a little over lat. 61°, though it must be allowed that they are deficient in point of sweetness. But this deficiency is more than counterbalanced by the delightful flavour which their increased aromatic properties impart.

The phenomena above mentioned can only be accounted for by the great influence the long days exert upon the vegetation in the far north, and by which oats will ripen under lat. 69°, rye under $69\frac{1}{2}$°, and barley under 70°; where also Scotch fir and birch may be found with stems three feet and one foot in diameter respectively.

The rapidity with which vegetable growth goes on is almost incredible. From observations made at Alten, lat. 64° 57′ 30″, it has been ascertained that barley will grow two and a half inches, and peas three inches in the twenty-four hours for several consecutive days; and this is the more remarkable when it is borne in mind that in Norway agriculture can be carried on successfully under the same parallel of latitude as that under which the ice-bound and desolate regions of Victoria-land, Disco Island, and Boothia Felix are situated.

Enough has been said to show that, to the botanist, Norway presents charms and attractions which are not to be met with in any other country; and affords an additional proof, if one were wanting, of that beautiful compensating principle which, to a greater or less degree, is observable in all the works of the Almighty Creator.

Before dismissing the climatic peculiarities of the Scandinavian Peninsula, the opinion (which very generally obtains in Norway) that the climate gradually assumes a severer character shall be briefly touched on. In support of this opinion different facts have been observed, which at first sight appear to have some weight. Thus, it is asserted that the glaciers gradually descend into the valleys; and legends are not wanting which speak of large extents of tillable land being completely buried beneath the ice. It is, moreover, well known that above the existing limit numerous remains of extinct trees have been found, which are said to have been unable to endure the gradually increasing severity of the climate. But the above theory will scarcely sustain a critical examination.

That the glaciers should have this constant descending tendency is a phenomenon which scientific observations do not justify. That they do have a periodic ascending and descending tendency has, however, been **frequently noticed** in the Alps of Switzerland, and has been shown **to depend on** the comparative warmth or cold **of the summers.** Neither does the discovery of the **remains of trees above** the now existing tree limit support the theory, **but is rather a** speaking testimony to the more or less sudden **upheaval of** the land in prehistoric times.

After the foregoing cursory description of **the** physical geography of Norway, a few lines must be devoted **to its inhabitants.**

From time immemorial two races essentially different in origin, civilization, and language have peopled the Scandinavian peninsula. In its northern parts we meet with the Lapp, whose short stunted statures, yellow complexion, flat faces, and squinting eyes, smooth and dark hair, betray unmistakeable signs of their Asiatic origin, an inference fully **borne out by** their wandering, **nomadic life. Protected against** the severity of the winter by their warm **reindeer skin** clothing, they pitch their tents in those places which afford the most nutriment for their large flocks of tame deer, in which, indeed, their sole property and wealth consists. During **the summer** and autumn they devote a good deal of time to the chase. It may be added that the tobacco pipe and the "brænde-viin" bottle are their inseparable concomitants. But in the southern parts of the country we meet with a totally different race of people, viz., the Gothic-Germanic. Their tall figures and fair features at once proclaim their Caucasian extraction; and wherever nature has not been on too imposing a scale, nor has isolated them from contact with their fellow-beings, they have to a greater or less degree kept pace with the general development peculiar to European civilizations.

In their warm, moss-covered log-houses the Norwegian peasants can defy the rudeness of the climate; and as they live frequently at long distances from towns or villages they are very much thrown upon their own resources to procure the necessaries of life. It is a rarity not to find the spinning-wheel busily humming during the long winter evenings, and to see the men carving useful or ornamental articles out of wood.

As has been stated above, but a small proportion of the country is adapted for agricultural purposes; and though the rich mountain pastures are well suited for the maintenance of sheep and cattle during the brief summer months; and though the silver, iron, and copper mines give employment to a fair number of hands in those parts in which they are found; and timber felling, and the care of the forest trees is, especially in the eastern parts of the country, the principal staple of wealth—yet all these, when compared to the employment the sea affords to their industry, occupy but a subordinate position in their national activities.

In olden times, when peaceful avocations were held in disdain, a sea-roving life, for which the peculiar formation of the western coast was extremely well adapted, was in high esteem; and there were few of the maritime countries of Europe but which suffered severely at the hands of the piratical Vikings.

During the dark and gloomy winters the heroes used to assemble in the banqueting-hall, while the "skjald," or bard, struck the lyre and sang of the glorious deeds of their forefathers. But as soon as summer returned they started off again anew, spreading terror and alarm through our own country, the Netherlands, France, and Spain, and indeed wherever anything was to be had. And even when laid to his last long sleep, provided that he died at home, the Viking was scarcely disunited from his favourite element, on which by far the greater portion of his life had been passed; for his men would bury him close to the sea-shore, together with his vessel, beneath a lofty *tumulus*.

Still, commerce was not entirely repudiated, for many old Arabic coins bear testimony to the commercial relations that existed between Scandinavia and eastern countries.

At a later period, when the spirit of the age became changed, the former manner of living altered too; but not even then did the sea become a less important means of national prosperity than before. On the contrary, its extensive fisheries along the western coast, added to the increasing commerce which year by year augmented, and is augmenting still, have proved to the country an inexhaustible mine of comparative wealth.*

The Norwegian has an innate love for commerce; while a hardier, more daring sailor than the Norwegian fisherman cannot possibly be found.

The Scandinavian now-a-days, as before, often wanders far away from his native land; but that love for the home of his birth, which is so exquisitely expressed in the words of King Harald:—" Jeg spörger de smaa Fugler hver en Morgen, som flyve did—vil I vel hilse Dovre fra Harald Harderaade,"† has by no means died out, and the recollection of the noble hills and grand valleys of "gamle Norge" never fails to touch a chord in his heart, so as often to excite the astonishment of the foreigner.‡

* Next to England and France, the mercantile navy of Norway is greater than that of any other European country.
† " I ask the small birds every morning as they fly thither—Will ye salute Dovre from Harald Harderaade?"
‡ A portion of the above remarks has been collated from a work by Dr. Schübeler, Conservator of the Botanical Gardens at Christiania, entitled 'Die Cultur pflanzen Norwegens.' For a further account of this work the reader is referred to a review which I wrote for the April number of 'The Journal of Botany, British and

The following description of the distribution of the vegetable products of Norway, will, I think, be found interesting. I cannot, therefore, do better than follow the same plan adopted by Dr. Schübeler in his synopsis of the 'Vegetable Products of Norway,' which I translated for him from the original MSS., at request, and which was solely intended for distribution at the late International Exhibition.*

The Norwegian name of each plant will be found appended, for the especial benefit of those who have some slight acquaintance with the Norsk language.

I.—FRUIT TREES AND SHRUBS.

ALMOND (*Amygdalus communis*, L. "Mandel").—Ripen as standards in warm summers between lat. 58° and lat 59¾° in the south.

APPLE (*Pyrus Malus*, L. "Æble").—Grow wild in lowlands up to Throndhjem, lat. 63° 25', in a cultivated state up to lat. 65°. Probably no apple-trees are found higher than this at any other place in the world. There are 346 known varieties in Norway. Apples weighing as much as 25¼ ounces have been known; and an apple-tree in Hardanger has been known to yield 38 to 39 bushels. The following remark taken from the 'Belgique Horticole' (1859, Février, pp. 153, 154, and Juillet 1860, pp. 317–319), "Notre pomologie nationale ne peut donc que gagner en recrutant les meilleures variétés issues du rude climat de la Norvége," is well worthy of notice.

Foreign,' 1863, by Dr. B. Seemann. I am also indebted to a little pamphlet, 'Den Skandinaviske Halvö,' by E. Löffler, of Copenhagen, for much valuable information.

* I have in the following made several additions from his larger work, 'Die Culturpflanzen Norwegens.'

There is what the French call a peculiar *précocité* in the vegetation of the north to ripen; and it requires some little time before this peculiarity is lost by transplanting into a more southern climate. The same writer remarks that from experiments made with apples from the north of Europe, "qu'elles se montrent plus précoces que les mêmes plantes, qui sont restées dans leur situation première, bien qu'elles soient cultivées l'une à côté de l'autre." And he therefore adds that it will be wise to look to the north for some of its vegetable treasures. There can be little doubt, I think, that our pomology would be considerably improved by introducing some of the best Norwegian kinds into our gardens and orchards. There are, I believe, about 18 varieties peculiar to Norway.

APRICOT (*Armeniaca vulgaris*, L. "Apricos").—Will ripen in average summers as far north as lat. 61°. Usually grown against walls.

BRAMBLE (*Rubus fruticosus*, L. "Björnebær")—With other species grow as far north as lat. 66°. "The Arctic bramble" (*Rubus Arcticus*, "Aakerbær") grows in great quantities on the banks of Tysfjord, lat. 68°, and is found as far north as lat. 70°, where in warm summers it will ripen. The delicate aromatic flavour of its fruit renders it worthy of cultivation.

CHERRY (*Prunus avium*, L. "Kirsebær").—Doubtful whether found wild in the southern parts of the country. In Urnæs parish, one of the interior arms of the Sogne Fjord, lat. 61°, there is a regular forest of these trees about 2½ miles in length. When cultivated, the cherry will grow as a standard as far north as lat. 66°. There are 22 varieties of cherries under cultivation.

CHESTNUT (*Castanea vesca*, Gürt. "Castanie")—Grows on the south coast up to Christiania, where it ripens in warm summers.

CLOUDBERRY (*Rubus chamæmorus*, L. "Multebær").—Grows everywhere on marshy places. Great quantities come annually from Nordland and Finmark for sale in Christiania. These have a finer aroma than is the case with those growing more to the south. Formerly the Norwegian government used to farm the "multer" marshes in Finmark; and even now they are held in such importance that the Storthing of 1854 made a special enactment concerning them, to the effect "that no one may pluck the berries on the 'multer' lands in Finmark and Nordland, unless to eat on the spot. And that if the owner of the lands refuses to give permission, they may not even be plucked for immediate use, under a penalty of 1 to 20 dollars."

CORNELIAN CHERRY-TREE (*Cornus mascula*, L. "Cornel Kirsebær").—Only cultivated in the neighbourhood of Christiania.

COWBERRY (*V. Vitis Idœa*, L. "Tytebær").

BILBERRY (*V. Myrtillus*, L. "Blaabær").

BOG WHORTLEBERRY (*V. Uliginosum*, L. "Blokkebær").—Grow wild over the whole country. The "Tytebær" figures now rather largely in the exports of Norway, large quantities being annually sent to Germany and England. This and the "Blaabær" are much used in Norwegian households for preserves, &c. A preparation from the latter is often used as a preventive against diarrhœa by the peasants. The "Tranebær" are found ripe in early spring, having remained the winter through beneath the snow. A most refreshing and acid syrup is made from them.

CRANBERRY (*Vaccinium Oxycoccos*, L. "Tranebær").

CURRANT, RED (*Ribes rubrum*, L. "Ribs").—Grows wild as far north as Finmark, and produces shoots 20 inches long under lat. 70°. Red and white varieties are cultivated as far north as Finmark. "Nowhere have I seen finer currants, both as to size and flavour, than near Christiania."

(*Ribes nigrum*, L. "Solbær").—Occasionally to be found growing wild in the south up to lat. 63° about. It is said also to have been found growing wild, and to ripen (?) in Svanevig, East Finmark, close to the Russian frontier. In a cultivated state it will ripen in favourable summers in West Finmark, lat. 68° 49'.

The MOUNTAIN CURRANT (*R. alpinum*, L.).—Grows wild as far north as Finmark.

ELDER (*Sambucus nigra*, L. "Hylletræ").—It is scarcely possible to say whether this tree is indigenous to the country. It is very probable that it was introduced by the monks in the middle ages. It is found, however, both in a wild and cultivated state in several parts along the coast up to lat. 64°, nearly. The fruit will not ripen further north than Throndhjem. On Hovedö, in the Christiania Fjord, close to the town, it is found in plenty. On this island may be seen the ruins of an old Cistercian cloister, which was destroyed by fire in 1532.

VEGETABLE PRODUCTIONS OF NORWAY. 261

GOOSEBERRY (*Ribes Grossularia*, L. "Stikkelebær").—Is found wild here and there in lowlands up to lat. 63°. In a cultivated state it will ripen up to lat. 66¼°.

GRAPE (*Vitis vinifera*, L. "Viinranke").—Many varieties are grown against walls in the south of Norway. In average summer's grapes will ripen as far north as lat. 61°. Bunches weighing one pound have been known near Christiania. The flavour is rather inferior. The most favourite varieties are the Isabella and Catawba.

(*Vitis Labrusca*, L.).—In some old Norwegian documents relating to events that took place in the year 1000, mention of American grapes is made. It appears that some of the Norwegians had discovered that continent; and penetrating as far as Massachusetts, found vines growing there. They called the country "Viinland."

HAZEL NUT (*Corylus Avellanea*, L. "Hassel").—Grows wild, and is found ripe as far north as lat. 66°; under lat. 63° it attains an altitude of 1,000 feet above the sea.

The cob-nut and red and white filbert are only to be found in the south.

MEDLAR (*Mespilus germanica*, L. "Mispel").—In places near Frederickshald and Christiania. The fruit ripens in average summers.

MULBERRY (*Morus alba and nigra*, L. "Morbærtræ").—Both thrive near Christiania, but the latter only yields ripe fruit.

PEACH (*Persica vulgaris*, D.C. "Fersken").—Will ripen against walls up to lat. 61°.

PEAR (*Pyrus communis*, L. "Pære").—Does not grow in a wild state. About 66 different varieties of the finer sorts are cultivated in the country. Near Sörfjord, in Hardanger, there is a "Bergamotte rouge" 48 feet high, and measuring in circumference (3 feet above the ground) 4 feet 2 inches. It has been known to yield 11 to 12 bushels.

PLUM (*Prunus domestica*, L. "Blomme").—Does not grow wild. About 22 varieties, probably more, are cultivated, some of which will ripen (*e.g.*, the greengage) as standards, and against walls as far north as lat. 64°. It should be borne in mind that the word "ripen" is used in a botanical sense, viz., that the fruit is perfectly developed. In the usually accepted sense, a ripe plum at this latitude would not perhaps be all that could be desired!

Perhaps no other fruit varies so much in taste, according to latitude, as does the plum. Thus, there is a striking difference between a ripe plum at Christiania and at Throndhjem.

QUINCE (*Cydonia vulgaris*, Pers. "Kvæde").—Is cultivated at a few places on the south-eastern coast between lat. 58° and lat. 60°. The fruit ripens in hot summers.

RASPBERRY (*Rubus Idæus*, L. "Bringebær").—Grows wild everywhere up to lat. 70°, where the red variety will ripen. The yellow raspberry is not found above lat. 67°. On the fjelds it attains rather a higher altitude than the fir.

STRAWBERRY (*Fragaria vesca*, L. "Jordbær").—Is found wild up to lat. 70°. Many of the finer varieties are cultivated in gardens, and will even ripen, I believe, at Alten.

WALNUT (*Juglans regia*, L. "Valnod").—Is not uncommon along the coast from Christiania to Throndhjem. It will ripen in average summers as far north as lat. 61°. The most northerly walnut-tree in Norway (probably in the world) stands in the parsonage garden at Frosten, lat. 63° 35′, some miles north of Throndhjem. In very warm summers the fruit will ripen. A few miles south of Bergen there is a walnut-tree 58 feet high, measuring in girth $6\frac{1}{2}$ feet, at a distance of 4 feet from the ground.

II.—FOREST AND ORNAMENTAL TREES AND SHRUBS.

AILANTHO (*Ailanthus glandulosa*, Desf.).—Some specimens, raised from seed, may be seen in the Botanical Gardens, Christiania.

ALDER (*Alnus glutinosa* Willd. "Or," "Older," "Svartor," &c.).—Is common on the banks of rivers, &c., in the south. It does not attain a higher altitude than 800 to 1,000 feet above the sea; nor does it extend further north than lat. 63°. In the parish of Indvigen, in "Nordre Bergenhuus," lat. 61° 47′, there is a very fine specimen of this tree. It is 40 feet in height, and is divided into three main branches, each about 18 feet in circumference; between the ground and the fork the trunk measures 40 feet in girth. It is popularly believed that it is very lucky to have one of these trees growing on one's property.

The WHITE ALDER (*A. incana*, Willd. "Or," "Older," "Hvidor," &c.).—Grows as far north as Finmark. Its limit on the mountains is intermediate to that of birch and fir. In Finmark its altitude is about 1,200 feet above the sea. There are about six known varieties.

Amelanchior ovalis, D.C.; *A. sanguinea*, D.C.; *A. vulgaris*, Mönch, are only found in gardens near Christiania.

AMERICAN ARBOR VITÆ (*Thuja occidentalis*, L.).—Is found in gardens as far north as Throndhjem, where it stands the winter very well. Near Christiania there are trees 24 to 25 feet high.

Anpelopsis hederacea, Mchx, or FIVE-LEAVED IVY, "Vild Viin."—Is common as an ornamental plant in the south of Norway, and grows as far north as Throndhjem. It stands the winter without protection.

ASH (*Fraxinus excelsior*, L. "Ask")—Is common in lowlands as far north as lat. 62½°. It does not attain a higher altitude than 1,500 feet in the south, nor more than 100 to 200 feet under lat. 62°, where also it will attain a growth of 80 feet in height.

ASH-BERBERY (*Mahonia Aquifolium*, Nutt).—Found in gardens in the south up to Christiania. It is not covered up during the winter.

ASPEN (*Populus tremula*, L. "Asp" or "Osp").—Is very common up to lat. 70°. At Aarnæs, in Romsdal, lat. 63°, there is a tree 60 feet high. Its limit on the mountains is about the same as that of the Scotch fir. The Norwegian peasant adopts a very practical way of getting rid of the troublesome shoots, which spring up even at long distances from the tree, and which are very difficult to eradicate from the soil. After the tree has been felled or sawn asunder, at about 4 to 5 feet above the ground, he strips all the bark off the stump. In about two years' time the root loses all power of throwing out suckers.

BASTARD INDIGO (*Amorpha fruticosa*, L.).—Is cultivated near Christiania. The tops are generally frozen off in the winter.

BASTARD MOUNTAIN ASH (*Sorbus hybrida*, L. "Rognasal").— Is very common in lowlands in the south, and grows up to Throndhjem. On the eastern frontier it is not found higher than lat. 60°. In Hardanger it is very common to use stocks of this tree for grafting pears on. The fruit thus obtained is said to be better than by using common pear stocks.

BEAM-TREE (*Sorbus Aria*, Crtz. "**Asal**," or "Hasal").—Is found here and there in valleys up to lat. 63½°, and probably grows further north.

BEECH (*Fagus sylvatica*, L. "Bög").—Only to be found wild in the south of Norway, where woods of this tree may be found. It scarcely attains a higher altitude than 800 feet above the sea. The northern limit for the wild beech is a few miles above Bergen, where there is a small wood of it. Cultivated, it will thrive as far north as Throndhjem.

Near the town of Laurvig there is a beech-tree 80 feet high; the trunk measures 8 feet 4 inches in diameter. It is about 154 years old. As an instance of the quick growth of the beech, there is a tree near Frederickshald which was planted as a young sapling in 1829. In 1861 it had attained a height of 54 feet.

The PURPLE BEECH (*F. sylvatica purpurea*, Ait).—Is not uncommon in gardens.

BERBERRY (*Berberis vulgaris*, L. "Berberis").—Whether it is indigenous or not is rather doubtful. It was, not improbably, introduced by the monks in the middle ages. It is found in a wild state in several places in the south, usually in the neighbourhood of towns. Grows in abundance near Christiania. The fruit will ripen as far north as Throndhjem. There are about 14 varieties cultivated.

BIRCH (*Betula*, "Birk").—Of those species which form large woods, it is probably *B. verrucosa*, Ehrh, which is most common in lowlands. *B. glutinosa* is found furthest north. The birch limit is reckoned by this species.

			Feet above the Sea.
At Jerkin . . lat. 62°,	the limit of birch	is about	3,700
„ Alten . . „ 70°	„	„	1,657
„ Hammerfest . „ 70° 40'	„	„	828

The altitude, however, differs much from local causes. Thus, on the eastern side of the Folge Fond, lat. 60°, it is 2,100 feet, while it is 1,900 feet on the western side. In lat. 70° trees of 20 to 30 feet high may be found. Birch-trees 70 to 80 feet high, with stems 9 to 18 feet in girth, are found in several places in Norway. These generally belong to that variety called the weeping birch, whose delicate hanging branches will attain a length of 12 to 16 feet, and even more. They are peculiarly beautiful, and surpass in point of size and picturesque effect those found in more southern climes.

Ancient trees, especially birches, are regarded with great reverence and superstition in many parts of the country. It is often believed, for instance, that a treasure lies concealed beneath the roots of such a tree, under the protection of a dragon or monster. No man carves his name on its trunk, as would be the case in our country, nor is even a twig broken off, for fear that some misfortune should happen to his cattle or his house. Indeed, on Christmas Eve, in some parts of the country, the peasants offer a libation of beer or mead on its roots.* Dr. Schübeler relates that he has been himself informed by peasants who have such a tree on their property, that they yearly place round the trunk loads of manure at a distance of several yards from it, as an offering. This is probably the remains of Druidical superstition; and is the more probable when it is mentioned that even within the memory of some now living, a man, who resided in a lonely district, had a stone image in his possession (Thors?) to which in secret he used to pay devotion. It had been preserved in his family as a precious relic of bygone days. For even till long after the introduction of Christianity into the country, heathenish customs were retained.

A magnificent specimen of the weeping birch is to be seen at Slinde, on the north shore of the Sogne Fjord, lat. 61°; it is about 60 feet high. It is regarded with great reverence and superstition. A few miles south of Throndhjem, in lat. 63°, there is a still finer specimen; it is 80 feet high, and the trunk is 16 feet in girth.

The uses to which the birch-tree is put are numerous. Not only is it most valued as fuel, but it is used largely for articles of household furniture. The twigs are carefully collected as fodder for the cattle during winter, and the bark (Norsk "Næver") is used for making baskets, &c., and roofing houses. The method of employing it for this latter purpose is as follows:—Pieces 1—1½ foot square are placed on the framework of the roof in layers, as is the case with tiles or slates. A thin coating of earth is then spread over it, over which again turf is laid, so that the whole roof is about 1 foot in thickness.

* Miss Martineau, in 'Feats on the Fjord,' alludes to this custom.

It is not unusual to see goats feeding on the roofs of houses, where the grass grows luxuriantly. A well-made roof will, with occasional repairs, last 50 or 60 years. There are many other uses to which the "Næver" is adapted. Thus, near Kongsvinger, shoes of birch bark are frequently worn. In Gudbrandsdal, layers of thin bark are pressed together so as to form a compact mass, and are then made into handles for knives. Many years ago, also, it was used as papyrus for writing purposes. In 1819, one Claus Frimann, a poet, published the life of a noted peasant, Sivert Aarflot, from which it appears that the subject of the memoir had learned to write on thin sheets of this bark which he had prepared.

DWARF BIRCH (*Betula nana*, L.).—Grows everywhere in the alpine regions, and attains a much higher altitude than any other of the species. In the south it descends to about 600 feet above the sea.

BIRD CHERRY (*Prunus Padus*, L. "Hæg").—Grows wild over the whole country as far north as the river Tand. At Alten, lat. 70°, the fruit ripens. Its limit on the mountains is nearly the same as that of the birch. Near Laurdal Church, in Thelemarken, I have seen a tree measuring, according to Dr. Schübeler, 36 feet in height, and the trunk 5½ feet in circumference.

BIRTHWORT, TUBE FLOWERED (*Aristolochia Sipho*, L'Herit).—Is cultivated as an ornamental plant as far north as Throndhjem: it is not protected during the winter.

BLACK THORN SLOE (*Prunus opinosa*, L. "Slaape").—Grows wild on the south coast up to lat. 60°.

BUCKTHORN (*Rhamnus cathartica*, L. "Troldbær").—Grows wild in the south-eastern valleys up to lat. 60°. The ALDER BUCKTHORN (*R. Frangula*, L. "Brakal" or "Troldhæg") extends up to the polar circle.

DOGWOOD (*Cornus sanguinea*, L. "Cornel-Kirsebær").—Grows wild as far north as lat 60°.

ELM (*Ulmus campæstris*, L. "Alm").—Is common up to lat. 66°. No woods of elm, however, are found in Norway. It attains an altitude on the mountains intermediate to that of fir and birch.

GUELDER ROSE (*Viburnum opulus*, L. "Krosved").—Very common: up to lat. 69° has the same altitude as the spruce fir.

HAWTHORN (*Cratægus Oxyacantha*, L. "Hagtorn").—Grows

wild in low lands in the south up to lat. 63° on the western coast. It was formerly much more common, but on account of the excellence of its wood, it has been much sought after.

HOLLY (*Ilex aquifolium*, L. "Benved" or "Christtorn").—Grows wild on the south and western coasts up to lat. 62°. It thrives especially on the numerous islands off the western coast. On Stordö, an island a few miles south of Bergen, there is a tree 47 feet high, the trunk measuring 2 feet 9 inches in diameter.

HONEYSUCKLE (*Lonicera Periclymenum*, L. "Vedvendel").—Grows wild near the coast, up to lat. 62½°.

HORSE CHESTNUT (*Æsculus hippocastanum*, L. "Hestecastanië").—Is very common in avenues and gardens near the coast up to Throndhjem. Trees 60 feet high may be seen in the south of Norway.

IVY (*Hedera helix*, "Bergfletta").—Grows wild near the coast up to lat. 60°. At Mandal, about 20 years ago, two young plants were placed in the ground 4 feet apart under a perpendicular cliff. In 1862, the branches covered an area of 49 feet by 33 feet.

JUNIPER (*Juniperus communis*, L. "Ener").—Grows wild over the whole country up to Finmark; its altitude is the same as that of the birch. It often grows like the cypress, in a pyramidal form. The largest juniper-tree in Norway grows in Haabel parish near Christiania; it is 20 feet high. In many parts of the country a weak decoction of the fresh juniper is used instead of water in brewing beer, on account of the flavour thereby imparted.

LARCH (*Pinus Larix*, L. "Lærketræ").—Does not grow wild, but thrives admirably when planted. An experiment was made near Mandal 20 years ago of planting 5,000 two-years old larches. In 20 years they had attained such a height that a ladder 50 feet long was made from two of them.

LIME (*Tilia Europæa*, L. "Lind").—Grows wild in low lands up to lat. 62°. It seldom attains a respectable size, as the shoots, &c., are much sought after as fodder. In the parish of Gjerrestad there is a very remarkable specimen known by the name of "Melaas Linde." It is about 50 feet high, and stands on the extreme summit of a lofty hill. Its shadow towards sunset extends nearly 5 miles. There are many traditions current with respect to this tree; it is in all probability one of the Druidical trees.

MISSELTOE (*Viscum album*, L. "Mistilteinn").—Only found between lat. 59° 25′ 30″ and lat. 59° 29′ 40″ on the western shore of the Christiania, usually on lime or oak. The misseltoe figures in Norwegian mythology. "Freya had extorted a promise from all the plants on the earth not to injure Baldr. But alas! she had omitted the misseltoe. The crafty Loke found this out, and making an arrow from the wood of the misseltoe, he gave it to blind Höðr, who shot Baldr with it."

MOUNTAIN ASH (*Sorbus Aucuparia*, L. "Rogn").—Grows wild over the whole country up to Finmark; the fruit will ripen under lat. 70°. Its altitude is the same as that of birch.

NORWAY MAPLE (*Acer platanoides*, L. "Hlynr" old Norsk). Grows wild in low lands up to lat. 61½°. Near Laurdal in Thelemarken, there is a tree 62 feet high, the trunk 10 feet in circumference; it is 65 to 70 years old.

NORWAY SPRUCE FIR (*Pinus Abies*, L. "Gran").—This and the Scotch fir constitute the most extensive forests in the southeast of the country. On the western coast it is rare, and from Lindesnæs to lat. 62°, proximity to the sea seems unfavourable to its growth. This is probably owing to the fact that its roots penetrate but to a little depth below the surface, but run in a horizontal direction, and thus it cannot so well endure the stormy winds which sweep over the Atlantic. Forests of this tree appear up to lat. 67°, but never higher. A group of the *Pinus orientalis* is said to have been found in East Finmark near the Russian frontier. Their altitude is, in general, 2,700 to 2,900 feet below the limit of eternal snow.

OAK (*Quercus pedunculata*, Ehrh. "Eeg").—Grows wild in the eastern districts up to lat. 61°, and to lat. 63° on the west coast. Though in comparison with oaks in England the oak-tree in Norway attains a small size, yet occasionally specimens may be found which are remarkable both as regards height and circumference of the trunk. Thus at Valen in Söndhordland, lat. 59° 40′, there is an oak-tree which is 125 feet high, and the circumference of the trunk is about 26 feet, measured at a distance of 3 feet from the ground. A specimen of still larger dimensions had formerly stood on the same property, but was blown down about 70 years ago. It is said that "24 workpeople one day took shelter within its hollow trunk; 22 got inside," says the historian, naïvely, "*the other* 2 *remained outside.*"

Q. sessiflora is only found in one part near Lindesnæs; it reaches a respectable size, but not nearly so large as the common oak.

PRIVET (*Ligustrum vulgare*, L.).—Is only found in a wild state in some of the islands at the mouth of the Christiania Fjord.

ROSE (*Rosa*).—Many species are found growing wild as far north as lat. 66°. In a cultivated state they will thrive in warm summers up to lat. 69°.

SALLOW THORN (*Hippophäe rhamnoides*, L. "Tindved").—Grows wild up to lat. 67°. Near Throndhjem it will attain a height of 14 to 16 feet.

SCOTCH FIR (*Pinus Sylvestris*, L. "Furu").—The largest forests are to be found in the eastern districts. It grows as far north as East Finmark. Its altitude on the mountains is 2,600 to 2,400 feet below the limit of eternal snow. It requires from 200 to 250 years before a tree has attained its full maturity so as to be adapted for masts, &c. In exposed places near the sea, these trees assume a peculiar form, viz., they become flat or compressed on the crown, resembling the cedar.

SPINDLE TREE (*Euœrymus Europœus*, L.)—Has only been found in a wild state at one place in Norway, viz., in Fladdal in Thelemarken.

SPURGE LAUREL (*Daphne Mezereum*, L. "Tyved").—Grows wild in lowlands up to lat. 67°.

WILLOW (*Salix*, L. "Silje" or "Vidje").—About 30 species are found growing wild up to Finmark.

YEW (*Taxus baccata*, L. "Barlind").—Grows wild in places in the south of Norway, but is not found above lat. 61°.

III.—CEREALS.

BARLEY (*Hordeum vulgare*, L. "Byg").—The four-rowed barley is most generally cultivated in Norway. Of all the cereals, it can be grown further north, and at the greatest altitude. Indeed, its limit on the mountains is about the same as that of spruce fir, rather less. According to the last census, barley composed 24·1 per cent. of the whole corn produce of the country. At Alten, lat. 70°, barley has been known to grow

2½ inches for several consecutive days. The corn-limit is measured by this species.

OAT (*Avena sativa*, L. "Havre").—Is the most commonly cultivated. It is not grown quite so far north as barley, neither does it grow at so great an altitude. On an average, it requires about three weeks longer to ripen than barley.

Of all the cereals, oats are the most generally cultivated: according to the last census they composed 55·8 per cent. of the whole corn produce of the country. Comparatively, a very small quantity is used for horses. By far the greatest part is employed for human food; partly, in an unfermented sort of bread called "Flad-bröd," which in shape resembles the "oat-cake" of the north, and partly in porridge. A great quantity of mixed corn is grown, as much as 14 per cent. of the whole produce of the country. It consists of a mixture of oats and barley, and is very generally used for porridge.

In years of scarcity it was formerly not unusual to mix oatmeal with the bark of certain trees to eke out the supply. It may readily be imagined what a deleterious effect such food must have had upon the human frame.

RYE (*Secale cereale*, L. "Rug").—Winter rye is most generally preferred by farmers to summer rye. The former will ripen as far north as lat. 69° 34', the latter as 69° 3'. They will both grow nearly at the same altitude as barley. According to the last census, rye composed 4·7 per cent. of the whole corn produce of the country.

WHEAT (*Triticum vulgare*, L. "Hvede").—Different sorts of summer and winter wheat are cultivated; the latter is, however, most generally used. Hitherto, wheat has not been grown in fields further north than lat. 64° 40'. According to the last census it composed 1·4 per cent. of the whole corn produce of the country. Summer wheat has been known to ripen near Christiania in 75 days. The average time for the interval between sowing and the ripening of the corn for the south of Norway is about 110 to 120 days. Near the little town of Bodö, lat. 67°, there is an agricultural school, probably the most northerly in the world. In 1860 an experiment was made there with summer wheat: it ripened in 120 days from the time of sowing.

IV.—OTHER PLANTS CULTIVATED FOR ECONOMICAL PURPOSES.

ANGELICA (*Archangelica officinalis*, Hoffm. "Kvann") Grows wild over the whole country as far north as Finmark: on the mountains it ascends above the birch-limit. In olden times it used to be extensively cultivated, but now is very rarely so. The peasants collect the roots, and dry them on lines, for medicinal purposes, or to chew instead of tobacco.

ANISE (*Pimpinella Anisum*, L. "Anis").—Is occasionally cultivated in gardens as a curiosity. It was probably introduced by the monks.

ASPARAGUS (*Asparagus officinalis*, L. "Asparges"). Is very common in a cultivated state as far north as Throndhjem, and would probably thrive further north.

BEAN (*Vicia Faba*, L. "Baune").—Is cultivated in several places, but not to the extent it deserves. In average summers the Windsor bean will ripen at Throndhjem.

BORECOLE (*Brassica oleracea acephala*, D. C. "Grönkaal").—Is cultivated over the whole country up to lat. 70°, where it will attain a height of 9 to 10 inches, with a head in proportion, though not planted out, but raised from seed on fields in the open air. The Cow CABBAGE has of late years been much cultivated, and in Bergen Stift has yielded as much as 40 tons per acre.

BRUSSELS SPROUTS, "Rosenkaal."—Is very common; in warm summers it will ripen in lat. 69° 39'.

CARROT (*Daucus Carota*, L. "Gulerod").—Is very generally cultivated over the whole country up to East Finmark. The average crop in the south may be estimated at 10 tons per acre, though double this quantity has been occasionally obtained. Carrots weighing as much as 4½ lbs. have been grown near Christiania.

CAULIFLOWER, "Blomkaal."—Thrives well, and comes to maturity even in lat. 70°.

CELERY, TURNIP-ROOTED (*Apium Graveolens*, L. "Selleri").— Is, with few exceptions, the only sort that is cultivated. It is very common over the whole country, and will in the south attain a weight of 1½ lb. the root.

CHICORY (*Cichorium aristinum*, L. "Cichorie").—Grows wild

in places in the south; it is much used with coffee. More than 300,000 lbs. are annually imported into the country.

CLOVER (*Trifolium pratense*, L. "Rödklöver").— The red, white, and Alsike clover are to be found both in a wild and cultivated state nearly everywhere in the south.

CUCUMBER (*Cucumis sativus*, L. "Agurk").— In average summers, cucumbers can be grown in the open as far north as Throndhjem. They are grown in beds up to lat. 70°.

DRUMHEAD WHITE CABBAGE, "Hovedkaal."—Is the most generally cultivated of all the cabbage tribe. Cabbages weighing 17 lbs. have been grown under lat. 64°. They do not, however, thrive within the polar circle. The largest cabbage that has been grown near Christiania weighed 30 lbs. The average yield is about 40 tons per acre.

FLAX (*Linum usitatissimum*, "Lin.").—The cultivation of flax in Norway is probably as old as the cultivation of corn. It may be met with here and there in a cultivated state up to the polar circle; but it is grown less and less every year. Indeed, none of the plants which are cultivated for their uses in the arts and manufactures occupy an important place in Norwegian agriculture, as they can be obtained much cheaper from abroad; and as long as Norway has to import a considerable quantity of bread corn, it would be improper, as a rule, to grow other plants than those which are absolutely necessary to the sustenance of human life, and at the same time useful in re-invigorating the soil.

GARLIC (*Allium sativum*, L. "Hvidlog").—Is very rarely grown, and is seldom used. The peasants occasionally use it mixed in "Brændeviin" as a remedy in cases of illness.

HEMP (*Cannabis sativa*, L. "Hamp").—Occupies, probably, a smaller space than any plant in Norwegian agriculture, owing to the causes alluded to under the head of flax.

HOP (*Humulus Lupulus*, L. "Humle").—Grows wild in lowlands up to the polar circle. It is not very generally an object of cultivation. More than 300,000 lbs. are annually imported. Beer-drinking in Norway is probably of as old a date as in Germany; and as the importation of hops is never alluded to in any ancient documents, it must either have been cultivated or else the wild hop was used. In all probability, both was the case.

HORSE-RADISH (*Cochlearia Armoracia*, L. "Peberrod").—Is

common in a cultivated state up to the polar circle, and probably further north.

JERUSALEM ARTICHOKE (*Helianthus tuberosus*, L. "Jordæble"). Is cultivated as far north as Throndhjem. Formerly it was much more common, but is now, in a great measure, superseded by the potato. It has, however, of late years been a good deal more attended to in consequence of the potato disease, and is much used for cattle in many parts.

KIDNEY BEAN (*Phaseolus*, L. "Bönne").—Many sorts, chiefly of the dwarf varieties, will ripen in average summers as far north as Throndhjem.

LAVENDER (*Lavandula Spica*, L. "Lavendel").—Is very common in gardens up to Throndhjem. As is the case with all aromatic plants, the perfume of the lavender is more developed the further it grows towards the north.

LEEK (*Allium Porrum*, L. "Purre").—Is very common in gardens. At Christiania it attains the same development as in other countries.

LETTUCE (*Lactuca sativa*, L. "Salat").—Numerous varieties are cultivated. It is grown everywhere where human beings can live.

LUCERNE (*Medicago sativa*, L. "Lusern").—Is cultivated at places in the south. Near Christiania the seed ripens, and the plant will stand the winter, when the ground is covered with snow.

MANGEL WURZEL (*Beta vulgaris rapacea*, Koch).—Has of late years been grown here and there in the south. The largest crop known was $15\frac{1}{2}$ tons, and $7\frac{3}{4}$ tons of leaves to the acre.

MELON (*Cucumis Melo*, L. "Melon").—Is generally grown in hotbeds, and will attain a weight of $16\frac{1}{2}$ lbs. near Christiania, and of 6 to 8 lbs. at Throndhjem. Of late years melons have been grown in the open, like cucumbers, with good results.

ONION (*Allium Cepa*, L. "Rödlög").—Is cultivated over the whole country up to Finmarken. The seed will ripen at Throndhjem. Onions weighing 1 lb. have been grown at Christiania.

PARSLEY (*Petroselinum sativum*, Hoffm. "Persille").—Is very generally cultivated; the seed will ripen at Throndhjem.

PARSNIP (*Pastinaca sativa*, L. "Pastinak").—Is grown everywhere up to Finmark. Roots grown under lat. 68° 49' will weigh

T

as much as 4½ to 5 ounces, and have been known to weigh as much as 2½ lbs. near Christiania. The average crops in the south may be estimated at 9½ tons per acre.

PEA (*Pisum arvense*, " Ert ").—Is the most general field-pea grown in the country. In average summers it will ripen up to lat 64°. Many varieties of garden peas are cultivated.

POTATO (*Solanum tuberosum*, L. " Potet ").—Can be grown further north and at a greater altitude than barley. The potato was imported from England about the middle of the last century, but was not generally cultivated in the south till the beginning of the present century. Strange to say, the potato disease, which has been very prevalent of late years in the southern districts of the country, has never shown itself north of lat. 64°.

RADISH (*Raphanus sativus*, L. " Reddik ").—The common varieties are cultivated everywhere up to the Russian frontiers on the Arctic Ocean. Even on the north shore of Varanger Fjord, East Finmark, they usually attain the size of a common coffee-cup.

RAPE is not cultivated in Norway.

RED CABBAGE, " Rodkaal," is cultivated up to the polar circle.

RHUBARB (*Reum*, " Rhabarber ").—Thrives admirably up to lat. 70°.

RYE GRASS (*Lolium perenne*, L. " Engelsk Raigræs ").—Grows wild, or as a naturalized straggler at places in the south. It thrives under cultivation on the western coast where the winters are not so cold.

SAGE (*Salvia officinalis*, L. " Salvië ").—Is very generally cultivated up to Finmark.

SALSAFIE (*Tragopogon porrifolius*, L. " Havrerod ").—Is cultivated as far north as lat. 70°.

SAVOY, " Savoikaal."—Is cultivated up to lat. 64°, perhaps a little farther north.

SPINACH (*Spinacia oleracea*, L. " Spinat ").—Is cultivated as far north as lat. 70°.

SWEDE TURNIP, " Kaalrabi."—Is one of the most common root-vegetables in Norway. In Finmark, lat. 70°, it grows to a rather less size than a clenched fist. Roots weighing 18 lbs. have been know near Christiania. Though not generally a remunerative crop within the polar circle, in 1860, at Bodö, lat. 67° 17', a crop of 14½ tons to the acre was obtained. And this is about the average crop per acre in the south, exclusive of about 5 **tons** of leaves. Under favourable circumstances, however, this is occasionally doubled.

TARE (*Vicia sativa*, L. "Foderwikke").—Is very generally cultivated up **to the polar circle. Many** varieties are grown. The **seed of** the "**white-seeded tare**" **is much** used in soups, as the flavour is remarkably fine.

TOBACCO (*Nicotiana Tabacum*, L. "Tobak").—At the beginning of **the** present century, during the wars between England and **Denmark**, when the Norwegian coast was closely blockaded by English vessels, and it was next to impossible to import **anything** into the country, the tobacco plant was not **uncommonly** cultivated in the southern districts of the country. It is occasionally grown, but generally **as an** ornamental plant. Tobacco was first introduced into **Norway** about **the year** 1616; but its importation was forbidden **in 1632** by an **order of** Christian IV., who considered its use injurious **to his** subjects!

The consumption of the weed in Norway is rather extensive judging from the following statistics. In 1855 the population amounted **to 1,490,047 souls; and during the** five years that elapsed, **to 1859, the** imports of tobacco amounted to about 3,300,000 lbs. per annum!

TURNIP, "Næpe."—Is undoubtedly the most popular **and the most** generally cultivated of all vegetables in Norway. In fact, there is scarcely an inhabited spot in the country where **turnips** are not grown. It is found up to the Russian frontier. On the Dovre Fjeld, lat. $62\frac{1}{4}°$, at an altitude of 3,000 **feet** above the sea, **this** plant will attain **a size** equal to twice a clenched fist. At Vardöhuus, a little fortress, lat. 70° 22', which lies exposed **to** the fierce storms of the Arctic **Ocean, and to very** severe weather, a crop of $8\frac{1}{2}$ tons to **the acre is raised** one year with another. In the south the average crop **per** acre is estimated at about **$17\frac{1}{2}$** tons, with rather more than 5 tons of leaves per acre. Occasionally, 22 to 25 tons per **acre** may be heard of, and even double **this quantity has** been known. Turnips up to 20 lbs. weight are **tolerably common in** the south, and have **been** heard of **up** to **nearly 30 lbs. in** weight.

CHAPTER VIII.

BOTANICAL RAMBLES ON THE DOVRE FJELD.*

By the permission of the late Professor Blytt, whom I saw a few weeks previous to his death, I am enabled to lay before my readers a detailed list of the Flora of the Dovre Fjeld.

The Alpine plants of the north seem to have concentrated themselves in parts of this mountain range, as will be more expressly alluded to in a few tours which I have appended for the benefit of the collector. A short list of the Ferns of Norway will also be found in their proper place, many of which are very rare, and some quite unknown in our country.

Those stations where good quarters are to be had are printed in italics.

The plates referred to will be found in the 'Flora Danica.'

RANUNCULACEÆ.

THALICTRUM ALPINUM, L.; Fl. D. tab. 11.—Common up to 3,400 feet above the sea; rarely found beyond this.

T. SIMPLEX, L.; Fl. D. tab. 244.—Common on the heights about *Tofte*, by Bergsgaard, Rustgaard, Lie, *Drivstuen*, in Drivdalen; rarely found above the birch-limit.

"Drivdalen," remarks Professor Blytt, late Professor of Botany at the Christiania University, "is one of the richest localities on

---

* The following description of the Flora of the Dovre Fjeld has already appeared in the pages of the 'Field' newspaper.

the whole Fjeld in Alpine Flora; nearly all the Alpine Flora of the north seems to have concentrated itself in this valley." There is good fishing in the Driv. Good quarters.

The "birch-limit," under lat. 61°, is 3,750 feet above the sea; under 62° it is 3,700 feet above the sea. "The dwarf birch (*Betula nana*) grows everywhere in the Alpine regions, and at higher altitudes than any other of the tribe."—Dr Schübeler.

The limit of eternal snow under lat. 62° is about 5,500 feet above the sea. That of the larger willows, *e.g.*, *Salix lanata*, *limosa*, *glauca*, &c., under the same latitude, is about 5,000 feet. Whenever "corn-limit" is used the limit of barley is to be understood.

ANEMONE VERNALIS, L.; Fl. D. tab. 29.—Common over the whole Fjeld. At Storhoë above Tofte, and near Drivstuen, it reaches the limit of eternal snow.

RANUNCULUS REPTANS, L.; Fl. D. tab. 108.—Common up to and a little beyond the birch-limit, by Fogstuen; near *Kongsvold*, it apparently vanishes at the above limit.

Kongsvold is an excellent station for the botanist—good quarters. The station is over 3,000 feet above the sea. Good shooting and fishing here.

R. PLATANIFOLIUS, Fl. D. tab. 3.—Rather common in Drivdalen. On the heights by Drivstuen it is found up to the birch-limit.

R. GLACIALIS, Fl. D. tab. 19.—Varieties of this plant, with snow-white, light or dark rose-coloured flowers, are abundant on the edges of melting glaciers. It appears to be the advanced guard of the flower world towards the regions of eternal snow. Reindeer are extremely partial to it. The peasants call it the rein-flower; and wherever the sportsman finds this plant in great quantities untouched, he may feel sure of not finding deer. In places—*e.g.*, near Kongsvold—it is found below the birch-limit.

R. NIVALIS, Fl. D. tab. 1,699.—Is found scattered about near the highest parts of Vaarstien, on ascending the Fjeld from the right. On the road from Vaarstien to Knudshoë, and on this Fjeld, it is general. It is found in large quantities on the heights near to where the snow never melts, usually in company with the *Phippsia algida*, *Saxifraga oppositifolia*, *Draba alpina*, &c., and reaches even higher than *R. glacialis*. Its flowers are bright yellow; and, where they are found in large quantities, as above

Drivstuen, impart a yellowish tint to the dark boggy earth on which it grows.

R. PYGMÆUS, Fl. D. tab. 144.—General up to the birch-limit, and is found even up to the snow-patches, but not so high up as the last. It is a very diminutive plant.

R. HYPERBOREUS, Fl. D. tab. 331.—Found on marshy, boggy places; plentiful on the road over Harbakken; near Fogstuen and Kongsvold, west of the bridge over the Driv; and by the road between *Jerkin* and Jerkin sæter, in Hviddal. Its limit appears to be about 200 feet above that of the birch.

Jerkin is an excellent station for the botanist, and will at the same time afford ample employment for trout-rod and gun. First-rate accommodation.

R. AURICOMUS.—Common in meadows near Fogstuen and Kongsvold.

R. POLYANTHEMOS, Fl. D. tab. 1,700.—Here and there in Drivdalen, and on the Fjeld sides by Drivstuen up to the fir-limit.

The fir (*Pinus sylvestris*) limit has been placed at 2,950 feet under lat. 62°, at 1,800 feet under lat. 64°. The limit of *Pinus abies* is 2,600 feet to 2,800 feet under lat. 62°, 1,600 feet to 1,800 feet under lat. 64°.

R. ACRIS (common).—A variety, R. PUMILUS, found chiefly on high ground up to the snow patches.

R. REPENS.—At Jerkin it vanishes a little below the birch-limit.

R. AQUATILIS.—In the largest lake in Hviddal.

CALTHA PALUSTRIS, L.; Fl. D. tab. 668.—Is found in places above the birch-limit. At Harbakken it grows at a height of 4,297 Rh. F. A variety (β RADICANS) found occasionally in streams flowing from the glaciers on Knudshoë, Blaahoë, Nystuhoë, &c.

BATRACHIUM CONFERVOIDES.—Occasional in marshy places between *Jerkin* and *Fogstuen*.

ACONITUM SEPTENTRIONALE, Fl. D. tab. 123.—Disappears at about the birch-limit; flowers, blue, white, and sometimes yellow.

ACTÆA SPICATA, L.; Fl. D. tab. 498.—Grows between *Kongsvold* and *Drivstuen*, where it vanishes at about 100 to 200 feet above the fir-limit.

PAPAVERACEÆ.

PAPAVER NUDICAULE, L.; Fl. D. tab. 41.—Found in places on the northern parts of the Dovre; rare on Blaahoë; more general on Knudshoë on the descent to Vaarstien; on the banks of the Driv below Vaarstien, and in the small valleys running up from Sundal and Opdal to the Dovre, *e.g.,* as Svisdal, Druedal, Vinsterdal; in Stöldal, near the streams north-west of *Kongsvold*.

FUMARIACEÆ.

FUMARIA OFFICINALIS, L.; Fl. D. tab. 940.—Found up to the limit of corn at *Tofte*, and in Drivdal.

Tofte, or Toftemoen, is an excellent station; it is kept by a descendant of Harold Haarfager (Fair-haired). *Vide* 'Bennett's Handbook,' p. 5. Good quarters for shooting.

CRUCIFERÆ.

BARBAREA VULGARIS, or PARVIFLORA, Fl. D. tab. 904.—Found a little above the fir-limit, near Kongsvold; plentiful near Nystubæk, between *Kongsvold* and *Drivstuen*, on the west bank of the river.

TURRITIS GLABRA, L.; Fl. D. tab. 809.—As the last.

ARABIS ALPINA, L.; Fl. D. tab. 62.—Common over the whole Fjeld; found above the birch-limit.

A. HIRSUTA, Fl. D. tab. 1,040.—Rare; found in Drivdal up to the birch-limit.

A. THALIANA, L.; Fl. D. tab. 1,106.—Found in places between *Kongsvold, Tofte,* and *Drivstuen*.

A. PETRÆA, Fl. D. tab. 1,392.—Rare; found in the small valleys from Dovre to Sundal; flowers white, sometimes violet.

CARDAMINE BELLIDIFOLIA, L.; Fl. D. tab. 20.—Rather common over the whole Fjeld; grows up to the edge of the snow.

C. AMARA, L.; Fl. D. tab. 148.—In places near *Jerkin* and *Kongsvold*, up to and above the birch-limit.

C. PRATENSIS, L.; Fl. D. tab. 1,039.—As last, but not above the birch-limit.

DRABA ALPINA, L.; Fl. D. tab. 56.—Varies greatly in size, according to the altitude at which it is found. Near Fogsaaen, *Kongsvold*, &c., on the low grounds it is found from 4 to 5 inches in height; on the highest parts, as at Blaahoë, Knudshoë, near the lasting snow, from 1 to 1½ inches. Grows in compact masses; flowers, large yellow.

D. MURICELLA.—The rarest of all the tribe on the Dovre; has only been found at two places on Fogstuvola, near the highest part of Harbakken, and on Gederyggen, by Jerkin, in both places in company with *D. lapponica*, on the steepest and most exposed places. On Gederyggen a variety has been found with quite smooth flower-stalks. Flowers, 6 to 7, yellowish white.

D. BRACHYCARPA.—Found on Gederyggen, near Jerkin.

D. HIRTA.—The commonest of all the tribe on the Dovre, and has a great tendency to vary in appearance according to locality. On high and dry places it scarcely attains a height of 2 inches; in shady or grassy places, in birch or osier copses, it is found more than 1 foot high. Found up to the lasting snow.

D. INCANA, Fl. D. tab. 130.—Has a great tendency to vary. Common over the whole Fjeld; does not grow so high up as the last.

D. LAPPONICA, Fl. D. tab. 142.—Common from the low rocks by Kongsvold up to the snow-patches on Nystuhoë. It is one of the earliest flowering of the Draba tribe. At Nystuhoë, Professor Blytt remarks: "It was the last phanerogamous plant I found in company with the stunted mountain form of *Lycopodium Selago*." It is nearly always found in seed; even by the snow-edge it is rare to find a specimen in flower.

THLASPI ARVENSE, L.; Fl. D. tab. 973.—Common up to the birch-limit.

CAPSELLA BURSA PASTORIS.—As the last.

SISYMBRIUM SOPHIA, L.; Fl. D. tab. 528.—By *Tofte, Jerkin, Kongsvold,* and in Drivdalen, especially near inhabited places, and on the roofs of houses. Common.

ERYSIMUM HIERACIFOLIUM, L.; Fl. D. tab. 229.—In places from *Tofte* to *Drivstuen*; grows up to the birch-limit, near Jerkin.

E. CHEIRANTHOIDES, L.; Fl. D. tab. 731.—In fields near *Tofte*. Common.

CAMELINA SATIVA, Fl. D. tab. 1,038.—Rare: in fields by Bergsgaard. Flowers, pale yellow.

BRASSICA CAMPESTRIS, L.; Fl. D. tab. 550.—By *Tofte*, Bergsgaard, Rustgaard, and *Dombaas*. Common.

SINAPIS ARVENSIS.—In fields near *Dombaas*.

SUBULARIA AQUATICA, L.; Fl. D. tab. 35.—On the banks of the Vola lake, between *Fogstuen* and *Jerkin*: **has 7 to** 8 white flowers.

VIOLARIEÆ.

VIOLA PALUSTRIS, L.; Fl. D. tab. 83.—General **over the whole Fjeld, and found even** above the birch-limit.

V. UMBROSA.—Found in places through the whole of Agershuus province, Ringerige, Toten, and Gudbrandsdal. Disappears entirely on Harbakken above *Tofte*, about 200 feet above **the** birch-limit. Flowers 5 to 6, blue, sometimes white.

Ringerige is a district in the province of Buskerud, **north-west** of Christiania. Toten is a district of Christians **Amt (province), on** the western shore of the Mösen lake.

V. HIRTA, L.; Fl. D. **tab. 618.**—**Common** throughout Gudbrandsdal; disappears **on the heights above** *Tofte*.

V. MIRABILIS, L.; **Fl. D. tab. 1,045.**—Found here and there in copses and **in** shady **places on** Harbakken, **above** Rustgaard; in Drivdal **on the** Fjeld **sides** between Vaarstein and Drivstuen above **the fir-limit.** Flowers, bluish-white.

V. **CANINA.**—Rare, just by the birch-limit above *Jerkin*, **towards** Foldal.

V. MONTANA, Fl. D. tab. 1,329.—Common in coppices by *Tofte*, in Drivdalen, and by *Kongsvold*.

V. ARENARIA.—Common up to *Fogstuen*, *Jerkin*, **and** *Kongsvold*. At the **former** place it is found near **the birch-limit, on the** banks of Fogs-aa (brook).

V. BIFLORA, L.; Fl. D. tab. 46.—Very common over **the** whole Fjeld and above the birch-limit. Flowers yellow.

V. TRICOLOR.—A variety with oblong leaves and large flowers is found by *Jerkin* and *Kongsvold*. A variety, with minute odoriferous flowers, is found in the fields near *Tofte*.

DROSERACEÆ.

DROSERA ROTUNDIFOLIA, L.; Fl. D. tab. 1,028.—Grows sparingly near the birch-limit by the roadside over Harbakken.

PARNASSIA PALUSTRIS, **L.;** Fl. D. tab. 584.—Common over **the whole** Fjeld: is found **in a** stunted form above the birch-limit.

POLYGALEÆ.

POLYGALA VULGARIS, L.; Fl. D. tab. 516.—By Bergsgaard and *Tofte*, near the birch-limit; less frequent near *Jerkin*.

P. ULIGINOSA.—More frequent than the last; but rarely found above the birch-limit. Flowers, bluish and white.

CARYOPHYLLEÆ.

SILENE ACAULIS, L.; Fl. D. tab. 21.—Becomes first general about the birch-limit, and mounts up to the edge of eternal snow.

S. INFLATA.—Smith, Fl. Brit. 467; Fl. D. tab. 914.—Common near mountain cabins; but not found above the birch-limit.

S. RUPESTRIS, L.; Fl. D. tab. 4.—Common; and is found also above the birch-limit.

LYCHNIS VISCARIA, L.; Fl. D. tab. 1,032.—Disappears on the hilly meadows near *Tofte* and Rustgaard.

L. SYLVESTRIS.—General on the Fjeld till high over the birch-limit up to the limit of the larger willows.

L. PRATENSIS, Fl. D. tab. 792.—Near *Tofte* and *Kongsvold*. A variety with red flowers is also found near *Tofte*, and here and there in Drivdalen, below *Drivstuen*.

L. ALPINA, L.; Fl. D. tab. 65.—Common over the whole Fjeld. It first appears where *L. viscaria* vanishes, and is found up to the patches of snow. It is sometimes found with white flowers.

VAHLBERGELLA APETALA, Fl. D. tab. 806.—First appears a little below the fir-limit, by the road between *Dombaas* and *Fogstuen*, and is commonly found up to the continual snow. " I have found," says Professor Blytt, " a variety with 3 to 4 flowers, but only one specimen."

SPERGULA ARVENSIS, L.; Fl. D. tab. 1,033.—Near *Tofte*; not found above where corn is grown.

S. SAGINOIDES, L.; Fl. D. tab. 1,577.—Common over the whole Fjeld. On high grounds above the birch-limit it has a very stunted growth, scarcely half an inch high, is darker of colour, and with very short, roundish seed-capsules.

S. NIVALIS.—In places over the whole Fjeld, though not under 4,000 feet; frequent by the old road over Vaarstien, on Knudshoë, Nystuhoë, &c.

SAGINA PROCUMBENS, L.; Fl. D. tab. 2,103.—In places over the whole Fjeld, especially by roads and mountain cabins; it can scarcely be said to grow above the birch-limit, and, like *Sp. saginoides*, has a very stunted growth at high altitudes.

STELLARIA NEMORUM, L.; Fl. D. tab. 271.—In shady places over the whole Fjeld, up to the highest limit of *Salix lanata*, *S. glauca*, and *S. limosa*.

S. MEDIA, Fl. D. tab. 525.—By mountain cabins and sæters over the whole Fjeld. Common.

S. GRAMINEA, L.; Fl. D. tab. 2,116.—Disappears at about the birch-limit. Found sparingly on Jerkinshoë and near *Kongsvold*.

S. LONGIFOLIA.—Near *Kongsvold*, in shady places; apparently it does not extend beyond the birch-limit.

S. ALPESTRIS.—Very common over the whole Fjeld. Extends from the uppermost regions of *Pinus abies* (Norwegian spruce fir) in Gudbrandsdal to the limit of willow on Dovre.

S. CRASSIFOLIA, Fl. D. tab. 2,114.—In marshy places near *Jerkin*, and above Bergsgaard, near *Tofte*. Rare.

S. ULIGINOSA, Smith, Engl. Flora, 2, p. 303.—Has great similarity to the last. Found in low woody places in Drivdalen, near *Tofte* and *Dombaas*.

S. CERASTOIDES, L.; Fl. D. tab. 92.—Very common from the uppermost region of Scotch fir to the lasting snow.

ALSINELLA STRICTA.—First appears a little below the limit of Scotch fir, and is afterwards common over the whole Fjeld, in swampy places, up to the perpetual snow.

A. BIFLORA (STELLARIA BIFLORA of Lin.)—On dry places; with regard to altitude, as the last.

A. RUBELLA, Fl. D. tab. 1,646.—In Drivdalen, from *Kongsvold* to Vaarstien, and on the neighbouring heights; first disappears near the perpetual snow. Not common.

ARENARIA SERPYLLIFOLIA, L.; Fl. D. tab. 977.—On dry hilly ground, near *Tofte*; not found above the limit of corn.

CERASTIUM ALPINUM, L.; Fl. D. tab. 6. β GLABRATUM, L.; Fl. D. tab. 979.—Common over the whole Fjeld; β frequent near *Fogstuen*. Both are found up to perpetual snow. C. ALP. is often met with low down in woody places; the variety is only found on the high Fjeld.

C. VULGATUM, L.; Fl. D. tab. 1,645. Common by roads and mountain huts; rarely found above the birch-limit. A variety, with shorter leaves and petals twice the length of the calyx, is found on the road between *Dombaas* and *Fogstuen*.

C. LATIFOLIUM.—Found on Knudsboë, Blaahoë, Fogstuhoë, Nystuhoë, always above the limit of the larger willows.

GERANIACEÆ.

GERANIUM SYLVATICUM, L.; Fl. D. tab. 124.—Common up to and above the birch-limit; disappears near the edge of the lasting snow-patches. Flowers, light red and white.

G. PRATENSE, L.; Fl. D. tab. 124.—Disappears on the hills near *Tofte*. Not common.

ERODIUM CICUTARIUM, or GERAN. CICUTARIUM, L.; Fl. D. tab. 986.—In Drivdalen, near *Rise*, a little below the limit of Scotch fir. Flowers 4 to 7, red.

Rise is about 8 English miles from Drivstuen. Fair quarters. Good shooting may be had here, and trout-fishing in the rivers Driv and Vinstra.

BALSAMINEÆ.

IMPATIENS NOLI-TANGERE, L.; Fl. D. tab. 582.—In Drivdalen, below *Drivstuen*. Not common.

OXALIDEÆ.

OXALIS ACETOSELLA, L.; Fl. D. tab. 980.—Disappears near the limit of birch, at which altitude it is found in flower in the beginning of August.

LEGUMINOSÆ.

ANTHYLLIS VULNERARIA, L.; Fl. D. tab. 988.—Below Harbakken it disappears a little under the birch-limit. Flowers usually yellow.

TRIFOLIUM MEDIUM, L.; Fl. D. tab. 1,273.—Common up to *Tofte*, where it disappears a little below the birch-limit.

T. PRATENSE, L.; Fl. D. tab. 989.—Common up to *Fogstuen* and *Jerkin*. Vanishes as the last.

T. REPENS, L.; Fl. D. tab. 990.—Common; as the last.

LOTUS CORNICULATUS, L.; Fl. D. tab. 991.—Common up to the birch-limit.

PHACA FRIGIDA, L.; Fl. D. tab. 856.—In places tolerably frequent over the whole Fjeld. First appears a little below the fir-limit, and extends above the birch-limit.

P. OROBOIDES, Fl. D. tab. 1,396.—Plentiful on the hills about *Tofte*, by Bergsgaard, Rustgaard, Harbakken; rarer near *Jerkin*, *Fogstuen*; general in Drivdalen from **Kongsvold** to *Drivstuen*, and on the neighbouring Fjelds. Rarely found **above** the birch-limit.

ASTRAGALUS ALPINUS, L.; Fl. D. **tab.** 51.—Common over the whole **Fjeld.** Often found above the birch-limit.

OXYTROPIS LAPPONICA. Common from *Tofte* to *Drivstuen*; extends beyond the birch-limit to the limit of the larger willows. Flowers usually 7, bluish-red.

VICIA SYLVESTRIS, Fl. D. tab. 277.—Between *Kongsvold* and *Drivstuen*, a little above the fir-limit.

V. CRACCA, L.; Fl. D. tab. 804.— Over the **whole Fjeld up to** the birch-limit.

V. SEPIUM, L. : Fl. D. tab. 699.—Near *Tofte, Jerkin, Kongsvold*, and Drivdalen, up to the birch-limit.

LATHYRUS PRATENSIS, L.; **Fl. D. tab.** 527.—By *Tofte*, Rustgaard, **and** *Drivstuen*, below the birch-limit.

ROSACEÆ.

PRUNUS PADUS, **L.;** Fl. D. tab. 205.—Found in flower near *Drivstuen* towards **the** end of August, near the birch-limit; rarely found higher.

SPIRÆA ULMARIA, L.; Fl. D. tab. 547.—In Drivdalen, **near** to **and** a little above the limit of fir; also near *Tofte* and *Dombaas*. **Common.**

DRYAS OCTOPETALA, L.; Fl. D. **tab. 31.**—Rare on Gederyggen, **near** *Jerkin*; plentiful **in** meadows and on hills near *Kongsvold*. On Gederyggen and Knudshoë it extends above the birch-limit.

GEUM RIVALE, L.; **Fl. D.** tab. 722.—Common up to the limit of the larger willows.

RUBUS IDÆUS, L.; Fl. D. tab. 788.—Common in Drivdalen, below *Kongsvold*; blooms the latter part of August.

RUBUS SAXATILIS, L.; Fl. D. tab. 134.— Common over the whole Fjeld up to the birch-limit, at which altitude the seed does **not** ripen.

R. CHAMÆMORUS, L.; Fl. D. tab. 1.—In morasses over the **whole** Fjeld, near and above the birch-limit, where the fruit does **not ripen.** In Nystudal it has been found ripe.

R. ARCTICUS, L.; Fl. D. tab. 488.—First discovered on the Dovre in 1861, growing in swamps near *Fogstuen*.

FRAGRARIA VESCA, R.—Near *Tofte* and *Kongsvold*; the fruit does not ripen here. Found in Drivdal with ripe and half-ripe fruit in the month of August.

POTENTILLA NIVEA, L.; Fl. D. tab. 1,035.—Found in small quantities on the highest parts of Gederyggen near *Jerkin*. Common near Goutstiaa, *Kongsvold*, on Knudshoë, and through Drivdal in the region of fir between *Drivstuen* and *Rise*. Extends above the birch-limit.

P. NORVEGICA, L.; Fl. D. tab. 171.—Disappears with the cultivation of corn near *Tofte*.

Found on some of the islands in the Fjord near Christiania.

P. TORMENTILLA, Fl. D. tab. 589.—Common over the whole Fjeld; occasionally found above the birch-limit up to that of the larger willows.

P. AUREA, Fl. D. tab. 114.—Common over the whole Fjeld, up to the lasting snow-patches.

P. ARGENTEA, L.; Fl. D. tab. 865.—Near *Tofte*, Rustgaard, and between *Kongsvold* and *Drivstuen*; on all places below the birch-limit, but above that of fir.

P. ANSERINA, L.; Fl. D. tab. 544.—Disappears near *Tofte* and Rustgaard below the limit of birch.

P. COMARUM, or COMARUM PALUSTRE, L.; Fl. D. tab. 636.—Occasional in marshy places; disappears a little below the birch-limit.

SIBBALDIA PROCUMBENS, L.; Fl. D. tab. 32.—Common from about the fir-limit to the permanent snow-patches.

ALCHEMILLA VULGARIS, L.; Fl. D. tab. 693.—Frequently found above the birch-limit: general. A variety β MONTANA is found near *Tofte* and Rustgaard.

A. ALPINA, L.; Fl. D. tab. 49.—Found over the whole Fjeld, but more general on the northern side, up to the permanent snow.

ROSA VILLOSA, L.; Fl. D. tab. 1,458.—In Drivdal below *Rise* in the region of fir. Flowers, 6 to 7, red or white. Not common.

R. CINNAMOMEA, Fl. D. tab. 1,214.—On the south side of Dovre, towards *Dombaas*; on the north side in Drivdal; in both places below the fir-limit. Flowers, 6, red.

COTONEASTER VULGARIS, or MESPILUS COTONEASTER, L.; Fl.

D. tab. 112.—In places near Bergsgaard, *Tofte* on Gederyggen, by *Kongsvold*, and in Drivdal, nearly always up to the birch-limit. Flowers, 6, white or reddish.

SORBUS AUCUPARIA, L.; Fl. D. tab. 1,034.—Disappears between the limits of fir and birch in Drivdal. Flowers in August at its highest altitude; the berries rarely ripen so high up.

ONAGRARIÆ.

EPILOBIUM ANGUSTIFOLIUM, L.; Fl. D. tab. 289.—Common to *Fogstuen*, nearly up to the birch-limit.

E. MONTANUM, L.; Fl. D. tab. 922.—In Drivdal, a little higher than the fir-limit.

E. PALUSTRE, L.; Fl. D. tab. 1,574.—Near *Tofte* and in Drivdal, scarcely above the fir-limit.

E. ALPINUM, L.; Fl. D. tab. 322.—Common from the fir-limit to above the limit of birch.

E. ORIGANIFOLIUM.—Rare about *Fogstuen*; more general in Drivdal by *Drivstuen*. It is found below the fir-limit, and extends beyond the limit of birch, by springs, on banks of streams, &c. It varies greatly in size, and resembles E. MONTANUM so much as to be easily mistaken for it.

E. NUTANS, Fl. D. tab. 1,387.—A little below the fir-limit, on swampy places, between *Dombaas* and *Fogstuen*; also in places over the whole Fjeld, by *Jerkin*, *Kongsvold*, &c. It extends beyond the limit of birch.

CIRCÆA ALPINA, L.; Fl. D. tab. 1,321.—Common to the limit of birch.

HALORAGEÆ.

MYRIOPHYLLUM SPICATUM, L.; Fl. D. tab. 681.—Found in Vola lake. Flowers, 6 to 7, white.

CALLITRICHE VERNA, L.; Fl. D. tab. 129.—Common on low grounds. A variety, β *minima*, found only at higher altitudes.

C. AUTUMNALIS, L.—Found in Vola lake.

HIPPURIS VULGARIS, L.; Fl. D. tab. 87.—Near *Jerkin* in a swamp below the station; between *Kongsvold* and *Drivstuen* in a swamp by the road; in both places above the limit of fir, but a little beneath that of birch.

TAMARISCINEÆ.

Myricaria germanica, Fl. D. tab. 234.—Near *Tofte*, on the banks of the river Laagen, close by the mills, and in Drivdal.

PORTULACEÆ.

Montia fontana, L.; Fl. D. tab. 131.—Common in moist places that are often flooded, up to above the birch-limit; generally in company with Kœnigia islandica.

PARONYCHIEÆ.

Scleranthus perennis, L.; Fl. D. tab. 563.—By the birch-limit above *Tofte*.

S. annuus, L., Fl. D. tab. 504.—Near *Drivstuen*. Flowers, 6 to 7, green.

CRASSULACEÆ.

Rhodiola rosea, L.; Fl. D. tab. 183.—Common over the whole Fjeld; extends above the birch-limit. Flowers, 7 to 8, yellow.

Sedum album, L.; Fl. D. tab. 66.—Disappears near *Tofte*. Flowers, 7 to 8, white.

S. rupestre, L.; Fl. D. tab. 59.—Over the whole Fjeld, but rarely found above the birch-limit.

S. acre, L.; Fl. D. tab. 1,644.—Vanishes near *Tofte*.

GROSSULARIEÆ.

Ribes rubrum, L.; Fl. D. tab. 967.—In Drivdal to *Kongsvold*. Commonly called " Ulvebær," or wolf-berry.

SAXIFRAGACEÆ.

Saxifraga oppositifolia, L.; Fl. D. tab. 34.—Common up to the permanent snow-patches. Found in flower on Knudshoë, in company with Ranunculus nivalis, at the end of August. Flowers blue or purple, occasionally white.

S. cotyledon, L.; Fl. D. tab. 241.—Found in places in Drivdal from Vaarstien to *Drivstuen*; below the last-named place, plentiful. Found also near the largest in Kalvella Aaen.

S. cæspitosa, L.; Fl. D. tab. 71 and 1,388.—In places over the whole Fjeld. First appears at about the limit of fir, and is found up to the continual snow. It has a very decided tendency to vary. A variety with a long stalk and delicate leaves, bearing a great similarity to S. HYPNOIDES, is found growing on loose gravel near Blaahoë and other places. The little stunted form which has been named *S. grœnlandica* is common on dry places at high altitudes.

S. CERNUA, L.; Fl. D. tab. 22 and 399.—From the limit of fir up to the continual snow. It has, like the last, a great tendency to vary; sometimes being found more or less branched, with a single terminal flower, or with more; more or less hairy. Flowers white.

S. RIVULARIS, L.; Fl. D. tab. 11.—On high places on the Fjeld, commonly by snow-water streams, fissures in the rock, &c., up to the permanent snow. Scarcely found as low down as the limit of fir.

S. NIVALIS, L.; Fl. D. tab. 28.—In places over the whole Fjeld, especially by *Kongsvold* and in Drivdal. Flowers, 7 to 8, white or reddish. A variety, β *tenuis*, is found near *Fogstuen*, on Goutstifjeld and Blaahoë.

S. HIERACIFOLIA, Fl. D. tab. 2,301.—Nearly up to the snow-boundary (4,000 to 5,000 feet above the sea), on Storhoë, above *Tofte*, about 7 English miles from Tofte Gaard (house), and by Tveraa, which rises in Storhoë, near the lasting snow. Professor Blyth considered it was undoubtedly allied with *S. pennsylvanica*, L.

S. STELLARIA, L.; Fl. D. tab. 23.—Very common over the whole Fjeld, extending over the birch-limit to the snow-patches. A variety, β *comosa*, Fl. D. tab. 2,354, usually bearing one flower, is more rare. Found by Goutsti-aa, Goutstifjeld, and Volasöfjeld.

S. AIZOIDES, L.; Fl. D. tab. 72.—Common by brooks, roadsides, &c. Found in Gudbrandsdal, down in the region of spruce fir, and extends up to the snow.

CHRYSOSPLENIUM ALTERNIFOLIUM, L.; Fl. D. tab. 366.—Near *Kongsvold*, in damp and shady places. Flowers, 5, yellowish.

UMBELLIFERÆ.

CARUM CARVI, L.; Fl. D. tab. 1,091.—Disappears below the birch-limit by *Jerkin* and *Kongsvold*.

This is one of the most favourite and common plants in the country: it is found as far north as Finmarken. The Norwegians are extremely partial to it, and it enters very largely into their household economy. The rye bread is usually besprinkled with it before baked; and the "Throndhjemske aquavit" (which, by the way, is a remarkably pure and clean-tasting spirit, far better adapted for a dram than cognac or whisky, &c.), is strongly impregnated with it. The green shoots, in early summer, are used in soups, indeed, it is very generally used in Norwegian dishes. Much as habit does, I never could get reconciled to the flavour of caraway in bread, not to mention that the seeds looked so like *fleas* mixed with the dough.

PIMPINELLA SAXIFRAGA, L.; Fl. D. tab. 669.—As the last.

ANGELICA SYLVESTRIS, L.; Fl. D. tab. 1,639.—In Drivdal above the fir-limit.

ARCHANGELICA OFFICINALIS, L.; Fl. D. tab. 206.—Plentiful near *Kongsvold*, and in Drivdal on the Fjelds on either side of the valley. Extends above the birch-limit, and grows as far north as Finmarken.

HERACLEUM SIBIRICUM.—Near *Jerkin*, *Kongsvold*, and in Drivdal, below the birch-limit. Flowers yellowish green. Frequent.

ANTHRISCUS SYLVESTRIS, Fl. D. tab. 2,050.—Up to the birch-limit by *Tofte*, and in places over the whole Fjeld, occasionally above the birch-limit.

CORNEÆ.

CORNUS SUECICA, L.; Fl. D. tab. 5.—In Drivdal, at and below *Drivstuen*; beneath the limit of birch.

CAPRIFOLIACEÆ.

LINNÆA BOREALIS, L.; Fl. D. tab. 3.—Found in places nearly up to the birch-limit.

Linnæus selected this plant as being most appropriate to hand down his name to posterity, on account of its "humble and depressed appearance, and its early flower." "The flower-stalks are erect, and bear each two pendulous, bell-shaped pink flowers," which have a delicate odour of almonds. Common in shady places in fir woods.

RUBIACEÆ.

GALIUM ULIGINOSUM. L. Fl. D. tab. 1,509.—By *Fogstuen* and *Kongsvold*, a little below the birch-limit. Common.

G. VERUM, L.; Fl. D. tab. 1,146.—By *Tofte*, Rustgaard, and *Drivstuen*.

G. BOREALE, L.; Fl. D. tab. 1,024.—Common in meadows near *Jerkin*, *Kongsvold*, and in places over the whole Fjeld below the birch-limit.

G. APARINE, L.; Fl. D. tab. 495.—In fields near *Tofte*.

VALERIANEÆ.

VALERIANA OFFICINALIS, L.; Fl. D. tab. 570.—Near *Tofte*, *Kongsvold*, and in Drivdal, below the birch-limit.

DIPSACEÆ.

SCABIOSA ARVENSIS, L.; Fl. D. tab. 447.—Near *Tofte*, almost by the birch-limit, Rustgaard, *Jerkin*, *Kongsvold*, and in Drivdal.

COMPOSITÆ.

TUSSILAGO FARFARA, L.; Fl. D. tab. 595.—In places over the whole Fjeld; it extends beyond the birch-limit to that of the larger willow tribe near Fogsaaen.

NARDOSMA FRIGIDA, Fl. D. tab. 61.—In places over the whole Fjeld; not unfrequent by *Kongsvold* and the neighbouring heights up to the permanent snow.

ERIGERON ACRIS, L.—In places near *Tofte*, *Jerkin*, *Kongsvold*, and in Drivdal. A variety, β *glabratum*, remarkable for its larger growth, smooth stalks and leaves, and for its darker and somewhat larger flowers, is found at a rather higher altitude. Plentiful near Fogsaaen, above *Fogstuen*, *Kongsvold*, and in places in Drivdal, where it attains a growth of 2 feet in shady places. "This variety," remarks Professor Blytt, "is so striking, that one might almost be tempted to look on it as a separate species, but that forms of it bearing evident signs of transition to *E. acre* are found, *e. g.*, *E. Droebachense*, Fl. D. tab. 874."

E. ALPINUS, L.; Fl. D. tab. 292.—Common over the whole Fjeld, from the hills near *Tofte* to Drivdal, where it descends, perhaps, 200 to 300 feet into the region of fir. It varies greatly both in size, and in being more or less branched. Near *Tofte* it is usually one-flowered, and of diminutive growth, but more vigorous near *Jerkin* and *Kongsvold*, often many-flowered, and with larger and more downy flower-heads.

E. ELONGATUS.—Common in birch copses over the whole Fjeld. Flowers, 7 to 8, red or white.

E. UNIFLORUS, L.; Fl. D. tab. 1,397.—Common at high altitudes on the Fjeld, *e. g.*, Harbakken, *Fogstuen, Kongsvold, Jerkin*. It extends above the birch-limit nearly up to the lasting snow, and is never found in the neighbourhood of or below the limit of fir. Florets, red or white.

SOLIDAGO VIRGAUREA, L.; Fl. D. tab. 663.—Common up to and over the birch-limit. A variety, β *lapponica*, is also common at the same altitude.

ANTENNARIA DIOICA; Fl. D. tab. 1,228.—Common over the whole Fjeld; extends above the birch-limit. Grows in dry, rocky places.

A. ALPINA (Gærtner).—Bears a great similarity to the last. First appears at about 100 to 200 feet below the fir-limit by the roadside between *Dombaas* and *Fogstuen*, after which it is plentiful over the whole Fjeld. Found up to the edge of permanent snow.

GNAPHALIUM SYLVATICUM, L.; Fl. D. tab. 1,229.—In Drivdal below *Drivstuen*. A variety, *G. rectum* (?), is common over the whole Fjeld, and mounts above the birch-limit to that of the larger willows.

G. NORVEGICUM (Chr. Günther); Fl. D. tab. 254.—Common over the whole Fjeld; extends up to and above the limit of the larger willow. From experiments made in the Botanical Gardens at Christiania, Mr. Moe pronounces it to be a distinct species from the last. It has a denser spike and broader leaves.

OMALOTHECA SUPINA (Cassini).—Common in birch copses over the whole Fjeld; mounts up to the limit of the larger willows. Found in Opdal as low down as the limit of corn.

At the village of Opdal the road through Sundalen branches off to the north-west. At a short distance south of this, at the station Aune or Ovne, excellent accommodation may be had, and good opportunities for trout-fishing and shooting.

PTARMICA VULGARIS (De Candolle).—Very rare on Dovre; only noticed at one place about 4 miles north of *Drivstuen*.

CHRYSANTHEMUM LEUCANTHEMUM, L.; Fl. D. tab. 944.—Found by Vaarstien in small quantities below the birch-limit; occasionally in Drivdal below *Drivstuen* and by *Tofte*, in dry places.

MATRICARIA INODORA, L.; Fl. D. tab. 696.—Near *Tofte, Fogstuen, Jerkin, Kongsvold*, &c.; not found above the birch-limit. Grows in waste places.

ACHILLEA MILLEFOLIUM, L.; Fl. D. tab. 737.—Common; in places found above the birch-limit.

ARTEMISIA VULGARIS, L.; Fl. D. tab. 1,176.—By **Tofte**, *Kongsvold*, and in Drivdal; always below the birch-limit.

A. NORVEGICA (Fries), Fl. D. tab. 801.—Plentiful on the fjelds by *Kongsvold*, and in Drivdal, where it mounts from the river banks up to the permanent snow. Flowers, 8, yellow.

TANACETUM VULGARE, L.; Fl. D. tab. 871.—Between *Laurgaard* and *Tofte*, by *Kongsvold*, and at places through Drivdal; above the limit of fir. Found in dry places.

Laurgaard is an excellent station, about 13 English miles south of Tofte. Good accommodation can be had here, and shooting may be got on the neighbouring heights. Reindeer are generally plentiful, and excellent ryper-shooting may be had. Capital trout-fishing in Vaage Vand, a few miles to the west, especially at Lom, where the river Bœvra empties itself into it. Shooting well spoken of.

TANACETUM BOREALE (Fischer).—Probably only a variety of T. VULGARE; found in Drivdal and in Nystudal.

ARCTIUM LAPPA, L.; Fl. D. tab. 612.—In Drivdal.

CARDUUS CRISPUS, L.; Fl. D. tab. 621.—By *Tofte, Kongsvold*, and at places in Drivdal.

CIRSIUM PALUSTRE (Scopoli).—By *Tofte*. Common in damp meadows. Flowers, 7 to 8, violet.

C. HETEROPHYLLUM, L.; Fl. D. tab. 109.—Common in damp meadows nearly up to the birch-limit.

C. ARVENSE (De Candolle), Fl. D. tab. 644.—Near *Tofte*, in waste places. Common.

SAUSSUREA ALPINA (De Candolle), Fl. D. tab. 37.—Common up to about the birch-limit.

CENTAUREA SCABIOSA, L.; Fl. D. tab. 1,231.—By *Tofte*.

SONCHUS ARVENSIS, L.; Fl. D. tab. 606.—By *Tofte*, Rustgaard, and below *Drivstuen*, to the corn-limit. Common on waste places.

S. OLERACEUS, L.; Fl. D. tab. 682.—As the last.

MULGEDIUM ALPINUM (Lessing), Fl. D. tab. 182.—By *Kongsvold*, and at places in Drivdal.

CREPIS TECTORUM, L.; Fl. D. tab. 501.—By *Tofte, Fogstuen, Jerkin, Kongsvold*, and at places in Drivdal. Common on roofs of cottages; sometimes found above the birch-limit. Flowers, 6 to 9, yellow.

LEONTODON **TARAXACUM**, L.; Fl. D. tab. 574.—Common up to and above the **birch-limit**.

L. CORNICULATUM (TARAXACUM LÆVIGATUM of De Candolle).— On hills near *Tofte*, Harbakken, &c.

HIERACIUM PILOSELLA, **L.**; **Fl. D. tab.** 1,110.—In Drivdal below *Drivstuen* in the region of fir.

H. AURICULA, L.; Fl. **D. tab. 1,111.**—In **Drivdal** a little above the fir-limit.

H. COLLINUM (Blytt).—In places on **the** right hand of the **valley of** Drivdal by *Drivstuen*. It varies greatly in size. **The smallest** forms approach nearer to H. AURICULA. The larger **are 1½** feet high, with many flowers in tufts, and approach **very near to**

H. CYMOSUM (Hartman), Fl. D. tab. 810.—Near *Drivstuen*, in scrub on the mountain side, where it attains a height of 2 to 3 feet.

H. AURANTIACUM, L.; **Fl. D.** tab. 1,112.—Occasional in meadows south of *Drivstuen*, in company with *Satyrium nigrum*, L. Rare. Flowers not so deep an orange as those found in the southern parts of the country.

H. DOVRENSE (Fries).—Common by *Drivstuen* and in Vinsterdal.

H. **ALPINUM, L.**; β *H. alpinum parviflorum*, Fl. D. tab. 27; *j. Halleri*, δ *incisum*.—All the above-named, with many intermediate varieties, are to be found over the whole Fjeld, from the limit of fir up to that of the larger willows.

H. MURORUM, L.—*H. sylvaticum; H. nigro-glandulosum; H. incisum*. These three varieties are the most frequent of the **variable H.** MURORUM. Found near *Tofte, Jerkin, Kongsvold*, and *Drivstuen*, but do not attain so high an altitude as H. MURORUM. The *H. incisum* here named Professor Blytt considers to be different from δ *incisum* mentioned under H. ALPINUM.

H. PRENANTHOIDES (Villars).—Near *Kongsvold*, a little below the birch-limit. Rare. More pleutiful in low scrub near *Drivstuen*. Stalk many leaved, hairy. Leaves slightly toothed, and hairy beneath and on the edges. Flowers, 7 to 8.

H. BOREALE (Fries), with lanceolate-tooth leaves; β *latifolium* with cordate, sub-amplexicaule leaves. The latter of these two forms is very marked, and may be distinguished from the former by its smaller development (rarely 1 foot high), by the stalk-leaves being fewer (usually 3 to 4), and wider apart; by its ovate-lanceolate root-leaves, broader stalk-leaves, cordate, toothed, and often marked with brown spots. Flower heads, 3 to 5; not so downy as in H. BOREALE, but sparsely furnished with short stiff glandular hairs. Most probably the latter is a distinct species. Both are found in low scrub by *Drivstuen* and other places in Drivdal. The last-named reaches up to the birch-limit.

H. CORYMBOSUM (Fries).—Places in Drivdal. Resembles H. BOREALE.

H. CROCATUM (Fries).—As the last.

H. UMBELLATUM, L.; Fl. D. tab. 680.—In low scrub by *Drivstuen* and other places in Drivdal. Not found above the birch-limit.

H. PALUDOSUM, L.; Fl. D. tab. 928.—By *Fogstuen* and in Drivdal up to the birch-limit. Found in moist places in meadows. Leaves smooth and thin.

HYPOCHÆRIS MACULATA, L.; Fl. D. tab. 249.—By Bergsgaard, and on hills near *Tofte*, where it vanishes a little below the birch-limit.

* APARGIA AUTUMNALIS (Willdenow), Fl. D. tab. 1,996.—General over the whole Fjeld. A variety, β *asperior uniflora* (Wahlberg), Fl. D. tab. 1,523, very similar to it, is found up to and above the birch-limit.

CAMPANULACEÆ.

CAMPANULA UNIFLORA, L.; Fl. D. tab. 1,512.—Plentiful in some places on Knudshoë, near *Kongsvold*, and on the Fjeld by *Drivstuen*; less common on Gederyggen, near Jerkin. On Knudshoë it is found above the birch-limit on dry places which abound in lichens, such as *Cetraria nivalis, cucullata, islandica; Cornicularia ochroleuca*, and *Cladonia rangiferina*, &c. It apparently vanishes below the lasting snowdrifts.

C. ROTUNDIFOLIA, L.; Fl. D. tab. 1,086.—Common over the

whole Fjeld. When found above the birch-limit it is usually one-flowered, and of such stunted growth as to be easily mistaken for the last-named species.

VACCINIEÆ.

VACCINUM ULIGINOSUM, L.; Fl. D. tab. 231.—Up to and above the birch-limit; ripens near *Kongsvold*, in August.

V. MYRTILLUS, L.; Fl. D. tab. 40.—Common. Berries not found to ripen above the birch-limit.

V. VITIS IDÆA, L.; Fl. D. tab. 40.—Common over the whole Fjeld.

SCHOLLERA OXYCOCCUS (Roth); Fl. D. tab. 80.—On Harbakken, and by *Fogstuen*, up to the birch-limit, but rarely found higher. Does not ripen on the Dovre Fjeld.

ERICINIEÆ.

EMPETRUM NIGRUM, L.; Fl. D. tab. 975.—Found up to and above the birch-limit with ripe berries.

ARCTOSTAPHYLOS UVA-URSI (Spreng); Fl. D. tab. 35.—Up to the lasting snowdrifts.

A. ALPINA (Spreng); Fl. D. tab. 73.—As the last.

PYROLA ROTUNDIFOLIA, L.; Fl. D. tab. 1,816.—Common below, and occasionally found above the birch-limit.

P. MINOR, L.; Fl. D. tab. 55.—Common. Is found at higher altitudes than the last-named.

P. SECUNDA, L.; Fl. D. tab. 402.—Up to, and a little above the fir-limit in Drivdal.

MONESES GRANDIFLORA (Salisbury).—Extremely rare, and only noticed near *Dombaas*, at the foot of the Dovre. Stalk erect, one-flowered. Flower white, large, and fragrant.

ANDROMEDA POLIFOLIA, L.; Fl. D. tab. 54.—Up to about the birch-limit.

A. HYPNOIDES, L.; Fl. D. tab. 10.—From the birch-limit up to the lasting snowdrifts.

ERICA VULGARIS, L.; Fl. D. tab. 677.—Common up to and a little above the birch-limit.

MENZIESIA CÆRULEA (Smith); Fl. D. tab. 57.—Up to the lasting snowdrifts, and as low as the region of spruce fir in Gudbrandsdal (2,600 to 2,800).

AZALEA PROCUMBENS, L.; Fl. D. tab. 9.—Common up to the snowdrifts.

GENTIANEÆ.

MENYANTHES TRIFOLIATA, L.; Fl. D. tab. 541.—Up to *Fogstuen*.

GENTIANA NIVALIS, L.; Fl. D. tab. 16.—Common up to the birch-limit; rarely found higher. Occasionally found some way down in the region of Scotch fir.

G. GLACIALIS (Villars); Fl. D. tab. 318.—Though found below the limit of Scotch fir, this species does not extend so low down as the last. It is, however, found higher up on the Fjeld, nearly to the continual snowdrifts.

G. CAMPESTRIS, L.; Fl. D. tab. 367.—Up to about the birch-limit; varies much in size and in form of leaf. Often found with white flowers.

G. AMARELLA, L.; Fl. D. tab. 328.—Up to and above the birch-limit. That found on the Dovre is not so broad-leaved as is represented in Fl. Dan., but bears a greater resemblance to *G. obtusifolia* β *spathalata* (*vide* Reichenberg's 'Flor. German. Excursoria,' p. 424).

POLEMONIDEÆ.

POLEMONIUM CÆRULEUM, L.; Fl. D. tab. 255.—Between *Tofte* and *Dombaas*, by *Jerkin* and *Kongsvold*; in every place below the birch-limit.

BORRAGINEÆ.

LYCOPSIS ARVENSIS, L.; Fl. D. tab. 435.—Common up to *Tofte* in fields. Not found on the Dovre further north.

ASPERUGO PROCUMBENS, L.; Fl. D. tab. 552.—By *Tofte*, *Fogstuen*, and *Drivstuen*.

MYOSOTIS CÆSPITOSA (Schultz).—General up to *Tofte*, where it disappears below the birch-limit.

M. ARVENSIS, L.—In Drivdal, by *Drivstuen* and *Tofte*.

M. SYLVATICA (Hoffman); Fl. D. tab. 583.—General in dry shady places over the whole Fjeld. It is found above the limit of birch up to that of the larger willow tribe. It differs slightly from the plate in Fl. Dan.; has shorter and thicker leaves, flower-stalk with compressed hairs. At higher altitudes which are more exposed it is more stunted in growth, with shorter clusters.

ECHINOSPERMUM DEFLEXUM (Lehmann); Fl. D. tab. 1,568.—Near *Tofte*; in Drivdal between *Kongsvold* and *Drivstuen*. Resembles *Myosotis arvensis*, but is larger.

E. LAPPULA; Fl. D. tab. 692.—On hills near *Tofte*.

ANTIRRHINEÆ.

LINARIA VULGARIS (Miller); Fl. D. tab. 982.—By *Tofte*; not found higher than the limit of corn. Occasional in Drivdal, a little above the (Scotch) fir-limit.

RHINANTHACEÆ.

MELAMPYRUM PRATENSE, L.; Fl. D. tab. 2,238.—By *Jerkin*, *Kongsvold*, and other places, nearly up to the birch-limit.

M. SYLVATICUM, L.; Fl. D. tab. 145.—As the last.

PEDICULARIS PALUSTRIS, L.; Fl. D. tab. 2,055.—Common up to the birch-limit.

P. OEDERI (Vahl); Fl. D. tab. 30.—On marshy places over the whole Fjeld, from the limit of fir up to the lasting snowdrifts. This plant has a great tendency to vary. On low grounds it is often quite smooth; at high altitudes downy, especially on the upper parts. The spike is more or less compact, according to age.

P. LAPPONICA, L.; Fl. D. tab. 2.—Common over the whole Fjeld, from the limit of fir up to the snowdrifts.

RHINANTHUS CRISTA-GALLI, L.; Fl. D. tab. 981.—Common up to the birch-limit.

BARTSIA ALPINA, L.; Fl. D. tab. 43.—Common up to and above the birch-limit.

EUPHRASIA OFFICINALIS, L.; Fl. D. tab. 1,037.—As the last.

VERONICA SERPYLLIFOLIA, L.; Fl. D. tab. 492.—As the last.

V. ALPINA, L.; Fl. D. tab. 16.—From about the fir-limit up to that of the willow. A variety, β *lasiocarpa*, grows in Nystudal.

V. SAXATILIS, L.; Fl. D. tab. 342.—As the last, but descends lower down into forest tracts.

V. OFFICINALIS, L.; Fl. D. tab. 248.—Very common. Mounts up above the fir-limit nearly to that of birch by *Kongsvold* and elsewhere.

V. CHAMÆDRYS, L.; Fl. D. tab. 448.—By Rustgaard on Harbakken, almost up to the birch-limit.

LABIATÆ.

GALEOPSIS TETRAHIT, L.; Fl. D. tab. 1,271.—Disappears near *Tofte* simultaneously with the cultivation of corn.

G. LADANUM, L.; Fl. D. tab. 1,757.—Near *Fogstuen*.

G. CANNABINA (Willdenow); Fl. D. tab. 929.—As the last.

LAMIUM PURPUREUM, L.; Fl. D. tab. 523.—Common up to *Tofte*.

GLECHOMA HEDERACEA, L.; Fl. D. tab. 789.— Disappears entirely on the road between *Dombaas* and *Tofte*; grows below the limit of fir in dry places.

STACHYS PALUSTRIS, L.; Fl. D. tab. 1,103.—Not found beyond *Tofte*.

THYMUS ACINOS, L.; Fl. D. tab. 814.—By **Tofte**, and in Drivdal below *Drivstuen*.

DRACOCEPHALUM RUYSCHIANUM, L.; Fl. D. tab. 121.—Grows in dry meadows near *Tofte*, below the limit of fir. Flowers, 7, violet. Not common.

PRUNELLA VULGARIS, L.; Fl. D. tab. 910.—Common. Grows up to, and sometimes a little above the birch-limit.

LENTIBULARIEÆ.

PINGUICULA VULGARIS, L.; Fl. D. tab. 93.—Common. Mounts above the birch-limit, nearly up to the lasting snowdrifts.

P. VILLOSA, L.; Fl. D. tab. 1,921.—Near *Fogstuen*. Grows abundantly near the small lakes below the Gaard (farm-house); also near *Jerkin*, below Gederyggen.

PRIMULACEÆ.

DIAPENSIA LAPPONICA, L.; Fl. D. tab. 47.—Occasional in places over the whole Fjeld, which are exposed to wind and weather, *e. g.*, on the highest parts of Harbakken, on the heights above *Fogstuen* by Fogsaa; on Volasö Fjeld, by Volasö lake; near *Kongsvold*, where it descends below the birch-limit; on Knudshoë, on the highest part of Vaarstien, and on the Fjeld opposite to *Drivstuen*, where it is most plentiful. Everywhere found up to the limit of snow; flower-stalks, upright, bearing each one white flower.

ANDROSACE SEPTENTRIONALIS, L.; Fl. D. tab. 7. Near *Tofte*, *Kongsvold*, *Jerkin*, and *Drivstuen*. Scarcely found above the birch-limit; disappears immediately below it. Leaves lanceolate, toothed, nearly smooth. Flowers, 5 to 6, white.

PRIMULA SCOTICA (Hook); Fl. D. tab. 125.—Common over the whole Fjeld. In some places, *e.g.* Knudshoë, Volasoë, &c., found above the birch-limit.

P. STRICTA (Hornemann); Fl. D. tab. 1,385.—Occasional. Found on Harbakken, on the left side of the rode, between *Jerkin* and *Kongsvold*.

TRIENTALIS EUROPÆA, L.; Fl. D. tab. 84.—Common up to and above the birch-limit, where it has a very stunted appearance and rose-coloured flowers. A variety, β *alpina*, is common over the whole Fjeld, but always above the larger willow tribe.

PLANTAGINEÆ.

PLANTAGO MAJOR, L.; Fl. D. tab. 461.—Disappears at about the birch-limit on Harbakken, above Rustgaard.

P. MEDIA, L.; Fl. D. tab. 581.—Grows over the whole Fjeld, especially by roads and mountain-paths. Not found above the birch-limit.

CHENOPODIEÆ.

CHENOPODIUM ALBUM, L.; Fl. D. tab. 1,150.—Grows by inhabited places on rich soil near *Tofte*.

C. POLYSPERMUM, L.; Fl. D. tab. 1,153.—Occasional by the side of the new road in Drivdal.

POLYGONEÆ.

RUMEX ACETOSA, L.—Common. Mounts up above the birch-limit.

R. ACETOSELLA, L.; Fl. D. tab. 1,161.—Vanishes a little below the birch-limit by *Jerkin*.

R. DOMESTICUS, Hartmann; Fl. D. tab. 2,349.—Common up to *Jerkin* and *Fogstuen*. Grows near houses.

OXYRIA DIGYNA, Campdera; Fl. D. tab. 14.—Over the whole Fjeld, up to perpetual snow.

POLYGONUM VIVIPARUM, L.; Fl. D. tab. 13.—Up to and above the birch-limit. Flowers often rose-coloured.

P. AVICULARE, L.; Fl. D. tab. 803.—Disappears a little below the birch-limit by *Jerkin*, but found above it on Harbakken.

P. CONVOLVULUS, L.; Fl. D. tab. 741.—By *Tofte*, up to the corn-limit.

KŒNIGIA ISLANDICA, L.; Fl. D. tab. 418.—Occasional on boggy places over the whole Fjeld, *e. g.*, near the old high-road over Harbakken, by the road between Volasö and *Jerkin*; by *Jerkin*, *Kongsvold*, and in Drivdal. First appears a little above the fir-limit, and mounts up beyond the limit of birch.

THYMELEÆ.

DAPHNE MEZEREUM, L.; Fl. D. tab. 268.—On Harbakken, above Rustgaard, at about the birch-limit.

EUPHORBIACEÆ.

EUPHORBIA HELIOSCOPIA, L.; Fl. D. tab. 725.—Up to the corn-limit, by *Tofte*.

URTICEÆ.

URTICA URENS, L.; Fl. D. tab. 739.—By mountain cabins.

U. DIOCIA, L.; Fl. D. tab. 746.—As the last, but more common.

AMENTACEÆ.

BETULA GLUTINOSA, or *B. verrucosa*, Ehrh., Wallorth; Fl. D. tab. 1,467.—Professor Blytt places its limit at 3,241 feet on the Rondfjeld, adjoining the Dovre, and on Vaarstien at 3,193 feet.—N.B. The limit of birch is reckoned by this species.

B. ALPESTRIS, Fries.—Occasional on the Dovre; grows on Knudshoë. Rare.

B. HUMILIS, Hartmann.—Occasional on the Fjeld. First appears a little below the birch-limit, and mounts up to 100 feet above it.

B. NANA, L.; Fl. D. tab. 91.—Grows highest up of all the birch tribe, to the limit of lasting snow; has a very stunted and creeping form.

ALNUS INCANA, L.; Fl. D. tab. 2,301.—Mounts 200 to 300 feet above the fir-limit in Drivdal.

A. PUBESCENS, Tausch.—Found in moist places in Drivdal and Nystudal.

POPULUS TREMULA, L.—Grows as a bush, 2 to 3 feet high on the Fjeld side a little above *Kongsvold*. Near *Drivstuen* it attains a tolerable height, some 100 feet above the fir-limit.

SALIX PENTANDRA, L.; Fl. D. tab. 943.—Between *Tofte* and *Dombaas*, and by *Drivstuen*.

S. GLAUCA, L.; β *Lapponum* (Fl. D. tab. 1,058); γ *appendiculata* (Fl. D. tab. 1,056); δ *denudata*.—Grow over the whole Fjeld, under very different forms. They mount up towards the permanent snow in company with *S. lanata, S. limosa*, &c., but not quite so high as *S. herbacea* and *S. polaris*. The capsules are always covered with a thick white, or greyish-white wool (according to age). The catkins of the male and female vary in length, as also do the leaves, both in respect to colour, surface, and margin; but generally they are entire, and of a darker colour on the upper than on the under side.

S. LANATA, L.; Fl. D. tab. 1,057.—Found over the whole Fjeld, at the same altitude as the last. The catkins of the female are sometimes two to three inches long. Leaves generally broader, and of more uniform colour on both sides, than in the last. Professor Blytt found on Blaahoë a creeping willow scarcely one foot high, in company with *S. polaris*. The leaves were more elliptical, and nearly smooth, catkins shorter, and naked scales, bearing a striking resemblance to specimens found in Greenland. "Unfortunately," he writes, "I found but one fruit-bearing specimen of this apparently very early flowering form."

S. HASTATA, L.; Fl. D. tab. 1,238.—Common over the whole Fjeld; extends far above the birch-limit. The form of leaves is very variable—sometimes elliptical, lanceolate, or oval. The colour generally constant, dark on the surface, and a pale green below. The plant varies much in size. As a creeping bush it approximates to *S. Arbuscula*, but differs from it in the smoothness of the capsules.

S. ARBUSCULA, Fries.—In places abundant. At Bergsgaard, above *Tofte*, between *Dombaas* and *Fogstuen, Jerkin*, and *Kongsvold*, it is found above the birch-limit.

S. PHYLICIFOLIA, L. (Fl. D. tab. 1,052); β *nigricans* (Fl. D. tab. 1,053); γ *majalis*.—Besides these varieties a great many intermediate forms are found over the whole Fjeld. *S. phylicifolia* is found up to the birch-limit. β *nigricans* grows as a small tree near *Fogstuen*, and is found up to the limits of the larger species, *S. lanata, limosa*, &c.

S. CAPRŒA, L.; Fl. D. tab. 245.—Disappears below *Tofte*.

S. DEPRESSA, L.—On dry sandy places, near *Tofte* and *Jerkin*, but not above the birch-limit.

S. LIMOSA, Wahl.—Grows at same altitude as *S. lanata*, &c.

Common over the whole **Fjeld**; **form** of leaf varies as in *S. glauca*.

S. MYRSINITES, L.; Fl. D. tab. 1,054.—Common. Not found quite so high **up as** the last. Flowers early. Not so variable as the last. **The** leaves of **this** species found on the Dovre are shorter and **thicker** than in the sub-alpine specimens.

S. OVATA, Seringe.—Rare by Fogsaa above *Fogstuen*; **plentiful in** Nystudal.

S. RETICULATA, L.; Fl D. tab. 212.—Common up **to and above** the birch-limit.

S. HERBACEA, L.; Fl. D. tab. 117.—Common from **the** fir-limit up to the permanent snow.

S. POLARIS, Wahl.—Rare. First shows itself **above the birch-**limit. Found in small quantities near *Jerkin* on Gederyggen, on Volasö-fjeld; more plentiful **on** Blaahoë, **Gontsti**-fjeld, and Knudshöe. It mounts **up to the permanent snow, and** appears to flourish best above the limit **of the larger willows.**

CONIFERÆ.

JUNIPERUS COMMUNIS, L.; **Fl. D. tab.** 1,119.—Mounts high above **the** birch-limit; **at its** greatest altitude the leaves are very short. The whole shrub is frequently covered with a bluish-green **dew** that gives it a remarkable appearance.

PINUS SYLVESTRIS.—Reaches its highest limit between *Dombaus* and *Fogstuen*, and is not met with again before coming **to** *Jerkin*, where it covers the bottom of the valley in the direction of Foldal.

PINUS ABIES.—Is not found on Dovre; but in the neighbouring heights of Vaage it reaches nearly the same altitude **as the last.**

ALISMACEÆ.

TRIGLOCHIN PALUSTRE, L.; Fl. D. tab. 490.—Common up to and a little above the birch-limit.

POTAMEÆ.

POTAMOGETON PALUSTRIS, L.; Fl. D. tab. 222 (?)—Found in **Volasö.**

P. PUSILLUS, L.; Fl. D. tab. 1,451.—Near *Kongsvold*, and in Volasö.

P. NATANS, L.; Fl. D. tab. 1,025.—In Hviddal lakes.

P. gramineus, L.; Fl. D. tab. 222.—In Hviddal lakes, and in a small tarn immediately to the east of *Jerkin*.

P. rufescens, Schrader; Fl. D. tab. 1,450.—In Volasö, above the fir-limit.

P. alpinus, probably a variety of P. pectinatus.—In Hviddals Vand and in Volasö.

P. pectinatus, L.; Fl. D. tab. 186 and 1,746.—In the easternmost of the Hviddal lakes.

ORCHIDEÆ.

Orchis maculata, L.; Fl. D. tab. 933.—On boggy places up to and above the birch-limit.

O. cruenta, L.; Fl. D. tab. 876.—At Bergsgaad, at about the birch-limit, and by a brook between *Tofte* and Rustgaard on the right-hand side of the old road from *Tofte* to Harbakken; also near *Laurgaard*.

O. incarnata, L.; Fl. D. tab. 1,232 (?).—Near *Tofte*.

O. cordigera, Reichenbach.—Occasional on marshy places, *e. g.* near *Tofte*, above Berggaard, near Rustgaard between *Tofte* and Harbakken; 1,800 to 2,000 feet above the sea.

Satyrium albidum, L.; Fl. D. tab. 115.—Occasional on swampy places, up to and above the birch-limit.

S. viride, L.; Fl. D. tab. 77.—Common. Often found above the birch-limit.

Nigritella angustifolia, Richard; Fl. D. tab. 998.—Rare. Found in meadows south of *Drivstuen*, between the river and the high road.

Gymnadenia conopsea, Wahl.; Fl. D. tab. 224.—Common up to and above the birch-limit.

Ophrys alpina, L.; Fl. D. tab. 452.—Plentiful on the hills above *Tofte*, and by the road between *Tofte* and Harbakken. Less common near *Kongsvold*.

Corallorhiza innata, Brown; Fl. D. tab. 451.—Very rare. Has only been found in birch copses near Langsvold. Flowers a dark reddish-purple.

Serapias latifolia, L.; Fl. D. tab. 811.—Rare. Found in small quantities a little below the birch-limit near *Tofte*.

Listera cordata, Smith; Fl. D. tab. 1,298.—By Volasöberg a little below the birch-limit, and occasionally in Drivdal a little above the fir-limit.

NEOTTIA REPENS, Sw.; Fl. D. tab. 812.—Occasional below the birch-limit near *Tofte*.

ASPARAGEÆ.

PARIS QUADRIFOLIA, L.; Fl. D. tab. 139.—By *Tofte*, and between *Kongsvold* and *Drivstuen* at about the fir-limit.

CONVALLARIA MAJALIS, L.; Fl. D. tab. 854.—By *Tofte*, nearly up to the birch-limit above *Drivstuen*.

C. VERTICILLATA, L.; Fl. D. tab. 86.—In Drivdal a little above the fir-limit.

MAIANTHEMUM BIFOLIUM, De Candolle; Fl. D. tab. 291.—By *Kongsvold* and in Drivdal up to and above the fir-limit.

COLCHICACEÆ.

TOFIELDIA BOREALIS, Wahl.; Fl. D. tab. 36.—Common. Mounts high above the birch-limit.

JUNCEÆ.

JUNCUS ARCTICUS, Willdenow; Fl. D. tab. 1,095.—Very common. Found occasionally above the birch-limit.

J. FILIFORMIS, L.; Fl. D. tab. 1,207.—As the last, but not so frequent.

J. USTULATUS, Hartmann.—Common up to the birch-limit.

J. BIGLUMIS, L.; Fl. D. tab. 120.—Very common. Mounts above the birch-limit.

J. TRIGLUMIS, L.; Fl. D. tab. 132.—As the last.

J. TRIFIDUS, L.; Fl. D. tab. 107 and 1,691.—Very common. Specimens bearing one and many flowers found over the whole Fjeld. Mounts above the birch-limit.

J. BUFONIUS, L.; Fl. D. tab. 1,098.—Near *Tofte*, *Kongsvold*, and in Drivdal; up to the limit of fir.

LUZULA PILOSA, Willd.—Disappears at *Fogstuen* at about the birch-limit.

L. PARVIFLORA, Hornemann; Fl. D. tab. 1,929.—Rare. Found by Fogsaa above *Fogstuen*, Gederygen, Volashöe, Blaahöe Gontstifjeld, Knudshöe, Nystuhöe, Jerkindshöe, and on the fjelds on either side Drivdal. Generally first appears where L. PILOSA vanishes. Mounts up to the limit of the larger willows.

L. CAMPESTRIS, L.; Fl. D. tab. 1,333—β *erecta*; γ *coarctata*, δ *suedetica*. The first grows on low grounds near *Tofte*, and a

Drivdal; β, in shady places in Drivdal; γ, near *Kongsvold* and in Drivdal; δ, on high grounds, and mounts above the birch-limit.

L. HYPERBOREA, Brown.—Common over the whole Fjeld. First appears somewhere above the birch-limit, and mounts up to the limit of the larger willows.

L. ACRUATA, Hartmann.—Less common than the last. Only found on the very highest parts of the Fjeld, *e. g.*, Fogstuvola, Harbakken, Storhöe, Volasofjeld, Blaahoë, and Goutstifjeld. It seldom becomes fully developed, on account of the snow which lies on the ground nearly all the summer through where it grows.

L. SPICATA, Hornemann.—Very common. Mounts above the birch-limit, and vanishes where L. HYPERBOREA becomes general.

TYPHACEÆ.

SPARGANIUM NATANS, L.; Fl. D. tab. 360.—In Volasö.

S. OLIGOCARPON, Angström.—Occasional in brooks and ponds near *Kongsvold* and *Jerkin*.

S. HYPERBOREUM, Lœstad.—Not uncommon. Found, among other places, near *Drivstuen*.

CYPERACEÆ.

SCIRPUS CÆSPITOSUS, L.—Common up to and above the birch-limit.

S. BÆOTHRYON, Ehrhart; Fl. D. tab. 1,862.—Rare. Up to and about the birch-limit by *Fogstuen* and *Kongsvold*.

HELEOCHARIS PALUSTRIS, Brown; Fl. D. tab. 273.—Below *Tofte*, in a pond near the roadside.

ERIOPHORUM ALPINUM, L.; Fl. D. tab. 620.—Rare. Found on Harbakken, near *Fogstuen*, *Kongsvold*, *Jerkin*, *Drivstuen*.

E. CAPITATUM, Hoffmann; Fl. D. tab. 1,502.—Common. Mounts up to the lasting snow, and descends into the region of fir.

E. VAGINATUM, L.; Fl. D. tab. 236.—Over the whole Fjeld. Vanishes a little above the birch-limit.

E. ANGUSTIFOLIUM, Roth; Fl. D. tab. 1,422.—Occasional over the whole Fjeld. Altitude the same as last.

E. LATIFOLIUM, Hoppe; Fl. D. tab. 1,381.—As the last.

ELYNA SPICATA, Schrad.; Fl. D. tab. 1,529.—Occasional on high and dry places; *e. g.*, on Harbakken, Jerkinshöe, Gederyggen, *Kongsvold*, &c.

KOBRECIA CARICINA, Willd.—Rare. On peat-bogs near *Tofte*, on the hills above the Gaard, and on the marshes along the road between Harbakken and *Fogstuen*, by *Jerkin*, *Kongsvold*, &c.

CAREX DIOICA, L.; Fl D. tab. 369.—Common. Often found above the birch-limit.

C. PARALLELA, Sommerfeldt.—Less common than the last. Occasional on damp, grassy places—*e. g.*, Gederyggen, Sprænbækdal, and in meadows near *Kongsvold*. It bears a resemblance to C. RUPESTRIS, in company with which it is found.

C. CAPITATA, L.; Fl. D. tab. 2,061.—Not common. Grows in the marshes between *Fogstuen* and *Jerkin*, and in those below *Jerkin* on the right of the road near the Gaard. Less frequent near *Kongsvold*.

C. RUPESTRIS, Allioni; Fl. D. tab. 1,401.—Occasional in swampy places, and in clefts and crevices of the rock—*e. g.*, along the road over Harbakken, on Gederyggen, near *Jerkin*, *Kongsvold*, and *Drivstuen*.

C. MICROGLOCHIN, Wahl.; Fl. D. tab. 1,402.—Rather common in the marshes from Harbakken to *Drivstuen*.

C. LEUCOGLOCHIN, Ehrhart; Fl. D. tab. 1,279.—Very rare. Found in the region of fir between *Dombaas* and *Fogstuen*.

C. INCURVA, Lightfoot; Fl. D. tab. 432.—Occasional in swampy places a little below the birch-limit—*e. g.*, by Bergsgaard, *Tofte*, *Fogstuen*, *Jerkin*, and *Kongsvold*.

C. CHORDORRHIZA, Ehrhart; Fl. D. tab. 1,408.—Occasional in marshes up to about the limit of birch—*e. g.*, near *Jerkin*, *Kongsvold*.

C. LAGOPINA, Wahl.; Fl. D. tab. 294.—Up to and often above the limit of the larger willows. First becomes general at about the fir-limit.

C. LOLIACEA, L.; Fl. D. tab. 1,403.—In the region of fir between *Dombaas* and *Fogstuen*.

C. CANESCENS, L.; Fl. D. tab. 285.—Is common with the β *alpicola*, up to and above the birch-limit.

C. HELVOLA, Blytt.—Rather plentiful in Nystudal.

C. STELLULATA, Schreber; Fl. D. tab. 284.—Not uncommon in Drivdal.

C. FLAVA, L.; Fl. D. tab. 1,407.—Near *Kongsvold*, *Tofte*, and in Drivdal.

C. FILIFORMIS, L.; Fl. D. tab. 379 and 1,344.—Near *Fogstuen*, *Jerkin*, *Kongsvold*, up to the limit of birch.

C. ROTUNDATA, Wahl.; Fl. D. tab. 1,407.—Occasional. In company with C. PULLA, of which it is probably only a variety, near *Fogstuen*, *Jerkin*, and *Kongsvold*.

C. CAPILLARIS, L.; Fl. D. tab. 168.—Common up to and above the birch-limit.

C. USTULATA, Wahl.; Fl. D. tab. 1,590.—Very common from the fir-limit, up to the lasting snow.

C. FRIGIDA, Hart.—Occasional on high parts of the Fjeld, from the birch-limit to the lasting snow—*e. g.*, on Blaahoë, Gederyggen, Knudshoe. Probably the same as *C. misandra*, found by Brown in Melville Island.

C. PANICEA, L.; Fl. D. tab. 261.—Common, with β *sparsiflora* and γ *pauciflora*, up to and above the birch-limit. It has a great tendency to vary. The latter is found only in shady places.

C. ORNITHOPODA, Willd.; Fl. D. tab. 1,405.—On hills near *Tofte*.

C. ERICETORUM, Pollick; Fl. D. tab. 1,765—Common over the whole Fjeld. Often found above the birch-limit.

C. ALPINA; Fl. D. tab. 403.—As the last.

C. ATRATA, L.; Fl. D. tab. 158.—As the last.

C. BUXBAUMII, Wahl; Fl. D. tab. 1,406.—Not common. Found on marshy places near *Fogstuen*, *Jerkin*, and *Kongsvold*.

C. PALLESCENS, L.; Fl. D. tab. 1,050.—Less common than the last, and not found at such high altitudes. Near *Tofte* and in Drivdal.

C. LIMOSA, L.; Fl. D. tab. 646.—Rare near *Jerkin* and *Kongsvold*. β *rariflora* by the road between Harbakken and *Fogstuen*, and near *Kongsvold*; γ *irrigua* near *Jerkin*.

C. AMPULLACEA, Willd.; Fl. D. tab. 2,248.—Near *Kongsvold* and *Fogstuen*.

C. VESICARIA, L.; Fl. D. tab. 647.—As the last. Both species grow below the birch-limit.

C. AQUATILIS, Wahl.—In marshes below *Fogstuen*. More plentiful between *Fogstuen* and Harbakken.

C. SAXATILIS, L.; Fl. D. tab. 159.—Common up to the lasting snow. A variety has been found in grassy places near the banks of streams, &c., by *Kongsvold* and Nystuhöe, bearing a great resemblance to the last-named species.

C. CŒSPITOSA, L.; Fl. D. tab. 1,281.—Occasional over the whole Fjeld, up to and above the birch-limit.

C. VULGARIS, Fries.—Common. Grows up to and a little above the limit of the larger willows.

C. JUNCELLA, Fries.—Occasional in damp places. Not found above the limit of birch.

C. PULLA, Goodenough.—Very common from the limit of fir up to the permanent snow. This species has a great tendency to vary according to locality.

GRAMINEÆ.

ALOPECURUS GENIDULATUS, L.; Fl. D. tab. 861.—Common, especially along roads up to about the birch-limit. Seldom found higher. A variety, β *natans*, Wahl., Fl. D. tab. 1,801, occasional in flooded places. Found also in a little lake at the foot of Blaahöe above the birch-limit.

PHLEUM PRATENSE, L.; Fl. D. tab. 1,985.—Occasional at low altitudes—*e. g.*, near *Tofte* and *Drivstuen*.

P. ALPINUM, L.; Fl. D. tab. 213.—Very common, and found up to and above the limit of birch.

PHALARIS ARUNDINACEA, L.; Fl. D. tab. 259.—In Drivdal, on the river banks above *Drivstuen*, where it attains its highest limit.

HIEROCHLOA BOREALIS, Römer and Schultes.—Drivdal and near *Jerkin*.

VAHLODEA ATROPURPUREA, Fries.; Fl. D. tab. 961.—Rare. Found a little below the birch-limit—*e. g.*, near *Fogstuen*, Volaso, and by the road between the lake and Blaahöe, and on the river bank below *Kongsvold*.

ANTHOXANTHUM ODORATUM, L.; Fl. D. tab. 666.—Very common. Mounts high above the birch-limit, nearly up to the lasting snow.

MILIUM EFFUSUM, L.; Fl. D. tab. 1,143.—Occasional in shady places. Grows at about the birch-limit—*e. g.*, in Spræbækdal, and at many places near *Kongsvold*, and in Drivdal in copses near *Drivstuen*.

PHIPPSIA ALGIDA, Brown.—At the edge of eternal snow on Knudshöe and Nystuhöe. Probably common in similar localities, but is easily overlooked on account of its diminutiveness.

CATABROSA AQUATICA, Palisot de Beauvois; Fl. D. tab. 381. —Very rare on Dovre. Has only been noticed at two places— *e. g.*, between *Dombaas* and *Fogstuen*, and by the Driv about a mile and a half north of *Drivstuen*. Grows a little below the fir-limit.

AGROSTIS RUBRA, L.—Occasional below the birch-limit.

A. ALPINA, Scop.— Common over the whole Fjeld. Mounts up above the birch-limit.

A. CANINA, L.; Fl. D. tab. 1,443.—Near *Jerkin*, *Kongsvold*, and in Drivdal.

CALAMAGROSTIS HALLERIANA, De Candolle.—In Drivdal, by mountain streams near *Drivstuen*.

C. PHRAGMITOIDES, Hartmann.—Not uncommon. Mounts up to the limit of the larger willows.

C. EPIGEIOS, Roth.; Fl. D. tab. 2,165.—Grows below *Tofte* in a dry meadow, and between *Tofte* and *Dombaas* on a sandbank close by the road.

C. STRICTA, L.; Fl. D. tab. 1,803.—Common up to the birch-limit.

C. SYLVATICA, De Candolle; Fl. D. tab. 1,683.—In the fir-forest between *Dombaas* and *Tofte*, near the road. Common.

AIRA CÆSPITOSA, L.; Fl. D. tab. 240.—Common up to the birch-limit. Not frequent above.

A. ALPINA, L.; Fl. D. tab. 1,625.—Common from about the fir-limit till far above that of birch.

A. FLEXUOSA, L.; Fl. D. tab. 157.—Common over the whole Fjeld at low altitudes. A variety, β *montana*, Fl. D. tab. 1,322, is found up to and above the birch-limit.

A. SUBSPICATA, L.; Fl. D. tab. 228.—Common. First becomes general between the limit of fir and birch. Mounts far above that of the latter.

AVENA PUBESCENS, L.; Fl. D. tab. 1,203.—Disappears near Bergsgaard and *Jerkin*, a little below the birch-limit; but has been found high above the same, near *Kongsvold* and *Drivstuen*.

POA ANNUA, L.; Fl. D. tab. 1,686.—Common near inhabited places. A variety, β *supina*, is found on high and dry places— *e. g.*, near *Jerkin*.

P. LAXA, Hænke; Fl. D. tab. 2,342.—General on high parts of the Fjeld. First appears at about the birch-limit. Usually found growing under stones near brooks, &c. It grows up above the limit of the larger willow, and disappears in the region of the polar-willow—*i. e.*, *Salix herbacea* and *Salix polaris*. A variety, β *minor*, is also found.

P. STRICTA, Lindeberg.—An intermediate form of P. LAXA (?).

Common on Knudsöe, Blaahöe, Fogstuhöe, Nystuhöe, &c. First appears above the limit of the larger willows, and mounts up to the extreme limit of the Phanerogami.

P. FLEXUOSA, Wahlenberg.—Occasional on Goutstifjeld, Blaahöe, Knudshöe, and Nystuhöe. First appears at about the birch-limit, and mounts above the limit of the larger willow tribe. Found in company with *Salix polaris* on Goutstifjeld, and with *Campanula uniflora* on Knudshöe. Professor Blytt is of opinion that it is one and the same species with *P. arctica* found in Melville Island by R. Brown. A variety, *P. flexuosa* β *abbreviata*, is found in plenty on Blaahöe, Nystuhöe, and Knudshöe, always above the limit of the larger willows.

P. GLAUCA, Vahl.; Fl. D. tab. 964.—Common on low rocky ground over the whole Fjeld.

P. BALFOURII, Parnell.—On the sunny side of the highest part of Dovre—*e. g.*, on Blaahöe, Nystuhöe, Snehætten, and Knudshöe.

P. ALPINA, L.; Fl. D. tab. 807.—Very general over the whole Fjeld. Mounts above the birch-limit, but does not grow so high up as P. FLEXUOSA or P. LAXA. A variety, β *vivipara*, is found on Jerkinshöe and near *Kongsvold*. This plant varies much in appearance according to the dryness or fertility of the locality where it is found. Thus, in very dry places it assumes a dwarfish growth, and has so great a resemblance to *P. laxa* β *minor*, as to be readily mistaken for it.

P. TRIVIALIS, L.; Fl. D. tab. 1,685. Occasional in moist and shady places below the birch-limit—*e. g.*, near *Kongsvold*, and many places in Drivdal.

P. PRATENSIS, L.; Fl. D. tab. 1,444.

β. *humilis*.
γ. *rigens*.
δ. *iantha*.
ε. *angustifolia*.

The first is found on grassy places, nearly always below the birch-limit. β on dry places, by road-sides — *e. g.*, near Jerkin and *Kongsvold*; γ on dampish meadows. The variety which Professor Blytt has entered under the name of δ. *iantha* is found high up on the Fjeld, far above the birch-limit, on rather damp places; ε near *Tofte, Jerkin*, and in Drivdal. The Professor found two other varieties, of which the one he thinks may have been a luxuriant form of γ. *rigens*. The other bore a great similarity to P. GLAUCA. Vahl.

P. SCROTINA, Ehrb.; Fl. D. tab. 2,166. In the lower parts of Drivdal and Nystudal, in moist places. Not common.

P. nemoralis, L. ; Fl. D. tab. 749.
β. *firmula.*   ⎫ The first of these is common in shady places,
γ. *montana.*   ⎪ especially in Drivdal ; β also in Drivdal ;
δ. *glauca.*   ⎬ γ near *Kongsvold, Jerkin,* and *Drivstuen ;*
ε. *cæsia.*   ⎭ δ and ε over the whole Fjeld, chiefly on
the higher parts. Professor Blytt considers the variety δ. *glauca*
and P. glauca, **Vahl.** Fl. D. tab. 964, to be the same plant. He
is also of opinion that this **as well as** ε. *cæsia* **are** probably
varieties of the

Poa **cæsia,** Smith.—Very common near *Kongsvold.*

Glyceria distans, Wahl. ; Fl. D. tab. 251 and 2,222.—Grows near *Tofte* and *Jerkin.*

Catabrosa aquatica, Palisot de Beauvois ; Fl. D. tab. 381.—On boggy places near *Tofte.*

Melica nutans, L.; Fl. D. tab. 962.—Grows nearly up to the birch-limit near Kongsvold and in Drivdal.

Molinia cærulea, Mönch. ; Fl. D. tab. 239.—Near *Tofte*, and in Drivdal below the birch-limit.

Dactylis glomerata, L.; Fl. D. tab. 743.—Near *Tofte* and below *Drivstuen* in Drivdal. Hardly found above the fir-limit.

Festuca ovina, L.—Common in dry places over the whole Fjeld ; often mounts above the birch-limit. A variety, β *vivipara,* is common near *Kongsvold* and parts of Drivdal ; γ *curvula,* another variety, grows near *Jerkin*, has a bluish-green appearance.

F. rubra, L.—Common up to and above the birch-limit. A variety, β *subvillosa,* grows near *Fogstuen* and *Kongsvold.*

F. elatior, L. ; Fl. D. tab. 1,323.—Common. Disappears near *Tofte.*

Triticum repens, L.; Fl. D. tab. 748.—In Drivdal and near *Tofte.*

T. violaceum, Hornem ; Fl. D. tab. 2,044.—According to Professor Blytt this plant is probably a variety of the last. It is found in tolerable quantities on high grounds in Drivdal, near *Kongsvold* and *Jerkin.*

T. caninum, L. ; Fl. D. tab. 1,447.—Occasional in shady places in Drivdal, where it mounts above the limit of fir.

Nardus stricta, L.; Fl. D. tab. 1,022.—Common over the whole Fjeld up to and above the birch-limit.

EQUISETACEÆ.

EQUISETUM ARVENSE, L.; Fl. D. tab. 2,001.—Occasional in moist places, on clayey soil, over the whole Fjeld. It mounts very high up, and is found on the banks of streams up to the limit of the larger willows. A variety, *E. alpestre* (Wahl., Fl. D. tab. 1,942), of more delicate growth than the former, is found even at higher altitudes.

E. SYLVATICUM, L.; Fl. D. tab. 1,182.—In Drivdal, to the same height as E. ARVENSE. A variety, β *capillare*, has been noticed near *Kongsvold*.

E. UMBROSUM, Willd.; Fl. D. tab. 1,780.—In Drivdal, at same altitude as the last.

E. PALUSTRE, L.; Fl. D. tab. 1,183.—Occasional over the whole Fjeld, on moist and swampy places about the birch-limit. A variety, *E. tenellum*, grows near *Jerkin* and *Kongsvold*.

E. HYEMALE, L.; Fl. D. tab. 1,409.—Occasional on rather damp, sandy, or peaty soil, up to about the birch-limit. Grows near *Kongsvold*, *Jerkin*, and in Drivdal.

E. VARIEGATUM, Willd.; Fl. D. tab. 2,490.—Occasional up to and even above the birch-limit—*e.g.*, near *Jerkin*, *Kongsvold*, and in Drivdal. It is often washed down by the rivers, and may be found on the banks of the Miösen, only 400 feet above the sea.

E. SCIRPOIDES, Willd.—Common nearly up to the limit of snow. This, too, is frequently washed down by the rivers. Professor Blytt differs in opinion from Hook and Wahlenberg, who held that the two last forms were one and the same. "*E. scirpoides*," he adds, "is a genuine Norse growth, and, as far as I know, has never been found in S. Europe; neither in our own country is it found at such low altitudes as *E. variegatum*."

E. LIMOSUM, L.; Fl. D. tab. 1,184.—In a tarn between great and little Nystubæk. A more delicate, less branched form has been found in the easternmost lake in Hviddal, and in a tarn by the roadside between *Jerkin* and Jerkin-Sæter.

FILICES.

POLYPODIUM VULGARE, L.; Fl. D. tab. 1,060.—Grows on walls, stone fences, rocks, and in fissures. Common up to E. Finmark. Found on the mountains up to, and sometimes above, the birch-limit. Bears fruit the summer through, and found with ripe fruit from autumn to spring.

P. PHEGOPTERIS, L.; Fl. D. tab. 1,241.—In woods. Common up to Alten and Hammerfest; probably also in East Finmark. Grows on the mountains up to and above the birch-limit, and is found even at higher altitudes than the last. Bears fruit all the summer. Occasional in Drivdal and Vaarstien. A variety, *P. major*, has been found on Bogstadaas, near Christiania.

P. DRYOPTERIS, L.; Fl. D. tab. 1,943.—Common in shady places in forests up to East Finmark; on the mountains up to, and sometimes above, the birch-limit. Bears fruit from the beginning of the summer to August and September, according to the altitude. Grows in Drivdal up to and above the fir-limit. A variety, *P. tenerrimum*, of much more delicate growth, has been found on Grefsenaas, near Christiania.

P. RHŒTICUM, L.; Fl. D. tab. 2,607.—Common on the mountains from the southernmost part of Christiansand Stift (*e. g.*, on Hekfjeld) to East Finmark, where it descends to the sea-shore. In the south it is only found in the higher regions, scarcely under the limit of fir, and grows at altitudes of 4,000 feet above the sea. The nature of the subsoil does not seem to affect it.

P. ROBERTIANUM, Hoff.; Suppl. Fl. D. tab. 41.—Has a great resemblance to the last. Occasional in shady places from Porsgrund and Christiania to Snaasen in Throndhjems Stift. Professor Blytt remarks that he has never found it on the mountains, and scarcely at higher altitudes than 1,000 feet. Bears fruit from June to August and September. Grows always on chalky soil.

WOODSIA ILVENSIS, R. Br.; Fl. D. tab. 391 and 2,186.—Common in fissures in the rock from the southern parts of Christiansand Stift to East Finmark; on the mountains in osier copses up to and above the birch-limit. Grows in the lower part of Drivdal in the region of fir. Bears fruit at different times, according to altitude.

W. HYPERBOREA, R. Br., Fl. D. tab. 2,185.—Bears a great resemblance to the last. Habitat same as the last. Occasional in Drivdal, and more frequent than the last. It seems to thrive best on substrata of lime and slate.

Aspidium Lonchitis, Sw.; Fl. D. tab. 497.—Grows on rocky places and in forests throughout the whole country. Rather common; somewhat less frequent in the south of Norway. On the mountains it may be found up to the birch-limit, occasionally higher. It bears fruit at different times, according to the nature of the locality. It may be found here and there in Drivdal, and near *Kongsvold* growing up to the birch-limit.

A. aculeatum (L.) β angulare.—Very rare. Grows on shady and rocky places. Beitstaden, in Throndhjems Stift, is its known northernmost habitat in Europe. It bears fruit from midsummer, and is green the winter through. Always grows on low ground, below the limit of fir. Has been found on Kolsaasen, near Christiania; near Sandvigen, on Ullernaasen, and in Maridal; on Hovlandfjeld, near Modum; and by Holmestrand; near Eidsfoss, near Ruim and Brunkeberg in Thelemark; near Tvedestrand, Christiansand; Lervig and Frue Gaard on Storöe in Bergen Stift, on Sandvigs Fjeld and in Dörvedal, near Voss.

Polystichum Thelypteris, Roth.; Fl. D. tab. 760.—Grows in marshy places, especially in copses on the edge of swamps. Rather common in Aggershuus Stift; less frequent in other parts of the country. Nummedal, in Throndhjems Stift, is its known northernmost limit. Found generally in low-lying forests below 1,000 feet above the sea. Bears fruit in July and August.

P. Oreopteris, D.C.; Fl. D. tab. 1,121.—Not unfrequent from the southern parts of Christiansands Stift, *i. e.*, from Lillesand along the whole coast to the southern part of Nordland, *e. g.*, Helgeland. Less common away from the coast. Bears fruit from July to September. Not found at higher altitudes than 1,000 feet above the sea.

P. Filix mas, Roth.; Fl. D. tab. 1,346.—Common in shady places through the whole country to East Finmark. Grows on the Fjelds up to about the fir-limit. At Drivdal it has been found somewhat higher. A variety, *P. Erosum*, Professor Blytt has only found growing on Egeberg, near Christiania. Bears fruit from July to September, according to altitude.

P. cristatum, Roth.; Fl. D. tab. 1,591.—Has hitherto only been noticed in the low lands of the southern parts of Aggershuus Stift, never in mountainous regions. It grows at several places in the neighbourhood of Christiania, *e. g.*, Östensö, Lysaker,

Næsöen, at the foot of Grefsenaas, by **Kjænsrudkjærn**, near **Stabæk**. It bears fruit in June and July.

P. SPINULOSUM, D.C.; Fl. D. tab. 707.—Common on dry as well as moist and shady places up to **East** Finmark. Grows on the mountains up to about 3,500 feet above the sea. Found in Drivdal above the fir-limit. Bears fruit according to the altitude at which it is **found**.

P. DILATATUM, D.C.; Fl. D. tab. 759.—In shady places, in forests and mountains **to East Finmark**. Its greatest altitude is about 2,000 feet. **Bears fruit from June to** September, according to the **altitude at which it grows. Grows** in Drivdal at same height as the last. Professor Blytt remarks, that "the three last-named species are **so closely united to each** other by intermediate forms that it is **a matter of difficulty to** pronounce them separate species."

P. RIGIDUM, D.C.—Very rare. Found in marshy **places on mountain forest** tracts. Has been found in Sogendal, **in Christiansands** Stift. Professor Blytt does not seem to **think that** Hübner's assertion that "he had noticed it growing in several **places in Norway**," worthy of credit.

CYSTOPTERIS FRAGILIS, Bernh.; Fl. D. tab. 401.—Common in shady places up to **East Finmark under** different **forms.** Grows on the mountains to 3,500 feet above the sea. **Bears** fruit from **July to September.**

C. MONTANA, Bernh.; Fl. D. tab. 2,259.—Not uncommon in mountain valleys up to **East Finmark**. It grows in dark, shady, and dampish places **on the** high Fjelds, and **attains an** altitude of 3,000 feet. Common near *Kongsvold* **and in Drivdal.** Bears fruit generally late on in the summer.

ASPLENIUM CRENATUM, or CYSTOPTERIS CRENATA, Fr.—Occasional in shady places in Gudbransdal, at altitudes of 600 to 1,000 **feet above** the sea, *e.g.*, Kringelen, *Elstad* on the **other** side the river opposite the Gaard, and by the so-called Storstenuren, 1½ **miles south of** Vig. Bears fruit late in August. Grows on **a substratum** of schist. **A more** detailed description of this ex**tremely rare** fern may perhaps be interesting. "Rhizoma about the thickness of the finger, blackish, scaly; fronds 1 to 2 feet high, sometimes half a foot wide, triangular, light green; frond stalk dark-coloured below, **and** closely covered with lanceolate scales; destitute of fronds **till** half way up, **and more** or less bent between them; fronds alternate, lanceolate; pinnæ deeply serrate, obtuse; sori crowded in the middle, generally two-rowed, but finally confluent. It bears fruit late in August."

A. FILIX FEMINA, Bernh.; Fl. D. tab. 2,436.—Common on rather damp places in copses and forests to East Finmark. Grows on the Fjelds up to and a little over the limit of fir. A luxuriant form, frequently attaining a height of 3 feet, is found in small valleys near brooks and rivers. Bears fruit from June to September.

A. ADIANTUM NIGRUM, L.; Fl. D. tab. 250.—Occasional in clefts of the rocks. Has hitherto only been found on the western coast from Stavanger to Romsdal. Grows on Findöe and Rennesoe, in Stavanger Fjord, and also near Stavanger. It appears to thrive best on low grounds near the sea, and generally on a substratum of granite. It bears fruit in the autumn.

A. TRICHOMANES, L.; Fl. D. tab. 119.—Common in shady places in clefts of the rock, as far north as Salten in Nordland, probably higher. On the mountains it vanishes below the limit of fir, and scarcely attains a higher altitude in the southern parts of the country than 1,200 to 1,600 feet above the sea. Bears fruit from July to September.

A. VIRIDE, Huds.; Fl. D. tab. 1,289.—Bears a striking resemblance to the last. Occasional in clefts of the rocks, and in moist shady places from the south of Aggershuus Stift, *e.g.*, near Porsgrund, Brevig, and Christiania down to the sea. More frequent on Fjeld tracts up to East Finmark. It mounts up above the birch-limit to about 3,500 feet above the sea. Bears fruit at different times, according to altitude.

A. SEPTENTRIONALE, Sw.; Fl. D. tab. 60.—Very common on rocks, stone fences, walls, &c., up to East Finmark. Grows on the Fjelds to same altitude as the last. Bears fruit according to altitude.

A. BREYNII, Retz.—Not common. Grows on low ground, in clefts of the rock. In Aggershuus Stift, Professor Blytt found it near Laurvig, on Sandoë, Nordre Aaroë, Östre Bolleren, Dröbak, on Næsodden, near Helvig, near Bækkelag close to Christiania. In Bergen Stift it has been found in Lerdal; also in Romsdal, and on Korsvigberg, near Throndhjem. Generally found on substrata of granite, lime, or slate. Bears fruit in July and August.

A. RUTA MURARIA, L.; Fl. D. tab. 190.—Not uncommon in clefts of the rock, and on walls, especially in the eastern and southern districts. Less common on the west coast, but found near Stavanger, on the islands in Stavanger Fjord, near Bergen, &c. Professor Blytt also found it growing on the cloister ruins on Tutterøe, near Snaaren's parsonage house, on Alstenöe. Wahlenberg also has noticed it near Qvalvig in Lyngen, and Storvigsnæs in Alten. In the south of the country—*e.g.*, in Valders—it attains an altitude of 1,400 to 1,600 feet above the sea. Generally grows on limestone. Bears fruit in July and August.

PTERIS AQUILINA, L.; Fl. D. tab. 2,303.—In rocky places at the edge of forests. Very common to about Ranen, in Nordland. In the southern districts it scarcely attains a higher altitude than 1,400 to 1,600 feet above the sea. Professor Blytt found a hairy form near Gjællebæk on limestone, and near Tvedestrand on granite. Bears fruit from June to September.

BLECHNUM SPICANT, Roth.; Fl. D. tab. 99.—Grows in shady places, especially on peaty ground. Common in the western, but rare in the eastern parts of the country. On the mountains it grows up to the limit of fir. Generally on a substratum of granite. Bears fruit from June till September.

STRUTHIOPTERIS GERMANICA, Willd.; Fl. D. tab. 169.— Common on the banks of streams, and in damp, moist places in forest tracts up to East Finmark. Less frequent in the western parts of Christiansand and Bergens Stift. Grows on the mountains up to the fir-limit. Bears fruit from June till September.

ALLOSURUS CRISPUS, Bernh.; Fl. D. tab. 496.—Common on rocky places, and in fissures along the whole of the west coast, both on low lands and on Fjelds up to East Finmark. In the eastern parts it is only found on the mountains in places, *e.g.*, in Thelemark, on the Hallingdal Fjelds, Valders, &c. Grows at an altitude of 4,000 feet above the sea. Professor Blytt remarks that it apparently thrives best on primitive rock formation. Bears fruit according to altitude.

HYMENOPHYLLUM WILSONI, Hook; Fl. D. tab. 954.—Occasional in the lower parts of Christiansand and Bergens Stift on moist rocky ground, in company with some of the *Jungermannia*, *Mnium*, *Hypnum*, and other mosses. It has been found near Sognefæste, in Bergens Stift; near **Ous, in** Gaustalien; near Andressaa in Suledal, Svanöe, Sandvigslev near Bergen; and on Nordhuglöe, between this last place and Storöe. Generally on granite or old limestone. Bears fruit in July **and** August.

BOTRYCHIUM LUNARIA, Sw.; Fl. D. tab. ·18 (the fig. on the left).—Occasional on grassy **banks** and mounds from the extreme south up to East Finmark. **On** Hallingskarv, Fille **Fjeld, and** Dovre, **it attains an** altitude of about 3,400 feet. **Has been** noticed **on a substratum of** lime, slate, and granite. **It varies with regard to size, the form** of leaf, and its lower or higher place **on the stalk.** Bears fruit at different times, according to **altitude.** On the Dovre it grows near Kongsvold, in Drivdal, and **other** places.

B. MATRICARIOIDES BOREALE, Milde; *B. lanceolatum*, Fl. D. tab. 18 (fig. to the right); *B. tenellum*.—**Professor** Blytt found all three forms growing **together near** *Nystuen*, the highest station on the Fille Fjeld; near *Kongsvold* and *Fogstuen* on the Dovre, up to 3,500 feet **above the sea.** Substratum lime, schist, or granite. **Not common. Bears** fruit in July and August.

B. **RUTACEUM, Sw.;** Fl. D. tab. 18 (fig. 2).—Much less common than *B. lunaria*. It has been found growing in Salt-dal, its **known** northernmost limit. It has also been found near Abildsö, **about 3** miles from Christiania, and near Hövring Sæter, in Gud-**brandsdal,** 3,500 feet above the **sea; and near** Hunnerfoss, about **10 miles north of** Lillehammer; and also **at** Svinesund, on **the Swedish side. Grows** generally on limestone, schist, and granite. Bears **fruit in** July and August.

OPHIOGLOSSUM **VULGATUM, L.;** Fl. D. tab. 147.—Grows on moist places. **Very rare in the interior of the country.** Said to have been **found growing in** Ringerige, **near Toten** and Kongs-berg. Professor **Blytt found it near Vittingfoss,** between Laur-vig and Kongsberg; **also near Kjonrud works, near** Drammen; on Snaröe and Osteröe, near **Christiania;** on Nordre Aaröe, near Aaröesund; on Lövöe, **near Brevig,** near Krageröe; Arendal, **near** Espenæs, Grimstad, **on Mallöe,** &c. Alskuöe, on Helgeland, is its known northernmost **limit.** It appears to thrive best on **lime.** Grows nearly always on the shore. Bears fruit from June **to August.**

MARSILEACEÆ.

PILULARIA GLOBULIFERA, L.; Fl. D. tab. 223.—Very rare; grows on places that have been flooded. Said to have been found near Bergen. Professor Blytt found it near Christiansand on a substratum of granite. Bears fruit from June to August.

ISOETES LACUSTRIS, L.; Fl. D. tab. 191.—Grows in ponds, lakes in Christiansands Stift, in Aggershuus Stift towards Österdal; in Valders, e.g., by the Lille Mjosen and Utravand, on the Fille Fjeld, to an altitude of 3,000 feet.

LYCOPODIACEÆ.

LYCOPODIUM SELAGO, L.; Fl. D. tab. 104.—Very common in woods and on the Fjelds between bushes, &c., up to East Finmark. It mounts up to the limit of Phanerogamous vegetation, almost to the limit of snow. Professor Blytt found it on Nystuhöe towards the end of August, when the snow was lying thick on the ground, in company with *Draba lapponica* and *Catabrosa algida*, between 4,000 and 5,000 feet above the sea.

L. INUNDATUM, L.; Fl. D. tab. 336.—On damp places, especially on peaty ground, by the banks of lakes, &c. Common in Christiansand Stift, and occasional in the southern parts of Aggershuus Stift, e.g., in the Nordmarken forests, near Christiania, and in Övre Romerige. Attains an altitude of 1,000 feet.

L. ANNOTINUM, L.; Fl. D. tab. 117.—Common in forests to East Finmark. A variety, β *alpestre*, found only on the high Fjelds, up to the limit of the larger willows.

L. ALPINUM, L.; Fl. D. tab. 79.—Common. In the south it is never found below the limit of fir, but attains an altitude of 4,000 feet. Bears fruit from August to September.

L. COMPLANATUM, L.; Fl. D. tab. 78.—Occasional on dry heathy places, near the edge of woods, &c. On the Fjelds it attains an altitude of 3,000 feet, but is rare above the fir-limit.

L. CLAVATUM, L.; Fl. D. tab. 104.—Common on the Fjelds in the region of fir.

SELAGINELLA SPINULOSA, Braun., or L. SELAGINOIDES, L.; Fl. D. tab. 70.—Common over the whole Fjeld. Mounts up above the birch-limit.

HINTS TO BOTANISTS ON THE DOVRE FJELD.

Having now given a complete list of the phanerogamous plants of the Dovre Fjeld and of the ferns in Norway, I shall proceed to sketch out a few trips on the above mountain range which the gatherer of botanical specimens had best undertake, and which will be the most likely to afford him the richest returns. I need scarcely remind my readers that fishing and shooting may be very successfully combined with botanizing—not simultaneously perhaps, though even when out on the fjelds, or by the river side, rod in hand, many a specimen may be gathered which might otherwise have escaped notice.

Reindeer-hunting, as stated above, may be had in many parts, while at nearly every station on the Fjeld very fair grouse-shooting may be had.

Up to the year 1822 the Dovre Fjeld remained a *terra incognita* to the botanist. In that year, however, it was visited by Hisinger and Prof. Wahlberg, who published a very complete and detailed list of the mosses and lichens, the flora and ferns, many of which had previously not been known to exist in this part of the country, and others only occasionally in the adjoining fjelds of Österdal and Gudbrandsdal.

In 1824 and 1825 Prof. Blytt visited the Dovre, and made many and important additions to the list above referred to, both of mosses and phanerogamous plants. Amongst the latter may be mentioned the *Pinguicula villosa* (which had hitherto been considered to belong to the flora of Lapland), *Aira atropurpurea*, *Poa laxa* and *minor*, *Triticum violaceum*, *Luzula parviflora* (only before noticed by Smith near Grasvigsæter in Vaage), *Epilobium origanifolium, E. nutans, Stellaria alpestris* (before only found on the Fille Fjeld), *Draba lapponica* and *muricella, Orchis cruenta* and *Ophrys alpina, Carex parallela* (formerly only noticed in the northern districts), *Salix phylicifolia majalis, Salix norvegica-pyrenaica* (never found before), *Equisetum variegatum, Woodsia hyperborea*, &c.

In 1828 the Dovre was again visited by the German botanists Kurr and Hübner. These gentlemen added many names to the catalogue of the flora. Hübner collected a great variety of mosses, which are treated of in his 'Muscologia Germanica,' Leipsig, 1833.

In 1835 and 1836 Prof. Blytt again visited the Fjeld. In this latter year he paid great attention to the mosses. According to an estimate made by this distinguished and lamented botanist, the following is an approximate statement of the mosses, flora, &c., that may be found on the Dovre:—Mosses, about 200; lichens, about 150; algæ, about 50; phanerogamous plants and ferns, about 439.

Additions **have been made to this,** and undoubtedly **will continue to be made when** the Fjeld has been more thoroughly explored. Those who are desirous to make **fresh** discoveries would do well to direct their attention to the following districts, which have not been nearly **so** fully examined as other parts, viz. **the** districts adjoining Foldal, Vinsterdal, **Hviddal, and the** neighbouring heights; **the whole of that side** of the Fjeld towards Læssöe, **and the heights around** the numerous small valleys which **branch** off in **the** direction of Sundal.

As may have been seen **from** the above list of the Flora of the Dovre Fjeld, Kongsvold, and, in fact, the **whole** of Drivdal, are the most likely districts to enrich **the** collection of **the** botanist. Nearly all the alpine flora of the **North seems to** have centred itself in these parts, while at the same time it abounds in mosses and lichens.

As to the best time of the summer for visiting the Fjeld for botanical purposes, perhaps, from the beginning of June till the end of July is the very best. At this season the higher Fjeld plants are found in flower **from** Kongsvold Gaard, **and** along the whole extent of **road** through Drivdal. **But** to find some of the very rare ones—*e. g. Campanula uniflora, Ranunculus nivalis, Poa flexuosa, Agrostis algida, Diapensia, Salix polaris*—a clamber up the heights of Knudshöe is essential.

Those plants which are *not* to be found in the neighbourhood of Kongsvold are, *Saxifraga hieracifolia, S. stellaris β comosa, Pinguicula villosa, Salix pyrenaica-norvegica, Arabis petræa, Draba muricella, Orchis cruenta,* and **Luzula arcuata**.

The following remarks—which are almost a literal translation from the account the late Prof. Blytt gave of his visit to Kongsvold—will be found valuable to the botanist, and should therefore be borne in mind.

'A couple of days should at least be devoted to Tofte. On the first of these an excursion should be made on the hills surrounding the Gaard, and on the heights towards Harbakken. The following rare plants will be found here: *Ophrys alpina, Orchis cruenta, Kobresia caricina,* &c. On the following day a trip should be taken to Storhöe, to look for *Saxifraga hieracifolia*. A journey over Harbakken, along the old road to Fogstuen, will be found to repay the trouble. A great many of the common Fjeld plants may be gathered on both sides of the road. Neither must Fogsaa be left unexplored. To find *Pinguicula villosa,* the swampy banks of the small lakes, about three-quarters of a mile below the Gaard, must be visited; it grows in plenty hereabouts, but is comparatively rare along the road between Fogstuen and Jerkin. *Carex capitata, Epilobium origanifolium, E. nutans, Conostomum, Cinclidium*, with other marsh mosses, grow here.

'From Jerkin, where there are excellent quarters, and where good fishing and shooting may also be had, an excursion must be made on the neighbouring Gederyggen. Amongst others will here be found, of mosses, *Lecidea Wahlenbergii, Eremodon splachnoides*, **Didymon pilifer, Dicranum Sphagni, Catoscopium nigritum**, &c.; *Draba alpina*, **lapponica**, and *muricella* (the two last growing together close to the uppermost stone-beacon on the ridge), *Pinguicula villosa* (in the marshy ground at the foot of the Fjeld), *Salix Arbuscula* (plentiful on the swamp by the road immediately below the Gaard), *S. polaris* (in small quantities on a single point of the Fjeld, near the snow-patches), *Carex capitata* (in the bog below the Gaard), *C. fuliginosa* (on the slopes of Gederyggen, above the willow-limit), *C. parallela*, and *C. rupestris*, in the same places and at the same altitude.

'It is scarcely worth the trouble to continue to explore west or south of Gederyggen. I have been over the whole terrain, and found the vegetation to be poor in the extreme. With the exception of a couple of cryptogami, *Lecidea morio, Grimmia Donniana*, and *Saxifraga stellaris β comosa*, I have not found a single rare plant. Neither will it repay one to explore in the direction of Fold-dal. The attention of the botanist should at once be directed to Blaahöe, about three miles and a half from Jerkin. It is best to start early in the morning from the station, and, in order to husband one's strength, to take a carriole to Volasö, and from thence to walk by Volasö-sæter to Blaahöe. In a birch copse along the mountain-path the *Aira atropurpurea* will be found; and further on, near the foot of the Fjeld, the *Mnium turgidum* in abundance on the marshes. The steepness of the Fjeld must not damp the explorer's ardour; it is not really so formidable on approaching it closely. By boldly breasting the ascent, and clambering up the furrows which the snow-brooks and avalanches have ploughed into the mountain side above the willow-limit, he will find himself more than compensated for the hard work he has undergone.' "In no places," writes the Professor, "have I found more beautiful and more varied forms of the Draba and Saxifrage than here. Here, too, may be found *Papaver nudicaule, Carex fuliginosa, Luzula arcuata, Poa flexuosa, Poa minor, Poa abbreviata, Salix polaris,* &c." 'The same may also be found, but more spread out over the ground, together with *Saxifraga stellaris*, near Goutstiaa and Goutsti Fjeld, which bounds it on the north. On Volasöberg, which lies between Blaahöe and the lake, *Salix polaris* and

Luzula arcuata may be found here and there, and *Diapensia* in abundance.

'On both sides of the road from Jerkin to Kongsvold, over Jerkinshöe, the vegetation is remarkably interesting. Perhaps in no other part of the Fjeld are there such good opportunities for noticing the different forms and growths of the very variable willow-tribe. The *Primula stricta* grows in comparative abundance close to the road side. On approaching Kongsvold the *Alsinella rubella β hirta*, and **Artemisia** *norvegica* begin to appear. On arriving at Kongsvold, where excellent quarters are to be had, excursions should be made on the east side of the river. The vegetation of the western side is comparatively poor, although many interesting lichens and mosses may be gathered. Nystudal, a high-lying mountain valley, is situated about five miles west of Kongsvold. Amongst the rarer specimens that may be found here are *Grimmia apiculata* (a *Poa* having much in common with *Poa distichophylla*), *Poa flexuoso, minor*, and *abbreviata*, and a variety of *Carex saxatilis*. But, as just said, explorations on the eastern side will be far more remunerative. And first, there is a little valley called Sprænbækdal. It is best to follow the course of the stream till after passing the willow-limit, and then to steer in a northerly direction up towards the Knudshöe heights.

'On arriving at the Fonds* which cover the foot of the highest peak of Knudshöe, the direction of Vaarstien should be taken. In the neighbourhood of the Fonds the *Agrostis algida* and *Ranunculus nivalis* may be found, the latter in great abundance; and lower down, a little above the willow-limit, on dry, lichen-covered slopes, the *Campanula uniflora* is plentiful. Somewhat lower down again the *Papaver nudicaule* is found in small quantities. This plant, together with *Draba lapponica*, *Potentilla nivea*, *Tussilago frigida*, flower early in the spring, but at these altitudes will still be found flowering later on in summer. Also on Knudshöe will be found *Salix polaris*, many rare *Poa*, and *Carex fuliginosa*. The *Ranunculus nivalis* descends almost to Vaarstien. On the steep sides above Vaarstien, *Lecidea Wahlenbergii* grows rather abundantly.

'The following plants, &c., are to be found along the road between Vaarstien and Kongsvold: *Alsinella rubella β hirta*, *Carex parallela*, *Triticum violaceum*, *Aspidium montanum*, *Botrychium lunaria*, various species of *Cladoniæ*, *Biatosa cuprea*, *Lecidea caudida*, &c. *Umbilicaria atropruinosa* (found also on the heights of Blaaöhe, Knudshöe, in quantities),

---

* The Snee-fond, or Snee-bræ, is the snow of the higher regions, before it is condensed into the crystalline ice of the Iis-bræ, or glacier.

Splachnum angustatum, Mnium turgidum, Meesia demissa, &c., and several others too numerous to mention.

'Around Drivstuen, especially on the Fjeld slopes on the east side, the vegetation is very luxuriant. Most of the subalpine plants may be found here in abundance—*Ranunculus platanifolius, Thalictrum simplex,* **Viola** *mirabilis, Epilobium origanifolium,* **Saxifraga** *cotyledon* (more common between Drivstuen and Rise), *Erigeron* **acer** β, *Gnaphalium sylvaticum* β, *Sonchus alpinus,* and many interesting forms of *Hieracium* **cymosum, murorum, boreale,** *aurantiacum*, and *prenanthoides*, and forms of *H. umbellatum, Apargia Taraxaci,* **Polemonium** *cæruleum, Myosotis sylvatica* and ***deflexa*, Satyrium nigrum,** *Convallaria verticillata,* **Calamagrostis Halleriana,** *Equisetum* **hyemale,** &c. By clambering higher up on the same side, above the birch-limit, the same rich alpine vegetation is met with as occurs at Kongsvold. The same cryptogamous plants are found here, and in addition, *Lecidia decipiens*, high above the birch-limit, and *Parmelia oreina* on the rocky slopes and stones near Drivstuen. On the other side of the river, opposite to Drivstuen, the vegetation in the lower parts of the Fjeld is less luxuriant and varying. It is almost neck-breaking work to clamber up to the summit of the Fjeld, and will scarcely repay one for the trouble, unless to find the *Diapensia* in flower be considered a sufficient reward. "Nowhere have I seen it," writes Professor Blytt, "in such beautiful flower as here, on the edge of the Fonds. The *Campanula uniflora*," he adds, "is said to be found here; but I have searched for it twice in vain, because I was informed that it frequented the same habitats as *Carex fuliginosa*. On Knudshöe, however, it will not be looked for in vain."'

APPENDIX.

Pasvig Elv.—(p. 9.)

This river is rented by Mr. Clark and a Mr. Jordan, **also a** Norwegian, who will doubtless give permission to fish.

Tana Elv.—(p. 11.)

Half **way** between Seida-guoika and Galgo-guoika is Polmac Elv, a short river running from Polmac Javre or Vand. The lake is said to abound with fish; but there is no good fishable water where the **river debouches into the Tana.**

At Galgo-guoika there are three good pools and a fine reach.

At Utsjok there are two pools and **some** good rapids. The Levvojok and Valjijok rivers are mere mountain torrents.

At Wonda-guoika, near Valjijok-guoika, are two pools and a reach.

At Karasjok and Assebakte, which **is a few** miles higher **up, the bed of the river is pure** sand and the current smooth. **The natives say that they get but** few salmon there.

Staburs Elv.—(p. 13.)

There are about eight miles of poor fishing in this river. No river-boats can be procured, and the banks are for the most part densely wooded. A friend writes me word of this river: "We took one fish of seventeen pounds here, and other smaller ones. The whole country is densely wooded, with scarcely a habitation. It is very rough work."

Alten Elv.—(p. 14.)

I have since been informed that the nets and boxes are entirely removed from this river, a very high rent being paid for it. The season of 1862 was a wonderful one; one rod taking 4,700 lbs. in six weeks!

Loppenö.—(p. 17.)

The shooting on Loppenö and Hadselö is taken, the former yearly from Consul Aagaard, and the latter on lease from the five parishes of the island.

Ranen Elv.—(p. 20.)

The largest river in the Ranen Fjord is the Rytsaa, near the end of the Fjord. It is a very fine stream; but the only fishing is near Korgen, about half an English mile below the Foss. The Foss is magnificent, and worth a journey.

"The shooting about here," a friend informs me, "was some years ago very fine. I have not heard of its having been tried since. There is very good ryper-shooting on the land adjoining Vigholmen, a small station at the mouth of the Fjord; and late in the season (October) thousands of ptarmigan on the rocky mountains opposite."

Stordals Elv.—(p. 23.)

There is now a new road up Stordal, so that the ferry is avoided. The river, from the Foss to Kringen, is on lease; but whether the part from this place to the mouth is taken, I cannot say with certainty.

Namsen Elv.—(p. 28.)

The season of 1863 has been a very late one on this river, and even in the best parts there was no sport at all till nearly the middle of July, and then very partial, one or two of the best stations doing very little, one or two well enough. The lower fishings are, I am informed, worth next to nothing; and that there is nothing below Sæm worth the journey, or any rent at all. Below this place the river loses its grand character. There are some fine-looking pools and streams below that point, no doubt; but hereabouts the river begins to run among immense clay banks. When the water is high the clay crumbles in, and discolours all the lower part. For instance, at the beginning of July it would have been impossible to have seen a dollar-piece at a depth of three feet in the lower part, whereas above Sæm, though high, it was a beautiful colour.

The consequence may readily be foreseen. At the beginning of the season, when the big fish are coming up, the lower water is almost certain to be too thick for them to see the flies, and by the time the water clears the best fish have already run up. Consequently I would not give much for a fishing below Sæm. *Verbum sap.*

Still, no doubt, some fair sport might be had occasionally below Sæm, by trailing from a boat; but I do not believe it to be worth much.

There is a possibility of the Namsen losing its reputation as being a first-class salmon river. Below Fiskum Foss is a bay and eddy which catches a great quantity of the timber which comes down the Foss. Here thousands of logs lie churning and grinding against each other for months. Consequently a great quantity of timber is rendered useless for the market. In order to remedy this, the timber merchants talk of digging a cut from above the Foss, which will bring a rush of water into this bay, and so float the timber out.

But as this cut will have to pass through a clayey soil, it may be a question whether the water will not wash out quite a new channel, leaving the Foss altogether, and carrying down clay enough to spoil the fishing. Of course this may not take place; but when once water is let loose, there is no knowing what may happen. I regret to hear that some of the lower fishings on this river, as well as some Finmark rivers, have been taken by a London tackle-maker for the purpose of sub-letting. Such a system, in my opinion, will conduce more than anything else to spoil sport in the country. However, if fishermen will do so foolish a thing as to hire water without knowing anything at all about it, they richly deserve disappointment.

Torrisdal Elv.—(p. 61.)

This used to be a splendid river some twenty years ago. The fishing is nearly all close to the Foss. Excellent trout-fishing above.

The saw-mills have been the ruin of the fishing.

Reindeer Hunting.—(p. 94.)

A friend of mine who has lately returned from Norway gives me a very poor account of reindeer-hunting. The fact is, the Bönder now hunt themselves, and may be seen by scores scouring the fjelds in all directions, even in the most remote corners.

One day, he tells me, he saw a herd of nine hinds and calves at a distance of about four English miles high up on the "snee-fonds" of the Vaage Fjelds; but, as it was late in the evening, he was reluctantly obliged to decline stalking them. The following morning he purposed going after them, but found himself forestalled by a party of native hunters from Lom. "I grieve to find," he adds, " that this sport is now utterly destroyed everywhere by the natives. When first I hunted in the Vaage mountains, some years ago, it was a rarity to find a Norwegian who ever came up so far to hunt. Now there are dozens! It seems to be the same in the Österdalen and Reendalen districts. There were also about thirty of these fellows hunting on the Rundene this year. When I was there, in 1858, there were not more than two. Therefore good-bye, I fear, for the future, to anything like real sport in the way of reindeer hunting, except it were possible to find some remote spot beyond the region of Sæters or Bönder, and this, I fear, is scarcely to be found."

THE END.

LONDON:
PRINTED BY WILLIAM CLOWES AND SONS, STAMFORD STREET,
AND CHARING CROSS.

www.ingramcontent.com/pod-product-compliance
Lightning Source LLC
Chambersburg PA
CBHW030259240426
43673CB00040B/1009